GW00771782

Illustration 1. Sophia Jex-Blake aged twenty-five. Portrait by Samuel Laurence, bequeathed to the Royal Society of Medicine by Dr Margaret Todd. (Reproduced by permission of the Royal Society of Medicine.)

SOPHIA JEX-BLAKE

THE WELLCOME INSTITUTE SERIES IN THE HISTORY OF MEDICINE

Edited by W.F. Bynum and Roy Porter
The Wellcome Institute

SOPHIA JEX-BLAKE
A WOMAN PIONEER IN NINETEENTH-CENTURY MEDICAL REFORM

Shirley Roberts

London and New York

First published 1993
by Routledge
2 Park Square, Milton Park, Abingdon, Oxfordshire OX14 4RN

Simultaneously published in the USA and Canada
by Routledge
711 Third Avenue, New York, NY 10017

First issued in paperback 2014

Routledge is an imprint of the Taylor and Francis Group, an informa company

Transferred to Digital Printing 2005

© 1993 Shirley Roberts

Typeset in Baskerville
by Pat and Anne Murphy, Highcliffe-on-Sea, Dorset

All rights reserved. No part of this book may be reprinted or
reproduced or utilized in any form or by any electronic,
mechanical, or other means, now known or hereafter
invented, including photocopying and recording, or in any
information storage or retrieval system, without permission in
writing from the publishers.

British Library Cataloguing in Publication Data
A catalogue record for this book is available from
the British Library.

Library of Congress Cataloging in Publication Data
Roberts, Shirley, 1927–
Sophia Jex-Blake: a woman pioneer in nineteenth century
medical reform/Shirley Roberts.
p.cm. – (The Wellcome Institute series in the history
of medicine)
Includes bibliographical references and index.
1. Jex-Blake, Sophia, 1849–1912.
2. Women physicians – Scotland – Biography.
3. Health reformers – Scotland – Biography.
4. Women physicians – Education (Graduate) – History.
5. Women in medicine – History.   I. Title.   II. Series.
R692.J49R63 1993   610'.92–dc20   [B]   93-14890 CIP

ISBN 13: 978-0-415-08753-7 (hbk)
ISBN 13: 978-0-415-75606-8 (pbk)

Cover illustration: Samuel Laurence *Portrait of Sophia Jex-Blake*,
courtesy of the Royal Society of Medicine.

Contents

Illustrations

Acknowledgements

My work on this project was assisted by many whose expert knowledge of various aspects of the subject was invaluable. I offer my sincere thanks to Professor J. Melville Jones of the University of Western Australia; Dr Michael Barfoot and Mrs Jo Currie of the Edinburgh University Library; Mr William Schupbach of the Wellcome Institute for the History of Medicine; Miss Anne Fletcher, Librarian of the Royal Free Hospital; Mr David Doughan of the Fawcett Library; Miss Joan Ferguson, Librarian of the Royal College of Physicians of Edinburgh; Mr Ian Lyle, Librarian of the Royal College of Surgeons of England; Mr Geoffrey Davenport, Librarian of the Royal College of Physicians, London; Mr John Mitchell and Mr Callum Calder of Edinburgh University; Mr Andrew Scott of St Giles Cathedral, Edinburgh; Mrs Fitzgerald, Archivist of Queen's College, London; Mrs Pamela Haines of Hastings Central Library; Mrs B. Bradley of Lewes Library, East Sussex; and Miss Joan Thomas, Information and Special Services Librarian, Gwynedd County Council.

The project also introduced me to many new friends among people with similar interests. Some of these generously gave or exchanged information, thus adding to the pleasure and interest of the work. I am especially indebted to Mrs Carolyn Lincoln of Edinburgh; Mr Edward Preston of Hastings; Frau Erika Rettig-Freiensehner of Ludwigshafen; Mr Thomas Jex-Blake of Gisborne, New Zealand; Mrs Catriona Williams of Jersey, Channel Islands; Dr Anne Shepherd of Edinburgh; Mr and Mrs R. Williams of Burnley, Lancashire; and my friends of the Lyceum Club, Melbourne.

Table of events

The women students have difficulty in obtaining certificates of attendance at lectures.

Elizabeth Garrett is awarded the MD Paris.

The women students are denied entry to the Edinburgh Royal Infirmary.

The Riot at Surgeons' Hall occurs on 18 November.

1871 Sophia is sued for defamation.

1872 The Managers of the Royal Infirmary vote to admit women students, but their decision is challenged.

The women students succeed in their lawsuit against the University.

Sophia fails the First Professional Examination.

The women students at last gain entry to the Royal Infirmary.

1873 The University wins its legal appeal and the University is again closed to women.

1874 Opening of the London School of Medicine for Women.

1875 Defeat of Cowper Temple's bill to empower Scottish universities to admit women.

General Medical Council votes not to oppose registration of women doctors.

1876 Resignation of examiners in midwifery of the Royal College of Surgeons of England.

Passage of the Russell Gurney Enabling Bill.

The King's and Queen's College of Physicians of Ireland opens its examinations to women.

1877 Sophia obtains the MD Berne.

The London School of Medicine is affiliated with the Royal Free Hospital.

Sophia obtains the Licence of the King's and Queen's College of Physicians, and becomes a registered practitioner.

Isabel Thorne is appointed Honorary Secretary of the London School of Medicine for Women.

1878 Sophia returns to Edinburgh and begins medical practice.

1881 Death of Sophia's mother.

1882 Death of Sir Robert Christison.

1883 Sophia moves to Bruntsfield Lodge.

1886 Royal Colleges of Physicians and Surgeons in Edinburgh open their examinations to women.

Sophia's book *Medical Women* is published.

Sophia founds the Edinburgh School of Medicine for Women.

Sophia becomes an accredited lecturer in the extramural system.

The friendship between Sophia and Margaret Todd begins.

1889 The Misses Cadell bring their suit for damages.

1890 Death of Lucy Sewall.

Table of events

Introduction

In the mid-nineteenth century the Crown, Britain's symbol of majesty and power, was worn by a woman. But among Her Majesty's subjects the status of the average woman, regardless of her social class, was virtually that of a serf. Although political reformers from John Wilkes onwards had pressed for 'universal suffrage' they and their followers all understood the term to mean 'universal *male* suffrage'. It did not occur to any of them that women should also have a voice in the government of their country. In his *Social History of England* Asa Briggs traces the origin of this attitude back to the Middle Ages, and finds that it was well established by the twelfth century:

> The formal position of women within society, as laid down by law, had been considerably eroded since the Norman Conquest, due to both the introduction of land tenure based on military order, and Christianity. Women in both canon and civil law were deemed to be 'under the rod' of their husbands and canon law specifically permitted wife-beating.[1]

By the nineteenth century wife-beating was less overtly encouraged, but the lot of women was otherwise unimproved. Among the poorer working classes it was usually women and children who did the most dangerous and unpleasant jobs in mines and factories, and their wages were lower than men's. Men obliged to work at uncongenial tasks could cling to the hope that they might eventually be promoted to something better, but for female labourers promotion was never a likely prospect.

In more affluent middle-class society women faced different problems. There a measure of a man's worldly success was his ability to keep his womenfolk in idle luxury. It was his duty to provide for them, and his right to manage their affairs as he saw fit. At marriage a bride's financial assets became her husband's property, and thereafter she was financially dependent on him. In an ideal marriage this did not matter, but if there were clashes of personality the husband was armed with a powerful weapon.

The precarious situation of women was highlighted by the famous case of Mrs Caroline Norton.[2] Caroline, who was one of the three granddaughters of

1

Richard Brinsley Sheridan, inherited some of her grandfather's literary talent. By the age of 17 she had successfully published a satirical novel. In 1827, when she was 19 years old, she married the Honourable George Norton. Caroline was warm-hearted, flamboyant and indiscreet, while Norton was withdrawn, suspicious and calculating. Their incompatibility probably doomed the union to failure. They had been married for nine stormy years when Norton suddenly startled the British public by announcing that he was taking legal action against the Prime Minister, Lord Melbourne, whom he accused of committing adultery with Caroline. The case attracted enormous publicity. Without leaving the courtroom the jury decided that Norton's accusations were unfounded. There was even a suggestion that he had acted partly from political motives.

An important aspect of the case was its revelation of a husband's legal powers over his wife. In the months between the filing of the suit and the court hearing Norton was able to remove his children from the marital home and to deprive their mother of all contact with them. He also appropriated all her possessions, even her jewellery. The court ordered him to pay her an allowance, but he failed to do so regularly. Furthermore, he claimed for himself the money she continued to earn from her writing. In 1853 Caroline Norton brought a legal action against her husband to secure her financial rights. She also addressed to the Queen an eloquent plea for reform of the divorce laws to correct injustice to women. Her writings on this subject won support for a series of Parliamentary Bills that were passed between 1857 and 1882, and helped to make some progress in this regard.

The image of middle-class women as domestic ornaments shaped attitudes to the education of girls. Serious study was thought to be beyond the ability of any female, and even injurious to her health. Furthermore, it could spoil her marriage prospects, since no man would want a 'blue-stocking' for a wife. The harmful effects of enforced idleness and boredom were ignored, but they were none the less real. In an editorial note the *Lancet* of 20 December 1873 warned medical men to be wary when they attended female patients in their homes:

> Some women cannot live without an intrigue, if it be only to procure a new bonnet or a ticket for a ball, and the most platonic and professional attendance of a middle-aged medical man may be warmed up into a romance in the brain of a foolish novel-reading woman with no family cares.

Probably most of the novel-readers were content with their lot, but there were signs of rebellion. Not all middle-class women had menfolk to support them. Widows, spinsters and others in straitened circumstances had to find some means of earning a livelihood. The occupation of governess was the only respectable one open to them, but it was poorly paid and overcrowded. By mid-century there were moves afoot to provide better education for girls, and

2

to give vocational training to those who needed to earn their living. Florence Nightingale's historic achievements during the Crimean War were changing popular attitudes to nurses and nursing. In the early decades of the nineteenth century nurses were few in number, untrained and often illiterate. They worked in charity hospitals, where only the poor and homeless would come for treatment; when more prosperous citizens became ill, they were cared for at home by their families and servants. But now Miss Nightingale was transforming nursing into a skilled profession that could attract women of ability and character.

Soon women were asking why there should not also be women doctors. The Victorian Age placed great emphasis on feminine modesty, yet women who sought treatment for their most intimate health problems were obliged to consult male practitioners. Some women were so troubled by this that they delayed the consultation until they were seriously ill. Some even preferred to die untreated. A great deal of suffering could be prevented by training women for the medical profession.

Many people recalled a tragic episode that happened in the second year of the young Queen Victoria's reign. The Queen was then striving to free herself from domination by her strong-willed mother, the Duchess of Kent. The Duchess was supported by her maid-of-honour, the Lady Flora Hastings.[3] Court gossips were aware of the Queen's dislike of Lady Flora, so they were pleased to report to Her Majesty that the unmarried Lady Flora was obviously pregnant – they could think of no other explanation for her changing contours. Incensed at Lady Flora's apparent shamelessness, the Queen instructed Lord Melbourne to have the matter investigated. Melbourne questioned the Court physician, Sir James Clark, whom Lady Flora had recently consulted, but Sir James was unable to say whether or not the rumours were true. Lady Flora had refused to be examined by him, so he had merely prescribed some medicine for her indigestion. But the Queen would not let the matter rest. She insisted that Lady Flora be medically examined to determine whether she was indeed pregnant. Reluctantly the lady complied, and a medical report was issued jointly by Sir James Clark and the Hastings family's physician, Sir Charles Clarke. These gentlemen stated that Lady Flora was not pregnant, and never had been. She had the misfortune to be suffering from an abdominal tumour, which caused her death a few months later. Lady Flora's relatives protested vehemently at the anguish their kinswoman had been made to suffer, and the episode was soon common knowledge. The Queen, Lord Melbourne and Sir James Clark were all severely criticized for their part in it.

Now, more than a century and a half later, the story seems to reflect mainly the Queen's immaturity and the narrow-mindedness of the time, but thirty years after the event it served another purpose. Campaigners for the medical women's cause could quote it as an example of the suffering that could be prevented if only women were able to consult doctors of their own sex. If women doctors were needed, there were women who were prepared to answer the call.

This small but determined group was convinced that medical practice would satisfy their need for work that was both challenging and of service to humanity. Their aspirations seemed unexceptionable, but the opposition they met was almost overwhelming.

The majority of male medical practitioners strongly opposed the admission of women to their ranks. The motives of some of the men were frankly mercenary – they feared that women competitors would make large inroads into their practices. Others had less selfish objectives. Some believed that women lacked the emotional and intellectual stamina necessary for practice, even though they might be clever enough to pass the examinations. Such women would eventually be failures and would damage the profession. Others were shocked at the prospect of young women declining marriage and motherhood in order to enter the rough masculine world; society as a whole would suffer, these critics claimed.

Two women succeeded in slipping past the defences of their opponents and becoming registered medical practitioners. They were Elizabeth Blackwell, whose name appears on the first Medical Register in 1859, and Elizabeth Garrett, who joined her in 1865. The success of Miss Garrett prompted the closing of the only route by which women could hope to qualify, and twelve years were to elapse before another woman's name appeared on the Register.

The story of the opening of the British medical profession to women reads like a segment of military history. Terms such as battle, campaign, clash, defeat and victory keep recurring, because all these are applicable to the events that led to the triumph of the women's cause in 1877. The heroine of this story is Sophia Jex-Blake. Without her courage and tenacity women would probably have been debarred from the practice of medicine for several more decades.

While it is true that Sophia had the support of many able men and women, she was always the driving force of the campaign. She began it in 1869, little knowing what a struggle lay ahead of her, but each setback seemed to stimulate her to more determined effort. She could brush aside her fatigue and depression because she was fighting not just for herself, but for a cause. Only after the victory was won did she seem to falter. It was then that the diplomatic skills of Elizabeth Garrett Anderson (Miss Garrett had married Mr Skelton Anderson in 1871) were called upon to smooth the onward path. Elizabeth's subsequent success and fame were built on the foundation of Sophia's achievements.

Sophia's important role in medical and feminist history suggests that collections of her letters and papers would have been carefully preserved, especially as she is known to have been both a prolific letter-writer and a hoarder of letters. But a careful search fails to locate any such collection. A clue to this mystery is to be found in her will, in which she directed:

> I leave my papers, letters, diaries, letter books, case books and all other
> private documents to my residuary legatee, Dr Todd, but in case she

should not survive me, then I desire that all such books and papers should be burnt without examination in the presence of my executor or witness.[4]

Dr Margaret Todd was Sophia's friend for twenty-five years. She survived Sophia by six years, and was the author of her biography, in which she quotes extensively from these letters and diaries. The biography was published only a few months before Margaret Todd took her own life. It seems likely that she acted on Sophia's second instruction and burnt the papers when she had finished with them. Fortunately, there are other sources of information on Sophia's achievements, and enough of her writing has been preserved to portray her warm, impulsive personality.

Notes

1.   A. Briggs, *A Social History of England*, Harmondsworth: Penguin, 1985, p. 77.
2.   Lord D. Cecil, *Melbourne*, Indianapolis/New York: Bobbs-Merrill Co. Inc., 1966, pp. 297–303.
3.   ibid, pp. 343–4.
4.   Last Will and Testament of Sophia Jex-Blake, 20 March 1911.

1

Childhood in Sussex

Sophia Louisa Jex-Blake was born in Sussex, at 3 Croft Place, Hastings, on 21 January 1840. Her parents were prosperous gentlefolk, conservative in outlook and deeply religious. With such a background Sophia might well have grown up to take her place in middle-class society as a wife and mother, graciously presiding over a household in which servants and nursemaids protected her from life's harsh realities. But she was destined to play a very different role. Even as a child she startled her parents with her inability to conform to the pattern of behaviour expected of small girls in early Victorian times.

Thomas and Maria Jex-Blake were no longer young when Sophia was born; Thomas was 50 years old, Maria 39. Their first three children had died in infancy. Then there were three who survived – Thomas William born in 1832, Caroline born in 1834 and lastly, Sophia. Both parents came from distinguished Norfolk families – the Blakes of Swanton Abbots,[1] and the Cubitts of Honing Hall.[2] Three years before Sophia's birth, her grandfather, William Blake, obtained a Royal Licence to change the family name to Jex-Blake, in honour of his grandmother Elizabeth Jex, who was an heiress when she married Thomas Blake early in the eighteenth century.[3] During Sophia's childhood, she and other members of the family often used the old name of Blake, but by the time she reached adulthood Jex-Blake was firmly established as their family name.

Her father was a member of the legal profession, a proctor of Doctors Commons. This was a professional association of Admiralty and ecclesiastical lawyers; the barristers in Doctors Commons were known as advocates, the solicitors as proctors.[4] At the time of Sophia's birth Thomas Jex-Blake had already practically retired from his profession. He was a kindly, studious man, a stickler for etiquette and frequently perplexed by the high spirits of his younger daughter.

Thomas and Maria Jex-Blake belonged to the evangelical movement in the Anglican Church and applied its tenets to their family life. Although they provided well for their children they also encouraged them to practise

Illustration 2. Thomas Jex-Blake (1790–1868). Portrait by H.T. Wells, R.A., 1862. (Reproduced by permission of the State Reference Library of Victoria, Australia.)

Illustration 3. Maria Emily Jex-Blake (1801–1881). Portrait by H.T. Wells, R.A., 1862. (Reproduced by permission of the State Reference Library of Victoria, Australia.)

self-denial. The children were expected to save their pennies so that they could help the poor and contribute to the Church's missions in Africa and Asia. Sophia used to say that her mother could have managed quite well as the wife of a poor man, so expert was she in avoiding waste and extravagance.

Illustration 4. 3 Croft Place, Hastings, Sussex. Sophia's birthplace.

The children were encouraged to read serious books by religious writers. Their parents considered most novels to be 'trash'; *Punch* they thought was vulgar. When the girls were growing up they were not taught to dance, and theatre-going was discouraged. Yet Sophia did not think her parents unduly harsh or forbidding. Despite her austere views, Mrs Jex-Blake had a lively sense of humour to which Sophia responded with delight. Mr Jex-Blake was more serious, but soft-hearted and companionable. Sophia was much closer to her parents than she was to her brother and sister, who were away at school during much of her early childhood.

She learned to read and write at an early age, and used to exchange little notes with her parents, such as the following, written when she was about 7 years old.

Dear Mrs Blake,

       I wish you would be so kind as to come and see me every night in Bed-ford-shire at least tonight and on Sunday Monday Tuesday Wednesday Thursday Friday Saturday and next Sunday after tomorrow. I require an answer to this note (letter) even if you do come tonight. There are now so many railroads that you can get to Bedfordshire in one minute. Please send 'Madam Mary' with this and then come up.

GRANDAFLORER[5]

The name 'Grandaflorer', with slight variations, was one she often used in the imaginative writing that was one of her favourite amusements. When she was 8 years old she began to write about a fairy-tale realm, which she ruled as the 'Grand Mogul and Despotic Emperor Grandiflora'. She kept a little notebook in which she described the land of Sackermena and its people. Sometimes she wrote in verse, with an occasional mistake in spelling:

> Sweet Sackermena and her isles
> See how many yards and miles
> It takes to go round Sackermena! . . .
> See how pretily the sunbeams dance
> Upon the fair waves of Speed-the-lance
> See the Waters of Gold . . .[6]

She reverted to prose and wrote on foolscap pages when dealing with the serious subject of Sackermena's constitution:

The Despotic Emperor has authority that none may dispute and none may appear in his presence without his gracious permission save his sons and Lord Field Marshall, also the chief general the high Admiral the high Treasurer, high Chancellor, Secretary of state and the Chief Justice.

Succession to the Crown. It is at the option of the Reigning Despotic Emperor to name his successor but if he dies without making any choice it descends to the eldest son but if he has no son the crown is placed on the head of the eldest daughter unless 12 *strong* reasons can be urged to the contrary and accepted by Parliament. . . .

Robery shall always be punished by the culprits restoring four-fold or if utterly unable to pay this as many days imprisonment as there are shillings in the forfeit. Intentional murder and personal injury shall be punished by injuries precisely similar. . . .[7]

9

Sophia ceased to write about Sackermena when she was 10 years old, but memories of the fairy realm remained with her all her life. Most children who create an imaginary land for themselves are content to people it with beautiful princesses and the brave knights who rescue them from danger. But Sophia pondered on the laws governing the succession to the throne of her kingdom, and on the just punishment of its lawbreakers. Her Sackermena must have been partly the product of an older mind, although her notes, which were found many years later, were all in her own childish hand. No-one else had corrected or altered them. Sophia's father probably read to her the legends of the Knights of the Round Table and other beloved tales of medieval chivalry. With his legal background he would have enjoyed explaining how an ancient kingdom was governed. Most children would be bored by this diversion from an exciting story, but Sophia was enthralled.

Sophia was taught at home by her parents until she was 8 years old. Then, late in 1848, she was sent to her first boarding school, which was kept by 'Miss B'. On 24 November Miss B wrote to Mrs Jex-Blake:

Sophy is a dear child, shewing advancement in her studies, and often delighting me by a rectitude of principle emanating, I trust 'from the Father of lights'. A little native wildness (and that gradually softening down) together with the want of promptitude in setting about her duties, are the chief obstacles that could be picked out from a much longer list of things most prized by an earnest teacher. I have often thought of your wish that she should learn the Latin grammar, and quite agree with your view of its probable advantage; but I am afraid of breaking down in the long and short syllables. . . . For the next few months it appears to me nothing will be lost by our present system, in which I find parsing to be generally a subject of interest.[8]

But less than two months later Miss B was writing that other commitments made it impossible for her to keep Sophia as one of her pupils. In the next eight years Sophia changed boarding schools six times, sometimes going back to a school she had attended previously. Several of her teachers became very fond of her, and welcomed her back each time, but before long they would need a rest from her vigorous presence.

In the mid-nineteenth century governesses and the proprietors of girls' schools were expected to train their pupils to be ladylike, pious and 'accomplished'. The accomplishments that mothers approved, because they enhanced the marriage prospects of their daughters, consisted of a superficial knowledge of English literature and history, a smattering of French, and the ability to sketch, embroider and sing or play the piano. It was also important for a girl to have a straight back, good deportment and an eye for fashion.

Sophia learned quickly and hungered for much more knowledge than her teachers could provide, so she felt frustrated when they tried to fill her time with such trivial activities. She really needed the kind of education boys received – challenging classwork relieved by the rough-and-tumble of outdoor games. This was the life her brother Thomas William was then enjoying at Rugby School, but girls' schools were conducted very differently. Most had only a dozen or so pupils whose ages ranged from 8 to 18 years, so opportunities for friendship were limited. The teachers were 'impoverished gentlewomen', who were themselves so poorly educated that they had only a meagre store of knowledge to impart to their pupils. There was also a generally held belief that outdoor games, while beneficial for boys, were somehow harmful to girls. The only exercise permitted to pupils of most girls' schools was an occasional walk in the neighbourhood of the school. Suitably bonnetted and gloved, the girls walked two-by-two in crocodile formation, accompanied by a mistress who kept a watchful eye on her charges and made sure that there were no lapses in decorum.

Repression and boredom sometimes caused Sophia to vent her feelings in ways that disturbed the smooth running of the school. When in this mood she played practical jokes on the other girls and exasperated her teachers with her impertinence. One of her fellow pupils, Lucy Portal, later recalled the two sides of her personality:

> Being the junior of Sophy, as we always called her, she and I were not much in touch, though I never forgot her, for she had a strong personality, and was so clever – in fact, far above our schoolmistress in natural intelligence, and she made a lasting impression on those with whom she associated. Whenever I heard her name in after life the vision of a young capable girl who asked questions that bewildered her governess rose before me.
>
> One day when we were walking on the 'Downs' with an assistant governess in the rear, Sophy saw a large stone by the wayside and seated herself on it. 'What do you mean by this?' said the governess. 'I am tired and must rest,' replied Sophy. 'Get up at once,' said Miss –; 'Do you suppose we are all going to wait your pleasure in this way?' 'Impossible to do what is beyond one's capacity,' was the rejoinder, and threats had no effect. At last Miss – lost her temper and said 'Sophy, distinctly understand that if you do not get up, I shall leave you here, and send a policeman to fetch you,' 'Ah,' said Sophy, 'that is a kind thought. I am sure he would prove of great assistance to me. But could you manage to procure *two* policemen, for I don't believe one would be able to carry me, and two might do so.' I need not say that the battle of words was soon over after that.[9]

At one of her schools the pupils were asked to write frank commentaries on each other. One girl wrote: 'Sophy is certainly excessively clever but unfortunately knows it, and makes a point of showing it off upon every possible occasion. She is truthfulness itself and can really be trusted. Very passionate but very penitent afterwards. Affectionate.'[10]

Years later another contemporary recalled her memories of Sophia. After mentioning her tactlessness and quick temper she continued: 'And yet there was always something loveable with it all. She came bounding into a room, bringing with her an atmosphere of gaiety and glee that is indescribable.'[11]

From Miss B's school she went to one kept by a Mrs Teed and her daughter. She had several sojourns at each of these schools, and both Miss B and Mrs Teed continued to write to her when her schooldays were over. They probably realized that while Sophia was a 'difficult' pupil her own life was not as untroubled as it at first appeared. Mrs Jex-Blake's health was never robust, but it was particularly poor during Sophia's adolescence. There is no evidence that she had any serious physical illness, her symptoms being more suggestive of neurasthenia. Severe headaches, weakness and fainting spells, which were brought on or aggravated by the slightest emotional disturbance, would confine her to her bed for days or weeks at a time. The rest of the family would then have to tiptoe about the house and speak in whispers. The two older children managed to comply with these restrictions, but Sophia was unable to rein in her high spirits for long. Soon there would be a stormy scene, after which she would be banished back to school. It was shortly after such a crisis that Mrs Jex-Blake wrote one of many letters in which she reveals her capacity for self-pity.

> I received your letter, and very glad we were to hear of your safe arrival, – but, my own child, I could have cried over your words. They were nice and affectionate, but *the very opposite of your acts.* . . . Either my child means what she writes or she does not. Your conduct completely contradicts your assertions. More sad and foolish behaviour than yours it is difficult to imagine. You behaved so ill that I doubt if I could have borne another day without being laid on a bed of sickness, and I might never have recovered. Your ever being with us again for three weeks at a time is *quite out of the question* till you have the good sense to understand (as other children of your age do) that to be happy and comfortable and to enable me in my weak state to have you at all, you must be *good.* When you seem really to feel how ill you have behaved, we will some time hence have you home for a week, and if I find you keep your word (which you do not now) we will have you home very often; and Papa says that he shall then think that he can never do enough to make you very very happy; but you now destroy your happiness and my health, and the medical men will *not allow* us to be together. Think of your great folly and sin, my dear child.[12]

Each year Sophia looked forward eagerly to the long summer holidays, which the family usually spent in the country. In 1849 they went to the Lake District, the following year to Scotland. Sometimes they stayed in North Wales, at Bettws-y-Coed, where they owned a house. These holidays gave Sophia a taste of the free outdoor life she could not experience at any other time. She enjoyed the long walks on mountain paths, and carriage rides, when she could sometimes take the reins and improve her already considerable skill as a driver.

In 1854 the family holiday was cancelled; not only did Mrs Jex-Blake have a prolonged episode of her usual malady, but Caroline was seriously ill with a fever. Sophia was kept at school for a whole year during which, apart from one or two brief visits by her father, her only contact with the family was by letter. With desperate eagerness she looked forward to the next summer holiday, which was to be at Bettws-y-Coed. But as the holiday time approached, letters from her parents plunged her into anxiety. They suggested that she might not be allowed to share the holiday for fear that she would disturb her mother. In her diary she recorded how she learned of their final decision:

Thursday, May 24th (1855) My answer was to come about Wales. When I got my letter I prayed God to help me to bear it, for I was nearly sure it would be a refusal, and I was quite prepared for it and determined to keep my promise not to worry about it. I put my letter in my pocket and ran away from them all. Then I burst it open and read, 'Daddy and I have such a strong wish you should see Wales, and it is truly painful to deny you such a pleasure.' There, thought I, but I had expected it and didn't feel so dreadfully disappointed. Then I read on and oh, I found it *was not* so, that I should go. Oh, I got so excited and half began to cry. Then came Mummy's caution not to be excited, but it was impossible. Dropped down there and thanked God. Oh, then I trust He has granted my prayer. Glory to God in the highest. Oh, I was so thankful.[13]

It was doubly hard on the girl that at this time her own health was not good. She suffered from recurrent episodes of joint pains and weakness of the limbs. Her governesses took her to consult several doctors, but none made a definite diagnosis. In her diary Sophia mentions that at times she felt 'a great shortness and pain in taking long breaths', and that some irregularity of her heartbeat had been noticed. It is possible that she was suffering from rheumatic fever, which could have had serious long-term consequences. Yet her mother, preoccupied with her own health, was content to leave her sick daughter in the care of the governesses at her boarding school.

It would be wrong to conclude that Mrs Jex-Blake did not greatly care for her troublesome younger daughter. If she had a favourite among her three children, that favourite was Sophia. She was proud of her son, who achieved first-class honours at Oxford in 1853 and 1855. She approved of her older daughter, who was serenely supporting the work of the Church and never caused her parents any anxiety. But deep within Mrs Jex-Blake there was a spark of the same current that electrified Sophia. In the mother it had long been denied, but it enabled her to love her daughter more than ever, just when she was reproaching her most severely. Sophia probably sensed this. Even during her unhappiest times her affection for her mother never wavered. She accepted that her banishment from home was reasonable and was caused entirely by her own thoughtlessness.

Illustration 5. 13 Sussex Square, Brighton, Sussex. The family home during Sophia's later childhood and adolescence.

Late in 1851 the Jex-Blake family moved from Hastings to Sussex Square, Brighton.[14] Sophia left Miss B's care for the second time and went to a boarding school near her new home. Here she remained for two years, until once again her parents were asked to take her away. This time the fault may not have been entirely Sophia's, as there is some evidence that the teachers at this school were more inflexible than most. She returned temporarily to Mrs Teed; then, in August 1854, she was placed at a boarding school in Notting

Hill. This had a higher academic standard than any of her previous schools and was more suited to her needs. Sophia was delighted to be introduced to the study of algebra, and to find that she had a flair for mathematics. She took pleasure in devising problems for her friends and family to solve. Her sister Caroline, now a young lady of twenty, did not share her enthusiasm for mathematics. Caroline wrote: 'Many thanks for your letters and numerous sums; I think the latter are rather overwhelming to me. I think I ought to have a little more instruction when you come, so please don't send me any more at present.'[15]

Sophia remained at the Notting Hill school for nearly two years, working hard and enjoying her studies, despite the emotional problems associated with her mother's continued ill health. Then, for reasons that have not been recorded, she was taken away from the Notting Hill school and sent to one in Brighton. Here there was little attempt at serious teaching, and boredom made her at times depressed and introspective. She was rapidly maturing into a woman with a depth of insight that surpassed that of her teachers. This was demonstrated when they discussed with her the matter of her forthcoming confirmation. She wrote to her mother for advice:

This subject of confirmation has come up again, and I really must say that I am positively shocked at the way it is settled and talked about. It is 'How old are you?' 'Does your Papa wish you to be confirmed?' and never, 'Are you fit to be?' or 'Do you really wish it?' It is just as if it were a history lecture to be attended. I really think it is wicked. Miss H. took it for granted that I should be and stuck down my name. I said, 'No thank you, Miss H.,' to her great indignation. I assured her you wished me to do exactly as I liked on such a subject, which she did not choose to believe at all.

But I really do wish it, Mother. I think it would help me, and I long to take the Lord's Supper with you. Will you let me be confirmed from home? – that is, spend the actual day of confirmation at home, so that I may think of something besides how I am dressed and how good or bad an examination I passed, on the day I take those solemn promises on myself. . . .

I think I should have preferred waiting another year, but I don't think I can quite expect God's blessing on His child while I defer owning myself such.

Oh, Mother, Mother, how I wish you were here, but it seems as if He had expressly left me to myself each time confirmation has been spoken of. I do not think you will refuse either the permission I ask, or your blessing on the step I take, – unless it would be too great an excitement for you, – though it need not be, for you need not go with me.[16]

At the end of 1857 Sophia left boarding school for the last time. She knew that she had to find a useful vocation, but at this stage she had no idea what it would be. She had begun to write a book based on her experience at Mrs Teed's school, to test her ability as a writer. Her diary records her uncertainty:

1857. Dec. 17th. Thursday. Came home for good. For good? Who can tell? Oh, what would I give to look forward ten, aye five, short years, and see what I shall be. Just 18; half my life at school. . . .
Well, shall I be a great authoress as my day and night dreams prompt me to hope? . . . Shall I ever be a happy wife and mother? Shall I ere ten years, or half ten years have passed, be *dust*? . . . I sometimes think so.[17]

Three weeks later she questioned herself again:

I must begin to write again if I don't mean to lose the knack. . . . I want partly to write for the money, – now why, I wonder? Honestly, why? I have plenty of everything. In a handsome if not luxurious home, 6 servants all much at my orders, lots of rides, a most loving Mother, tender father, almost every wish gratified, £30 a year clear, and lots of presents, almost at will – why I should write for money unless I am avaricious or spendthrift I don't exactly know. Partly for the *pride* of earning it, – of knowing myself as well able to earn my bread as my inferiors.[18]

But writing did not seem to be her vocation. The news of the death of her friend Mrs Teed made her lose interest in the book and it was never finished. Most of the young women she knew expected to marry, but Sophia thought this was probably not her destiny:

Mother and I were talking about my marrying, – the chances pro and con. I said I did not fancy I should every marry, for I thought I should require too many qualities to meet in the man I could think of as my husband, for it to be likely that I should ever meet such a paragon who could be willing to marry me.
Let me see; the indispensables are I think: – A perfect gentleman, a sincere Christian, a liberal-minded broad-churchman; a lofty intellect to which it would be a pride to bow, a firm will which it would be a pleasure to submit to and concur in; a nice-looking fellow, – for I *could* not be happy with one whose face I could not love and admire in beauty of expression if not of form, and one whose means combined with mine would lift us above genteel poverty at least.[19]

At times she became severely depressed, doubting that she was capable of loving anyone for long, and fearing that she might become insane or meet an early death. Boredom was probably the cause of her unhappiness. She was saved by the visit of two Norfolk cousins she had not met before. Elinor and

Sarah Jex-Blake were guests at Sussex Square for several weeks, and their bright young company was just the tonic she needed. Sophia then visited Norfolk, staying first with Ellie and Sarah, and then with other relations on both sides of the family. She returned to Brighton two months later, refreshed in spirit and delighted that Ellie was to join the family holiday party at Bettws-y-Coed.

The Welsh holiday that year was an unqualified success. As well as enjoying the usual pleasures of the country, the young women interested themselves in the little school for the local children. There was no teacher in the village; the cobbler gave the children lessons whenever he could spare the time. The three holiday-makers gladly spent part of each day in taking classes at the school. Their efforts were greatly appreciated, and they enjoyed the experience. It was probably this holiday that implanted in Sophia's mind the idea that teaching could be her life's work.

Notes

1. *Burke's Landed Gentry*, 1972.
2. W. Rye, *A History of the Family of Cubitt*, Norwich: Samuel Butler, 1873.
3. *The London Gazette*, 25 August 1837.
4. *Encyclopaedia Britannica*, 1959 edn, vol. 13, 874Ab.
5. M. Todd, *The Life of Sophia Jex-Blake*, London: Macmillan, 1918, p. 5.
6. ibid., p. 7.
7. ibid., p. 7.
8. ibid., p. 12.
9. ibid., p. 26.
10. ibid., p. 33.
11. ibid., p. 33.
12. ibid., p. 25.
13. ibid., p. 45.
14. The terraces in Sussex Square were the work of the master builder Thomas Cubitt (1788–1858). Cubitt also built terraces in Belgrave and Tavistock Squares, London, and carried out extensions to Buckingham Palace. It is probably a coincidence that the Jex-Blake family lived in one of his houses, as there is no evidence that he was directly related to Mrs Jex-Blake.
15. Todd, op. cit., p. 38.
16. ibid., p. 47.
17. ibid., p. 52.
18. ibid., p. 54.
19. ibid., p. 56.

2

The student in London

When Sophia talked of becoming a teacher some of her relations were astonished, not at the occupation she chose, but at her intention to take up work of any kind. Why need she bother, when her father was perfectly willing to keep her in comfort? In any case, she would soon be married, and then her husband would provide for her. Mrs Jex-Blake used to say that when she was a girl the question mothers asked themselves was not *whether* their daughters would marry, but *whom* they would marry. Sophia was more realistic when she calculated that there was a good chance that she would remain single. Women outnumbered men, and not all men felt that marriage was *their* inevitable fate. Population statistics for England and Wales in the year 1851 showed that, of women between the ages of 35 and 44 years, almost 25 per cent were either unmarried or widowed.[1] Thus, there were many women who had to find something else to do with their lives, even if financial need did not force them to work for a wage.

In earlier times women had been better able to cope with adversity. Many craftsmen and artisans had worked at home, where wives and daughters could learn their skills and share their work. Thus, the womenfolk were often able to carry on the family business when illness or death overcame the male bread-winner. For instance, Hester Bateman (1709–94), who was the wife of a silver-smith, was widowed when she was middle-aged. Not only was she able to provide for herself and her family, but Hester Bateman became one of Britain's most famous silversmiths.[2]

Then the Industrial Revolution moved crafts and industry out of the home and into the factory, where women could not participate as equals. Working-class women could find employment only as unskilled factory hands or as domestic servants. The only respectable occupation for middle-class women was that of governess or school mistress. For this work they were paid a pittance; often board and lodging were considered ample reward for their services. They could hardly demand more, since the number of women seeking such work always greatly exceeded the number of vacancies, and the qualifications required were minimal.

This was certainly not the vocation that Sophia had in mind. Her own unhappy experiences as a schoolgirl had made her aware of the need for a much higher standard of education for girls. This would be attainable only if female teachers were themselves well educated and trained for their profession. Girls also needed larger, well-equipped schools, more like those provided for boys. But before she could begin to plan such a school Sophia *needed to* broaden her own education and gain teaching experience.

She first heard of Queen's College in the spring of 1858; it was then that she met Miss Ada Benson, the sister of the future Archbishop of Canterbury. Miss Benson also had a sister, who was attending Queen's College in London, and thoroughly enjoying the experience. Summer holidays interrupted the friendship, but when Sophia and Miss Benson met again in the autumn they continued their discussion of Queen's College. Sophia wrote for a prospectus.

She learned that the College was originally associated with the Governesses' Benevolent Institution, a charitable organization founded in 1841 to assist unemployed governesses.[3] The Institution's committee of management realized that the possession of formal qualifications would improve the status and financial prospects of women seeking employment as teachers, so in 1847 they founded Queen's College. Here 'ladies over the age of twelve years' could attend courses in a variety of subjects, which would be taught at advanced secondary-school level. Certificates of proficiency would be issued to those who passed the examinations held at the end of each course.

The syllabus was planned by a committee under the chairmanship of the Reverend Frederick Denison Maurice, Professor of English Literature and Modern History at King's College, London. All of the dozen or so lecturers recruited for Queen's were distinguished scholars. Although the fees were modest, there was nothing second-rate about the education now being offered to women. The College was in Harley Street, next door to the Governesses' Benevolent Institution, but five years after it was founded its administration was separated from that of the Institution. Its facilities were to be available to all women, not just those who intended to be governesses.

Sophia was convinced that Queen's College exactly suited her needs, but it was with some difficulty that she persuaded her parents to allow her to enrol for the term beginning early in October 1858. Then she had to look for accommodation in London, as the College did not have a residence. Several women who were already attending the College provided the ideal solution by inviting her to share their 'digs'.

When the term began Sophia found that there were some three hundred women enrolled, but most of them were taking only one or two subjects. She herself had a full programme of seven – mathematics, English, French, history, natural philosophy and astronomy, theology and Church history. In some subjects there were classes, as well as the formal lectures; in the classes students could ask questions and have difficult points explained by their teachers. Lectures and classes were held every day, except Sunday. They began at ten in the morning and continued until three in the afternoon, without a break for lunch. Sophia had to work harder than she ever had before, but she revelled in her new life. She was quite ecstatic when she wrote in her diary, a few days after the term began:

> Very delicious it is to be here. 'Oh, if there be an Elysium on earth, it is this, it is this!' I am inclined to say I am as happy as a queen. Work and independence! What can be more charming? Really perfection. So delicious in the present, what will it be to look back upon?[4]

Several weeks later she was writing more soberly, but still with complete satisfaction:

> I am so *thoroughly* happy in this way of life, hardly any other could suit me as well. So independent, yet so busy, so comfortable, yet not luxurious. Plenty, yet no superfluity. It is certainly *very* kind of the dear 'old folks' to let me have it so, and very wise. I should never, at least at present, have settled at home. I should have been ever longing for independence and work, and now I have all I want and may yet do good. Having, as Maurice would say, found my centre, other things will, I trust, grow up around it. I trust most fervently I may yet be a real comfort to my precious Mother and dear kind Father.[5]

The main reason for Sophia's happiness was that at last she was being taught by people who understood the true purpose of education. So many of her former governesses and teachers had thought their job well done if their pupils could recite by heart large sections of a textbook. At Queen's College learning by heart was actively discouraged; students were expected to think and reason for themselves. The opinions they expressed in their essays had to be their own, and not merely copied from a book. At the College's Inaugural Lecture Maurice had said:

> The teachers of a school may aim merely to impart information; the teachers of a college must lead their pupils to the apprehension of principles. . . . When I speak of leading our pupils to the study of principles, I think I mean something as nearly as possible the opposite of introducing them to an encyclopaedia of knowledge. . . . Study is not worth much if it is not busy about the roots of things.[6]

This was still the policy of the College in Sophia's time.

Half-way through the first term her contentment was shattered when she had a disagreement with one of her fellow lodgers. What began as a trivial dispute became serious when it disturbed the peace of the others. One of the disputants had to leave, and Sophia, the newcomer, was the one obliged to move. For several weeks she searched unsuccessfully for suitable lodgings. For the first time in her life she encountered dirty houses, drunken landladies and unsavoury fellow lodgers. Her knowledge of the world broadened rapidly. Then at last she found rooms well suited to her needs, and was able to feel safe and comfortable again.

Doubtless Sophia brought this trouble on herself, but she also extricated herself without assistance. Her parents felt concerned, but they did not come to London to help her. In one letter her mother wrote, 'I wish I were near, yet I don't think I could be of real help; it is not in my way.' Throughout their married life Mr and Mrs Jex-Blake generously assisted people reduced to living in conditions like those that had shocked Sophia. But while reaching out to help others they were able to remain within their own safe environment. They never had to come to grips with the ugliness themselves. Their sturdy, practical daughter was probably better able to survive the hazards of the city than they were.

Another episode that occurred during her first few months at Queen's College also reflected the difference in outlook between Sophia and her parents. The College offered tutorials to small groups of students who needed to correct deficiencies in their basic education before they could benefit from the lectures. Well-educated governesses would have been capable of acting as tutors, but they were not easy to find; the position of mathematics tutor had been vacant for months when Sophia joined the College. Because of her unusual proficiency in this subject she was offered the position, although she would be attending lectures as a student. If the class numbered four or more students the tutor was paid a small salary. Sophia was delighted to accept; it was an honour, and the salary would be welcome. Her father gave her a generous allowance, but it seemed to disappear rapidly. She wrote in her diary:

> In actual money I have about £200 a year and in money's worth another £100. Therefore I conclude about £300 a year to be about the happy medium of wealth for a single woman. Dear generous old Father! Few would, I think, give so much in so good a way to their children. I believe as regards happiness and satisfaction never was money better, if never more kindly, spent. I must try to pay back the 'labour of love,' and 'requite my parents,' dear, dear old things! Bless them both.
> I really believe as regards money I am honestly *quite contented*. I wish for no more. And as this is, they say, a somewhat remarkable fact, I specially note it down. Yet it sounds ludicrously tempting to reply to myself, Contented! Shame on you if you were not, I think. Yet for actual pocket money, I am horribly pinched just now, – only 9s. 9d. till next quarter, – nearly four weeks hence.[7]

To be paid for her work would prove that she was performing a useful and valued service, and this meant even more to her than the money.

21

Her parents were astonished at their daughter's rapid promotion at the College, but it was only after the exchange of several letters that her father realized that she might receive a salary. This he could not condone. He wrote:

> I heartily admire your readiness to turn your talents to good account, and employ them in a way so clearly beneficial to others, but believe me that if you take money payment, you will make a sad mistake, debase your standing, and place yourself in a position that people in general, including many relations and friends, will never *as long as you live* understand otherwise than as greatly to your discredit. You would be considered mean and illiberal, – tho' I am sure you are neither the one or the other – accepting wages that belong to a class beneath you in social rank, and which (it would be said) you had no right, under any circumstances to appropriate to yourself.[8]

Sophia's reply was long and impassioned. She pointed out that she would not be depriving anyone else of the money because the position had for long remained unfilled. She continued:

> You as a man, did your work and received your payment, and no one thought it any degradation, but a fair exchange. Why should the difference of my sex alter the laws of right and honour? Tom is doing on a large scale what I do on a small one, – I cannot recognize any fundamental difference in the matter. I cannot say 'I do not want this money, I have no use for it,' for in truth, tho' having an ample and generous allowance I should have plenty of use for it. Then there is the honest, and I believe, perfectly justifiable pride of *earning*. Did you not feel this when you received your first salary? Why should I be deprived of it? Then again you offer to give me the money if I refuse to take it from the College. But this would be a wholly false position, to get credit for generosity in refusing what I yet receive. I could not do this. In that case I must say to the Dean, not 'I am willing to work without payment,' but 'My Father prefers that I should receive payment from *him*, not from the College,' and I think the Dean would think us both ridiculous, or at least foolish.[9]

To and fro the letters went, neither writer convincing the other. After a week of debate Sophia offered, as a compromise, to forego payment for the first term only. Her father acquiesced. In the event, her class did not exceed three members during that first term, so she sacrificed nothing. The tone of the correspondence suggests that father and daughter quite enjoyed the battle of words. Mr Jex-Blake never threatened to suspend Sophia's allowance as a means of forcing her to comply with his wishes, not did she ever seem to fear that he would act in this way. Perhaps he realized that the world he had known was fast disappearing, to be replaced by one in which women like Sophia would play an important role.

Sophia did not allow these minor problems to distract her from her studies. Her teachers reported favourably on her progress, and she continued to enjoy her work as much as she had in the first few weeks. But work was not her only pleasure. She formed lasting friendships with a number of her fellow students and also strengthened her association with the Cordery family of Hampstead. The Corderys and the Jex-Blakes were old friends, but in 1857 Sophia's brother Thomas had married Henrietta Cordery, thus linking the two families even more closely. Sophia was made so welcome at Hampstead that she felt as though she had a second home there.

She also enjoyed the personal freedom that went with her new life. Although the administrators of Queen's College were conservative enough to provide a chaperone (a 'Lady Visitor') at each of the lectures, the students made their way to and from the College without such protection. They even went to theatres and operas unchaperoned! Sophia's parents did not approve of this, but did not forbid her from joining in. Sophia felt that as a matter of principle she must be a member of some of the theatre parties, but she was rather disappointed in the performances of some of the leading actors and did not become an avid theatre-goer.

Her cousins Ellie and Sarah, who were still living at home in Norfolk, were greatly intrigued with the accounts they received of Sophia's activities in London. Ellie wrote:

> You seem to be spending rather a jolly time of it, but still it seems to me rather queer that a lot of girls should walk about London when and where they please. I don't think you would come to any harm, but I am sure there are many that would.[10]

When Ellie soon afterwards visited Sophia she was favourably impressed with the changes she observed in her cousin. She wrote to Sarah:

> When I first saw her that evening, I thought she did not look so well, but since then I think the contrary – She is much thinner, but in such good spirits, and so happy. I think she quite likes everyone to know that she has been made mathematical tutor, for it is considered a great honour.[11]

In July 1859 Sophia took the examinations that marked the end of her first year as a student. She acquitted herself well, passing in all subjects 'with great credit'. Her certificate to this effect was signed by three of the College's most distinguished teachers – F.D. Maurice, E.H. Plumptre and R.C. Trench.

After her summer holiday Sophia returned to London. She resumed her post as tutor at Queen's College and also became an unpaid teacher at several organizations providing education for impoverished women and children.

One of these was the Society for Promoting the Employment of Women, founded by Jessie Boucherett in 1858. Miss Boucherett had observed that many destitute women were unable to obtain work as shop assistants or clerks because they lacked a knowledge of simple arithmetic; they could not calculate change for a small cash transaction or add up a column of figures. With a little educational assistance many learned very quickly and showed good business aptitude. The Society also helped to find employment for these women.

Sophia's work brought her into contact with many cases of hardship, and she could never turn a deaf ear to a cry for help. She would give practical aid to a woman stressed by overwork, sometimes sending the sufferer to complete her recovery at her parents' home in Brighton. This was one of Sophia's interests that her parents understood and shared. Her friends also knew that if they called on her for help when they were in any kind of difficulty she would respond at once, no matter how hard-pressed she was at the time. Sophia once said of herself, 'I think I am very like a life-boat – valueless in itself, yet useful enough in saving better things alive.'

In January 1860 Sophia found a new friend. Miss Octavia Hill came to dine with her and afterwards gave her a lesson in book-keeping. Sophia recorded the event in her diary and summed up her guest in a few words, 'Nice, sensible, clever. Very good worker, I expect.' By the time the book-keeping course was finished, a few weeks later, they had become firm friends.

Octavia Hill was only a year older than Sophia, but vastly more experienced in surviving hardship.[12] She was one of five sisters who had been brought up by their mother and maternal grandfather, Dr Southwood Smith, since their father, James Hill, had suffered a mental breakdown from which he never fully recovered. Their mother, Caroline Hill, was a highly intelligent woman who, before her marriage, had studied and written on the subject of education. Although the family was constantly short of money, Mrs Hill was thus able to give her daughters a first-rate education. She was ahead of her time in believing that girls should be free to enjoy outdoor games and to devise their own hobbies and amusements. In the semi-rural environment of Finchley, where Octavia and her sisters spent the greater part of their childhood, it was possible for them to enjoy this freedom and to be unaware that they were poor.

Octavia knew that her grandfather spent much of his time working to improve the living conditions of the city's poor, but she had never seen slums and could not fully understand his concern. Then, when Octavia was 13, Mrs Hill was offered the position of manager of the Ladies' Co-operative Guild in London. The Guild had been founded by the Reverend Frederick Maurice, who was also the founder of Queen's College. Its main purpose was to help needy women find employment. The manager's position was a resident one, so when Mrs Hill accepted it she and her daughters exchanged the wholesome environment of Finchley for the starkness of a London slum.

Octavia's carefree childhood ended with the move to London. At 13 she

Illustration 6. Octavia Hill (1838–1912). Sophia's views on women's role in society were influenced by her brief friendship with Octavia. Portrait by Edward Clifford. (Reproduced by permission of the Ruskin Gallery, Collection of the Guild of St George, Sheffield.)

herself became a teacher in the Ladies' Co-operative Guild. The following year she was asked to take charge of a ragged school for poor children.[13] Here the children were taught to make toy furniture, which they could sell to help support themselves. Although still little more than a child herself, Octavia became a second mother to the children at her school.

When she was 17 she met the writer John Ruskin. He came to inspect the work of the Guild and was impressed with Octavia's artistic ability. He suggested that, to improve her skills and as a means of earning some money, she should paint for him a series of copies of famous paintings. They would be used to illustrate a book he was preparing for publication. So, in addition to her teaching, Octavia committed herself to a heavy burden of art work.

In 1856 a deep rift developed in the managing committee of the Ladies' Co-operative Guild. Maurice's religious views were not as orthodox as those of some influential committee members, who were prepared to close the Guild rather than work with him. Mrs Hill resigned out of loyalty to Maurice, shortly before the Guild ceased to exist. She lost not only her salary, but also her home. She returned to her father's home in Finchley and her daughters were scattered. Octavia remained in London, working long hours each day at her painting, as well as continuing to manage the ragged school. Fatigue began to undermine her health; she developed a severe, debilitating fever, which forced her to rest for several months.

When she recovered, Octavia persuaded her mother and sister Emily that the three of them should pool their resources and live together in London. With hard work and improvisation they transformed a very small house into a comfortable home. Here Mrs Hill was again able to earn by teaching, and Emily could study at Queen's College, where she had been awarded a scholarship. Octavia resumed her painting for Ruskin. She also worked at another of Maurice's projects, the Working Women's College, where she was both a teacher and the secretary.

It was at this stage of her life that Octavia Hill met Sophia. Perhaps it was inevitable that the two young women should be strongly attracted to each other, for although they came from very different backgrounds their lives were converging on a single path. Each was searching for a worthy cause to which she could devote all her ability, energy and courage; service to humanity would be an essential part of her life's work, but the satisfaction of personal achievement was almost as important. They were both still without a clear sense of direction, and were therefore subject to periods of self-doubt and depression. At such times an understanding confidante was sorely needed. Their friendship filled this need; Sophia's exuberance and vigour complemented Octavia's reserve and sensitivity.

Soon they were enjoying outings together; visits to art galleries and an occasional day in the country were a welcome relief from the routine of work. They shared their books and their knowledge, each giving the other lessons in subjects in which her own studies were more advanced. Sophia's generosity impressed Octavia, who described her new friend in a letter to one of her sisters:

> I have been giving some book-keeping lessons to Miss J-B. She is a bright, spirited, brave, generous young lady, living alone, in true bachelor style. It took me three nights to teach her, and she begged me to come to dinner each time. She has a friend who is killing herself by hard work to support her younger sisters. I gather she would gladly give her friend help, for she speaks most sadly of the 'modern fallacy' 'that the money must be earned.' She thinks it might be given when people are dear friends: she says they've given the most precious thing and what difference can a little money make?[14]

When Sophia went home to Brighton for Easter, Octavia accompanied her. Mr and Mrs Jex-Blake approved of their daughter's friend, of whom they had already heard a great deal. The success of this visit prompted Sophia to invite Octavia to join her and her sister Caroline on their summer holiday at Bettws-y-Coed; Sophia's diary records that they were both deeply moved, 'She sunk her head on my lap silently, raised it in tears, and then such a kiss!'

The three young women had a memorable holiday. The Welsh mountain scenery was new to Octavia, who thoroughly enjoyed the long walks and country drives. They also gave lessons to the pupils at the school and, as the holiday came to an end, they held a party for the children. On her return to London Sophia wrote to her mother:

> All over, darling, now, and such a happy time without a single blot I never remember in my life. Everything has been better than any anticipation of it. We have done everything we wanted to do. We have been everywhere and have had no mischance, no annoyance of any kind. Octa looks five years younger, and as bright as a sunbeam. And I am in so thoroughly happy a state of mind as hardly to know myself. I really almost think I should be good-tempered now. We came home by Llangollen on Saturday, 40 miles coach and 194 miles rail. Not a bad journey for one day. We went up that morning to your high mound. The view was glorious. I took poor old Ellen Jones some squills for her cough, but she looks very ill indeed. She sent so very much love to you, and wished she had something to send you.
>
> The treat came off excellently on Thursday. It was grand fun to see Octa playing with the children. . . . Well, how strange it is to find this all over, and probably never to return. . . . I cannot say I am glad our tour is over, for I do believe I was never so happy for so long in my whole life, but neither can I say I am sorry to see dear old London again, – I am sure I could come back to no other place – as a place – with near so much pleasure. . . .

Just fancy Octavia's energy, – after that tremendous journey not reaching home till 10.30, she was off to Lincoln's Inn at 7 a.m. the next morning for the early communion, and went again, and I with her in the afternoon. Her mother and sister were so delighted with her account of all her doings, and a glorious one she gave certainly. I had tea with them last night. Goodbye, my darling, for the present. Not so very long now, I trust, before we meet.[15]

In September Mrs Hill learned that two of her daughters, Florence and Miranda, were returning from Italy. She wanted them with her, but there was not enough room in her small house. Sophia heard the discussions and suggested a solution – she could give up her own lodgings and share a larger house with Mrs Hill and her daughters; she would gladly contribute rather more than her share of the expenses. At first Mrs Hill and Octavia were reluctant to accept her offer, but her enthusiasm persuaded them.

Sophia's parents had their misgivings. The move would entail a large amount of work, and they knew their daughter well enough to foresee that she would drive herself relentlessly. They also knew that under these circumstances she could become short-tempered and 'difficult'. They did not object to the extra expense; they even offered to send their trusty maid Alice to help with the work. So the plan began to take shape.

Mrs Hill and Octavia, who were temporarily out of London, left the task of finding a suitable house to Sophia. She found that the rents being asked were higher than they had expected, especially in the locality favoured by Mrs Hill. Octavia wrote to Sophia:

> Thanks for all the trouble that you are taking about the houses, I am quite ashamed it should all fall to your share. Is a Harley Street house quite out of the question? I received a letter from Mama, earnestly desiring that we should keep near the park; she would not at all like Bentinck Street. Don't weary yourself with searching. I will certainly return on Thursday (probably much before) then we will look together again. . . . If it would secure the Harley Street house by all means let us pay all the taxes whatever they may be. . . . Mama has an affection for Harley Street now.[16]

When an attractive large house was found, not in Harley Street but at 14 Nottingham Place, they decided to reduce the expense by letting part of the house to a lodger. The problem seemed to be solved, until Mr Jex-Blake learned that his daughter was to become one of the joint proprietors of a lodging house. He wrote at once to veto the plan:

> You cannot surely mean to take a house and let lodgings in direct opposition to your dear Mother and me. It would be quite disgraceful

and we can never consent to it. I will not believe, my dear child, with all our love for you, that you will so directly disobey us, or that Miss Hill, knowing our feelings on the subject, can be a party to it.

When you spoke of the other house, you said a lawyer was to look over the lease, and take care of the Hills, and I firmly believed, till the last few days, that you were to hire rooms. I had no more idea of your becoming a lodging-house keeper than of your keeping a shop. You cannot suppose that I would assist Miss Hill in such an exceedingly blameable transaction. I would *with real pleasure* assist her in all possible ways, . . . but no Father or Mother who love their daughter, in your position, could consent to her joining in it. I trust, dearest child, you will give up all idea of such a thing, which, once done, you would repent as long as you lived.[17]

A compromise was reached by having Sophia share the house as a lodger herself, rather than as a proprietor. Mr Jex-Blake was satisfied and considered the episode closed. But Mrs Hill had been grievously offended; evidently Sophia's parents thought that their daughter was descending to a lower plane in her friendship with the Hills. She could no longer feel any pleasure in Sophia's company.

Octavia returned to London and together the two friends set about making the house ready for occupation. Emily wrote to Miranda:

Ockey is immensely busy, and quite in her element, buying things, reading over schedules of fixtures and examining plans and carpentering. We have not yet fixed what rooms we are to keep; it must depend on the lodgers. . . . We are close to the Park, so the air is very good, and we are about ten minutes' walk from Queen's College. The back of the house is delightfully quiet, because it looks out on Marylebone Church Schools.[18]

By mid-December they were able to move in, although there was still much to be done in the house. They all had other commitments as well – Emily to her studies at Queen's College, and the others to their work as teachers. When two of the sisters became ill, the burden of work was even greater. Fatigue made them impatient with each other, so the peace of the household was frequently disturbed by brief, but sharp, disagreements. It was often Octavia who played the role of peacemaker but, unfortunately, she was also the least robust. In May 1861 she had reached the limit of her endurance when she wrote, some-what melodramatically:

I am like a broken thing, thin and pale, with aching back and hands . . . well enough till I feel or do anything, then feeling like a shadow, a queer feeling as if a slight touch would push me over the brink, however, it is no use talking about it, no one knows but there may be some years of life for me, at any rate, my way is clear, to rest if I can, not to frighten myself anyway.[19]

Octavia's release came shortly after this when she received a request to stay with an old friend, Mary Harris, who lived in Cumberland. Miss Harris was recovering from a serious illness, and needed help and companionship in her convalescence. Having previously thought herself indispensable at Nottingham Place, Octavia now went away for a holiday that was to last for five months.

The household became even more troubled in her absence. Despite her enlightened views on education, Mrs Hill still regarded herself as the matriarch who had to be consulted and obeyed at all times. Her daughters were accustomed to this, but Sophia's independent spirit rebelled. Octavia received numerous letters from her mother, her sisters and Sophia, all calling on her to return home and restore peace. But she was reluctant to leave the haven of Mary Harris's home. In July she wrote to Sophia:

> I hold myself prepared to come when it seems right, sure to be given strength to do my duty, but certainly not longing for anything that will bring me again into a world of contention. I can't bear to think how pained you would be if you could know the strength of this feeling, for I know you would feel it a failure of love. I tell you all this because I am sure you will feel it in my letters, because I am sure such a cloud hurts less when frankly confessed, because I am sure such a friendship as yours and mine need not fear it, remaining untouched and immoveable, based on what can neither change nor know fear. . . . All my life long this dread and misery about even the slightest contention or estrangement has taken the form of misery, continually saying in itself, 'I can*not* bear it.' Since physical strength has left me so far this wretched dread has increased tenfold. . . .
>
> How delightfully kind and good you are to everybody. I can fancy I see you, brightly kind, good and energetic, going about among all the people, entertaining monitors, inviting my sisters to tea, giving club dinners, learning about examinations, arranging the play, talking to Miss Boucherett, delighting to plan work and holiday for them all. . . .
>
> When I have thought, as I often have, that it is probable that I may never have the strength to work any more, you cannot think how I have clung to the thought of your ever ready and powerful help and care.[20]

The situation at Nottingham Place did not improve. In October Mrs Hill virtually commanded her daughter to return home. Octavia complied, probably having already decided on the action she would take. The frail young woman who quailed at the prospect of 'even the slightest contention' now acted with remarkable resolution. She refused to discuss the problem with Sophia, declaring that their friendship was permanently ended, and that

Sophia must arrange to leave Nottingham Place. Octavia's sisters knew that the fault was not all Sophia's, but they could only watch sadly as she packed her possessions and moved to hastily secured lodgings. She could not go home to Brighton until her teaching responsibilities at Queen's College finished with the end of the term.

Sophia felt as if she had suffered a bereavement. Once she had thought that only death could end her friendship with Octavia Hill; now it was as though that death had occurred. She poured out her anguish in long letters to her mother, and sought solace in her religion. Always she would remember this as one of the unhappiest periods of her life. For nearly two months she managed to carry on with her usual activities, outwardly unchanged, although privately suffering from severe depression. Then the resilience of youth began to assert itself. On a Sunday night in mid-December she sat up until midnight making notes in her diary; when these were finished she wrote to her mother:

> Don't chide me for writing late, Mother. I must speak to you. If I could give you an idea of the peaceful, happy evening I have had – sending me to bed with a heart full of love and joy and thankfulness. No, nothing has changed in outer things. I have no other news. But perfect peace has come. I can hardly tell you how happy I am, Mother.
> I have had such a happy, holy evening with two or three of the girls. . . . And God seemed to give me such a wonderful power to help them, and I believe He has helped them. And in all – I know not how, but I wake up at their departing . . . to find that somehow God has rolled away my burden utterly.
> I had forgotten it and myself altogether, and now I can find neither. I can hardly believe in the pain and misery of the morning, it seems a dim, far-off memory.[21]

Although Sophia had regained her serenity, the sense of loss always remained. For years she clung to a faint hope that Octavia would relent and they would be reunited, but this never happened.

Both women were later to find their true vocations, which differed so greatly that their friendship probably would have weakened even if the dramatic break had not occurred. Octavia continued Dr Southwood Smith's work for the improvement of housing and social amenities for the poor. Her approach to the problem was both enlightened and business-like; the results she achieved were so striking that in later years she became a national authority on the subject.

Sophia applauded Octavia's success, although they held opposing views on some aspects of the feminist movement. As proof of her continuing regard, for many years Sophia named Octavia as a beneficiary in her will. But all this lay in the future. In the closing months of 1861 all Sophia could feel was the pain of a lost friendship. A few days before Christmas she completed her various tasks in London and gladly left the city that once had given her so much pleasure. At home in Brighton she could make fresh plans for the future.

Notes

1. B.R. Mitchell and P. Deane, *Abstract of British Historical Statistics*, Cambridge: Cambridge University Press, 1962.
2. J.P. Fallon, *The Marks of the London Goldsmiths and Silversmiths, Georgian Period (c. 1697–1837): A Guide*, New York: Arco Publishing Co., 1972.
3. E. Kaye, *A History of Queen's College, London*, London: Chatto & Windus, 1972.
4. M. Todd, *The Life of Sophia Jex-Blake*, London: Macmillan, 1918, p. 64.
5. ibid., p. 66.
6. Kaye, op. cit.
7. Todd, op. cit., p. 66.
8. ibid., p. 67.
9. ibid., p. 68.
10. ibid., p. 73.
11. ibid., p. 73.
12. E. Moberley Bell, *Life of Octavia Hill*, London: Constable, 1942.
13. These charitable institutions existed throughout England and Scotland in the first half of the nineteenth century; ragged schools rapidly disappeared after 1870, when the system of national compulsory education was introduced.
14. C.E. Maurice, *Life of Octavia Hill as Told in Her Letters*, New York and London: Macmillan, 1913.
15. Todd, op. cit., p. 86.
16. ibid., p. 89.
17. ibid., p. 88.
18. Moberley Bell, op. cit., p. 56.
19. ibid., p. 57.
20. Todd, op. cit., p. 90.
21. ibid., p. 97.

3

The student abroad

Work was usually Sophia's cure for depression, but she could not face an early return to London, with all its unhappy associations. She made enquiries about other educational opportunities for women, and was advised to go to Edinburgh. The highly successful Edinburgh Ladies' Educational Association was not established until 1868, but there were already some teachers holding classes for women, in a variety of subjects including mathematics. So early in 1862 Sophia, accompanied by her maid Alice, travelled to Edinburgh and went through the now familiar routine of finding lodgings and settling in.

The classes were profoundly disappointing. The mathematics master was incapable of teaching algebra; he was accustomed to students who had barely mastered the multiplication tables and had come to him to learn basic arithmetic. Feeling that her journey had been wasted, Sophia was about to return home when her new-found friends in Edinburgh came to her aid. She had arrived in their city almost a complete stranger, but a letter of introduction to Miss Margaret Orr and a slight acquaintance with Mrs Burn Murdoch had been enough to win her the capable support of these two ladies. They introduced her to Mr Begbie, Mr Weisse and Miss de Dreux, who agreed to give her private tuition in mathematics, German and English. These teachers were able to provide the intellectual stimulation Sophia needed and they, in turn, were delighted to have a pupil with so much ability and enthusiasm. So, after a disappointing beginning, Sophia found herself among friends and assured of a useful sojourn in Edinburgh.

The letters she exchanged with her mother from this time onward show how their relationship had improved. Sophia shared her thoughts about religion and the life that lay ahead of her. Mrs Jex-Blake's replies conveyed her concern for her daughter's wellbeing. She had come to realize the importance to the young of mental relaxation and physical exercise.

I suppose your work in Edinburgh has been very intense while it lasted, and proportionately exhausting, – and then you don't, as a schoolboy does, get any reaction the other way. You have no one to play with, *no* positive recreation. I always think the games and perpetual 'outings' in public schools such a fine arrangement; and then an Oxonian or Cantab., has his boat or his ride. My darling has positively nothing.[1]

She also appreciated the importance to Sophia's wellbeing of working for others: 'Remember, as a help, how many bless you for having sped them on their way. Your want just now is for someone to be helped and braced for usefulness.' Mr Jex-Blake offered his support for any of her efforts to help others.

In addition to studying German and her favourite mathematics, Sophia was reading more widely than she had before. She read *Jane Eyre* for the first time, and was deeply moved by the story of the gentle governess who showed courage and initiative in adversity. She defended Charlotte Brontë's novel against the criticism that it would undermine the moral standards of its readers because the heroine falls in love with a married man. Some readers were doubly shocked because the lovers are a governess and her employer; the virtue of governesses had to be above suspicion. Sophia rejected these criticisms:

How people *dare* speak ill of such a book, – I suppose they simply can't understand it. Its grand steadfastness and earnestness and purity, is something glorious. I read and re-read it as I never could another novel, and how it helps one![2]

Mrs Jex-Blake did not agree:

Well, darling, you and I must wait to talk it out about *Jane Eyre*. I shall never be able to write it out. . . . I don't at all ask a different code of morals for men and women. But I do wish a woman to be refined and pure, not because I am conventional, but because I think it essential to self-respect and dignity. . . . I don't believe high-toned governesses fall in love with their employers.[3]

In May 1862 Sophia received an interesting letter from a young woman she had previously met in London. The writer was Miss Elizabeth Garrett, and the occasion of their meeting was the first of a series of public lectures on human physiology given by the famous scientist T.H. Huxley. Sophia thought that teachers should understand basic physiology and hygiene, so she had persuaded two of the Hill sisters (probably Emily and Miranda, Octavia being then in Cumberland) to accompany her. Elizabeth Garrett and her friend Miss Drewry were the only other women in the very large audience. At the end of the lecture the women were eager to share their impressions. Elizabeth was staying at the home of her married sister, Louisa. She invited the others to walk back with her to the house in Manchester Square, so that they could continue their conversation.

That night Elizabeth wrote to her friend Emily Davies, describing the evening she had just spent, and commenting on the idiosyncrasies of her companions. Miss Drewry seemed not to understand Sophia's conversation, and the Hill sisters were shocked by Miss Drewry's radical views. Elizabeth herself was not greatly taken with the Hill sisters:

> I should like them much more readily than I do, if they spoke more agreeably. They have a peculiar drawl which is very unpleasant to me, but they seem very good and I should think they are superior in many ways. I have not seen the one who draws for Ruskin's books.[4]

Sophia seems to have made a satisfactory impression at her first meeting with Elizabeth, who was missing the companionship of her sister Louisa and her family:

> Louie and James are in Paris now and the children are at Aldbro' so I am still entirely alone. I shall be very glad to work with Miss Blake for the sake of having some one to talk to; it is very bad to live such a silent life as I am tempted to do, especially when as in my case, I do not make up by thinking a great deal more.[5]

The opportunity for working together was lost when Sophia left London, but Elizabeth remembered her when, a few months later, she herself planned a visit to Edinburgh. She wrote to Sophia telling her of her intention to apply for admission to Edinburgh University to study medicine, and asking her help in arranging the necessary interviews. The letter reminded Sophia of all she had heard of Elizabeth's unusual ambition and of the difficulties she was encountering.

Elizabeth Garrett, who was nearly four years older than Sophia, was like her in being determined to find a worthy vocation. Three years previously she had attended a lecture by Dr Elizabeth Blackwell, the first woman to obtain a medical degree in the United States; this lecture convinced her that a career in medicine was the answer to her search. Her parents were at first quite dismayed at her decision. Society accepted that working-class women could be midwives, and Miss Nightingale was beginning to achieve for nursing the professional status that would make it a vocation for ladies, but no women had yet attempted to undergo a course of training in a British medical school, with the intention of entering the medical profession.

When Elizabeth Garrett tried to enrol as a medical student, the responses of officials ranged from incredulity to frank hostility. Fortunately her father, Newson Garrett, became her strongest supporter, and was willing to pay for her to receive much of the tuition privately. But this did not solve all her problems. The Medical Act of 1858 marked an important advance in the organization of the profession; it was also the basis of many of Elizabeth's difficulties.

Before the passage of the Act anyone at all – trained or untrained – could claim to be a medical practitioner. The public had no easy means of distinguishing between a charlatan and a professionally trained man. The Act provided for the annual publication of a register that listed the names of all practitioners with approved qualifications. Qualifications in this category were the medical degrees or diplomas that were awarded by nineteen bodies – the universities, the Colleges of Physicians and Surgeons, the London Society of Apothecaries, and the Apothecaries' Hall of Dublin. Degrees awarded by foreign universities were not recognized unless they had been obtained before 1858, and the holders had also been practising in Britain before that date. The Act left members of the public free to choose unregistered medical advisers if they so desired, but only registered practitioners could sign medico-legal documents, or take legal action to recover unpaid fees. Appointments to medical positions in government service were also restricted to registered men. Regardless of the level of his knowledge and skills, an unregistered man's legal status was the same as a charlatan's.

Each of the institutions that awarded medical qualifications required its candidates to have completed a prescribed programme of lectures and practical training, under the supervision of its approved teachers. Signed certificates for each section of the programme had to be produced by candidates presenting for examination. The men who had drawn up the charters of the various institutions did not for a moment think of the possibility that some future candidates could be women. The wording of their regulations and application forms thus implied that all candidates were men, although women were not expressly excluded. Elizabeth Garrett had to accept the personal interpretations of the rules by the officers in charge at the time. Because her prospects were so uncertain, she was advised that before making any applications to be enrolled as a future candidate she should work as a hospital nurse for six months. This would prove to sceptics that she had the physical and emotional stamina needed to withstand the rigours of medical training.

With the help of a family friend who was a governor of the Middlesex Hospital she was accepted as an unpaid probationary nurse at that hospital. During the six months that she spent in a busy surgical ward she was exposed to every situation that could frighten or offend a lady of delicate sensibility. Elizabeth worked steadfastly, fulfilling all her nursing duties and using every spare moment to study her medical books.

At the end of her term as a nurse she had won the respect of the medical staff, with the result that they granted her request to be allowed to work in the students' dissecting room and to attend the chemistry lectures. A few weeks later she was given permission to attend ward rounds, when the physician or surgeon in charge of the ward would move from bed to bed, elucidating the features of each case for the benefit of the students who accompanied him. Most of the medical staff of the Hospital accepted her presence and were impressed with her intelligence and industry, but these same qualities were soon to bring about her downfall. Many of her fellow students began to resent her ability. When she was able to answer questions that had left them tongue-tied they felt humiliated. The School Committee received a memorandum from the students claiming that the presence of a woman in their classes prevented the lecturers from dealing with 'delicate' subjects, and that they were being deprived of important teaching. They also claimed that Miss Garrett's sojourn among them had made the Middlesex Medical School a laughing-stock, and soon no self-respecting student would be associated with it. Alarmed at the prospect of a dying school, the Committee voted in support of the petition, and Elizabeth Garrett had to leave the Middlesex. It was shortly after these events that she had her meeting with Sophia Jex-Blake at Huxley's lecture.

In addition to finding new teachers, Elizabeth had still to be accepted as a future candidate by one of the examining bodies. Of all the registrable qualifications, university degrees had the highest academic status, so in April 1862 she applied to London University for permission to take the matriculation examination. Elizabeth wrote to each member of the University Senate, setting out clearly her reasons for thinking herself eligible, but at the subsequent Senate meeting the motion supporting her application was lost by one vote. The closeness of the decision justified optimism when a second opportunity arose almost immediately. A month later the University would adopt a new Charter, so Elizabeth and her friends canvassed vigorously for the inclusion in the Charter of a clause that would acknowledge the rights of women. This time the vote was even closer; on the first count it was evenly balanced, but then the Chairman, Lord Granville, gave his casting vote against the admission of women.

Elizabeth then decided to test the attitudes of the Scottish universities, starting with Edinburgh. She thought at once of Sophia as a source of advice on planning her application. Sophia had no personal interest in medicine as a career, but she was delighted to be able to help Elizabeth. Her friends the Burn Murdochs and Mr Begbie provided the names of influential people who should be canvassed. Shelving her own work, she scurried from one address to another, explaining Elizabeth's aspirations and arranging appointments for her. For several days a painful foot caused her to limp, but this did not curtail her activity. On 29 May Sophia wrote in her diary:

> E. G. coming tomorrow, – sent her off a telegram this afternoon in case she might stay another day for the report I promised, and so lose tomorrow's appointment with Balfour, whom I saw today with that splendid man, Begbie, who went down last night and this morning with me, and is to arrange with Newbiggin tonight for an appointment for her. My sore foot quite lame and not helpful for this bustle. However I believe I shall have done a bit of real work for her, and as I said to Begbie, if there *are* such people, ready to face such an ordeal let's help

them in God's name. One great obstacle the (sometimes) 'faux air' of consideration for ladies' delicacy. People don't seem to see how that is *her* affair. Besides she *has* faced it: it's a day too late.[6]

Elizabeth spent two weeks in Edinburgh, staying with Sophia at her lodgings at 3 Maitland Street. Together they visited all the people with whom Sophia had made appointments, stating the case for women's admission to the University. The two young women made an interesting contrast in their appearance and personalities. Elizabeth was petite, auburn-haired and with a quiet manner that belied the strength of her determination. Sophia was sturdily built, with black hair and strong facial features, but it was her expressive brown eyes that people noticed and remembered. At their interviews Elizabeth was rather reserved, so it was Sophia who took the lead in explaining their mission. Some of their hearers at first thought it was Sophia, rather than Elizabeth, who was seeking admission to the University.

Sophia had written to a local newspaper, seeking support for their campaign; the letter was published. For her own amusement she also drafted a 'reply', in which she satirized an imaginary bigoted opponent. She showed the letter to Elizabeth, who enjoyed the joke and encouraged her to submit it to the *Daily Review*, using a *nom de plume*. But overnight both Elizabeth and Sophia had second thoughts. Next morning they agreed that to send the letter would be against their principles of honesty and sincerity, principles to which they both adhered steadfastly through the difficult years that followed.

Elizabeth's twenty-sixth birthday occurred half-way through her sojourn in Edinburgh. To celebrate the occasion Sophia arranged a weekend visit to the Trossachs. After the anxieties of the previous week they were refreshed by the beauty of the mountains. They spent their days climbing rocky paths, sometimes sheltering from sudden showers of rain, and enjoying the views when the sun shone again.

On their return to Edinburgh they threw themselves into the final phase of Elizabeth's campaign, for which her father had come to lend his support. Their reception throughout had been favourable enough to justify optimism, but again, as in London, the outcome was disappointing. Sophia wrote to Dora Burn Murdoch, telling her the news:

I do not know whether we are to look upon the result of the Physicians' meeting most as a defeat or as a triumph, – the motion 'to consider the question of admitting Miss Garrett' was negatived by 18 votes to 16, – very disappointing as regards immediate results, but very much as a victory for the principle, just as at London University. You see they have *not* refused to admit, – only postponed the question indefinitely, so that, when time and opinion have been brought to bear, they can again entertain it without inconsistency.[7]

Elizabeth then decided to try for admission to St Andrews University. At first it seemed that there she would be readily accepted, but then suddenly this door was also slammed in her face. Elizabeth Garrett then accepted that for her a medical degree was unattainable. She would have to be content with the lowest of the registrable qualifications, the Licence of the Society of Apothecaries. But even for this she still had a great deal of study and preparation to complete, so, with her objectives redefined, she spent several months taking private lessons from some of the best teachers at St Andrews, and then returned to London.

The shared experience did not result in a deep and lasting friendship between Sophia and Elizabeth. Each saw much to admire in the other, but their differences in temperament made them ill at ease in each other's company. Despite all the help Sophia had given her, Elizabeth may even have wondered if her application to Edinburgh University would have been more successful if she had managed it by herself, in her own less forthright manner.

Sophia felt the need to widen her educational experience by travelling abroad. She had been investigating opportunities for study in France, Germany and the United States, before Elizabeth's visit had become her pre-occupation. With Elizabeth gone her plans began to take shape, despite some opposition from her father. Mr Jex-Blake's worst fear was that in Europe she could be converted to Roman Catholicism! He regarded Germany as less hazardous in this regard than France, so to please him Sophia decided to look for a teaching position in Germany. In a long letter to her mother she defended her decision to travel:

> God has, I believe, given me this work. . . . So now my whole intention and bent is to go anywhere in the world where, as it seems to me on sufficient grounds, I may expect to learn most for my work, – to learn what will make me myself a better scholar and to learn what will most help me to organize (if organization falls to my lot) a better system here in England.[8]

Sophia's tutor and friend, Miss de Dreux, arranged for her to board with a family at Göttingen while she looked for a position as a teacher. On 21 July 1862 she made a night-crossing from London to Antwerp, describing it as a 'delicious, cool and pleasant passage'. From Antwerp she travelled to Cologne, spent the night there, and arrived in Göttingen the next day. She was given a warm welcome by her hosts, and although she was not fluent in the German language she soon settled into the life of the German family. She remained with them for nearly two months, studying German, teaching English to the daughter of the family and making enquiries about educational institutions for girls. It appeared that the Grand Ducal Institute at Mannheim was the one best suited to her needs.

The Institute was founded in 1819 by the Grand Duchess Stephanie of

Baden, a lady of great wisdom and goodwill. Her aim was to provide advanced education for girls who had reached the age of 14 and had completed the basic school curriculum. In a two-year course they would be taught a wide range of academic subjects, and would also be introduced to the appreciation of the arts. Girls of all Christian sects would be accepted; the religious services at the Institute would be ecumenical.

Under a succession of gifted principals, the Institute won a reputation for excellence. It attracted pupils not only from Germany, but from many other European countries, and even from as far afield as Australia. It usually had between thirty and forty pupils, most of whom were boarders; a few girls whose families lived in Mannheim attended as day scholars.

One of the outstanding principals of the Institute was Fräulein Amalie Jung, who presided over it from 1834 to 1860. The year of Fräulein Jung's retirement was also the year in which the Grand Duchess Stephanie died. The Grand Duchess Luise became the next patroness, and Fräulein von Palaus was appointed the new Principal. Sophia's enquiries revealed that under its new directors the Institute was fully maintaining its founder's objectives, so she wrote to Fräulein von Palaus, applying for a position as a teacher of English. But at this time the Institute was experiencing financial difficulties and pruning its expenses, so she was unsuccessful. Sophia decided to go to Mannheim and apply again, in person. If she failed again she would ask to enter the Institute as a pupil, so eager was she to observe its teaching methods.

At five o'clock one September morning she began the 200-mile journey southwards, taking with her the good wishes and farewell gifts of her friends at Göttingen. At Mannheim she found a hotel that was 'clean, cheap, and civil', and at the end of a long day's travel sank into her bed, wondering at her own temerity in coming so far with no certainty of succeeding. With some amusement she thought of the adventures of Lucy Snowe, the heroine of Charlotte Brontë's *Villette*. Next morning she dressed with special care before presenting herself at the Grand Ducal Institute.

Fräulein von Palaus was reserved and dignified, but there was a kindliness in her manner that Sophia appreciated. The interview was conducted in French. Fräulein von Palaus explained that she could not increase the permanent staff, but one of her teachers had been obliged to take sick leave for six months, so there was a temporary vacancy. She warned Sophia that the teachers' rooms were very plainly furnished, and that the food was simple. She reminded her that although the Institute did not favour any one denomination, all the teachers and pupils were expected to attend the daily religious services. Sophia assured her that she found these conditions completely acceptable. After a little more discussion it was agreed that Sophia would become a teacher at the Institute for six months. She would receive her board and lodging, but no salary.

She hastened back to her hotel, collected her possessions, and an hour later had moved into the teachers' quarters at the Institute. She was elated. For the first time in her life she would be earning her keep; the allowance from her father would pay for 'extras' and leave enough over to help the school at Bettws-y-Coed and her other projects.

For the first week or two Sophia did not have to take classes, but merely supervised the students at their music practice. She was a little nervous about her responsibilities as a teacher. In London she had taught small groups of older girls and young women who were all eager to learn; discipline was unnecessary. Now she had classes numbering twenty-five or so, and they were younger girls who easily became bored and inattentive. To her relief and pleasure the first English class went very well.

> Today I have had one lesson, and am just going to give another, – delicious! It's really like oats to a horse who has been kept a year on hay. Miss Garrett was right enough when she said, 'Get teaching!' I quite laugh at myself to feel how radiant I am with delight at being again in harness.[9]

To her friend Lucy Walker, whom she had taught at Queen's College, she wrote:

> I am much pleased on the whole with the kind of tone I find between teachers and pupils, and with the general principles, which, if not the very highest, are yet greatly superior to what you find in most English boarding schools.[10]

Sophia found the ecumenical approach to religion very much in accord with her own views. She wrote to her mother:

> [This union] struck me very much in its beauty tonight as Miss von Palaus pronounced, – 'There is but one name given under heaven among men whereby we may be saved', and we all received it on our knees, – Protestants and Romanists, Unitarians and Trinitarians, – each 'in his own tongue.' Was it not beautiful how just that name bound us all together, – Christians, – seeking at least the spirit of Christ who loved us all, – our Master, – that we might 'love one another'.[11]

The Principal won Sophia's respect and affection, 'That good Frl. von Palaus! Well might I today liken her to a sunbeam! How she lights up the very house, – how bright burns her lamp, – yet how simply!'

This ecstatic mood could not last indefinitely. At the Grand Ducal Institute, life was taken very seriously. Although it aimed to promote the physical health of its pupils, the Institute was less successful in this aspect of its policy. Most of the girls had very little outdoor exercise. They were astonished at Sophia's enjoyment of long walks and at her preference for open windows. There were no term holidays or other regular intervals of relaxation. The Principal took only one week's leave in a year, and in some years she missed even this. The girls were permitted to go home for a few days only, at long intervals. It was little wonder that the pupils became fractious and their teachers irritable. Half-way through her appointment Sophia's joy turned to depression and self-criticism:

> I don't know why especially, but I seem so oppressed with a sense of the greatness, the weight of my work, – and of my own miserable insufficiency for it. Oh, so weak and stupid and unfit! And it isn't humility, – it's just truth.[12]

At first her pupils had been awed by their new English teacher, but when she was no longer a stranger they were tempted to test her ability to impose discipline. Sophia was conscious of her deficiency in this regard; she could not establish a set of simple rules and apply them consistently.

> As my sky is bluer or greyer, as I see, or think I see, more or less into a child's character, the scale varies. Justice is blind no longer, but gives a chuck to one side or the other.[13]

The girls taunted her with her inability to sing, paint and embroider; they even laughed at her for weeping with emotion during the church services. All of this was childish nonsense, but hurtful to a young woman who was far from home and family. Sophia could have impressed her pupils by buying expensive clothes and playing the 'grand lady'. But she had chosen to live austerely and she would not act a part that was foreign to her nature. She was determined to stay on for the full six months, longer still if a replacement had not been found for her, but she yearned for home. It was a comfort that her pupils, despite these difficulties, were making excellent progress in their studies and Fräulein von Palaus seemed well satisfied with her work.

The situation improved considerably after an event so insignificant that it served to show how trivial was the cause of her unhappiness. At the School Carnival Ball, she wore a beautiful gown. It was not new, having been her bridesmaid's dress for the wedding of a friend in England, but even the critical pupils pronounced it 'ravissant'. It seemed to convince the schoolgirls that their English mistress really did appreciate the things that mattered to them; from that time their attitude to her improved. Sophia's term was extended by two months, but these last weeks were much happier. Just when she was about to leave she contracted scarlet fever, which delayed her departure for three weeks. Then at last she was able to make the journey home, and another segment of her life was ended.

Sophia took a holiday from work and study, while she completed her convalescence and visited old friends whom she had not seen for several years.

42

Thus months passed in what was, for her, an unusually leisured existence. But, as always, she was ready to give up her own pursuits if others needed her help. To her friend Lucy Walker she sent the sad news of the death of a young woman they had both known well:

> I heard of it on Thursday and went up to London directly, and I never was more heartily glad of having done anything in my life, for both Mrs B. and E. seemed *so* glad to see me, and you can hardly believe the peaceful happy few hours we had together, – indeed there came to me (and I think to them too in some degree) such an intense realization of what the joy and light was into which she had entered, that no room seemed left for any pain for oneself. I did love L. very much, – more perhaps than any of you knew, – but when I stood looking down on that calm pale face, the only words that would come into my mind were, – 'He was not, for God took him'. . . .
> Just before she died, L. finished a story at which she had been working to compete for some magazine prize, – if it does not win this, we hope to get it published separately, as a memorial that will be beloved of many, – and indeed I hope it may come out in this form. I have offered to undertake the whole business. It is very pleasant to me that she has left this, – is it not to you?[14]

Sophia was gradually winning her parents' acceptance of her plan to visit schools in America, when she received a letter that drove from her mind all thoughts of foreign travel. It came from the Reverend T.D.C. Morse, Rector of Stretford, Manchester.

> I have had some correspondence with Professor Plumptre of Queen's College about establishing a Ladies' College in this locality, and he has referred me to you as likely to help me in this good work. Notwithstanding the fact that the movement for the improvement of female education has now been for some time set on foot, this populous neighbourhood is still very destitute in this respect. I have two girls, 12 and 13 years of age, and after making enquiries in very competent quarters, I have been told that there is only one Ladies' School 'worth a farthing' in or near Manchester, and that is the Ladies' College on the north side of the city at Higher Broughton. We are living on the south side and are surrounded by a large number of wealthy people who must necessarily miss such educational facilities. I wish therefore to *try* whether a good Ladies' College can be founded on this side of Manchester, and I would be glad to know whether you could introduce me to a lady qualified to act as Principal of such an Institution. Mr Plumptre was not quite sure whether you might be disposed to undertake such a work yourself or not, but, if you were so, I feel sure from what he has told me that the matter

could not be in better hands. . . . You will understand, of course, that the matter at present is only in the phase of a project.[15]

Here was an invitation to establish her Sackermena and to be its Grandiflora! She wrote back at once to express her interest in the project and a fortnight later, with much preliminary work already done, Sophia was in Manchester as the guest of the Morses. She found Mr Morse to be 'clear, energetic and practical; a little "trammelled" by clerical bonds, but in the main wide and satisfactory'.

With so much at stake, Sophia might have been expected to tread warily, but in her usual forthright way she took the first opportunity to broach a contentious subject – her unconventional religious views. She told Mr Morse how she frequently attended the Unitarian Church and received help there. A practical issue of importance was the question of daily prayers at the proposed school. Mr Morse expected that a Church school would have at least one daily religious service for the assembled staff and pupils. Sophia told him she believed that prayer should be private and spontaneous; even family prayers seemed to her to be artificial. This attitude seems at variance with her appreciation of the ecumenical services at the Grand Ducal Institute. Sophia's religious views were very personal. She read widely and formed her own opinions, but these were being modified constantly in the light of experience or further reading. Perhaps her reluctance to commit herself indefinitely to presiding over daily services stemmed from a dread of having to go through a ritual that had become meaningless or abhorrent to her. Mr Morse must have thought highly of Sophia's qualifications for the position, since he decided to let this awkward question remain unanswered until planning of the school was more advanced.

Sophia visited established schools in the Manchester area, and sought advice from many sources. Aware of the financial difficulties that threatened the project, she observed the strictest economy in her plans for the conduct of the school. She proposed that, like Queen's College, her school would have its 'Lady Visitors'. One eminent lady who agreed to be a Visitor was the author Mrs Gaskell. At a public meeting Manchester citizens were told of the plans for the school, and the newspapers gave it publicity. Everything depended on generous financial support by the people. Unfortunately, this was not forthcoming. After three months of hard work Sophia learned that the scheme would have to be abandoned because of lack of funds. She accepted the loss philosophically. It was gratifying to have been offered the position of Principal, and the experience she had gained in formulating her plans was invaluable.

Now her thoughts returned to the proposed visit to America. She persuaded her parents to give their approval, her arguments strengthened by the fact that she had found a travelling companion; Miss Isabel Bain, a friend and former Queen's College student, would accompany her.

Sophia hoped to visit a number of the leading colleges and schools in the eastern states. Friends gave her letters of introduction to American academics, and helped her to plan her itinerary, but the final arrangements could not be made until she arrived in Boston. During these last busy weeks before sailing Sophia received a pressing invitation to visit a friend who lived in Yorkshire. This was Lucy Walker, who had married in November 1864 and was now Mrs Unwin. Lucy wished Sophia to meet her husband before setting off on her trip. Sophia replied:

> I should like exceedingly to see you if it were possible before sailing for America, and your letter has made me wish more than ever to do so.
> If I found it just possible to come to you for one day and night, would you think it worthwhile to have me? I do not know what the possibilities are, – are you *in* the town? – or would it be an undertaking to get to you from the station? Would it upset you all terribly if I came and went at unearthly hours as I might have to do?
> I should like to see you exceedingly, and I should like *very* much to see your husband, – if my coming in such a rush and making such a fuss wouldn't make him hate me.
> Thank you very much for your photograph. There are no decent ones of me, but I will see if I can find you up one of the least bad.[16]

The visit took place and, although brief, it was a happy and memorable event, particularly for Lucy. She was expecting her first child, and Sophia was like an elder sister to whom she could confide her joy and anxiety. It may have been Sophia's fruitless search for a photograph of herself that prompted her parents to have her portrait painted by the noted artist Samuel Laurence. The portrait is known to have been painted in 1865; she probably sat for it shortly before her departure for America.

On 27 May 1865 Sophia and Isabel Bain sailed from Liverpool in the steamship *Africa*. The crossing took twelve days, and for most of the time the weather was bitterly cold. The highlight of the voyage was the sighting of icebergs, 'great cliffs of white rearing themselves out of the waves that beat into spray at their base, looking so strong and grim and beautiful'. The *Africa* reached Boston at midnight on 8 June. Early next day the two young women disembarked and had their first taste of life in the United States.

Notes

1. M. Todd, *The Life of Sophia Jex-Blake*, London: Macmillan, 1918, p. 112.
2. ibid., p. 108.
3. ibid., p. 113.
4. Elizabeth Garrett Anderson Papers, Fawcett Library, City Polytechnic, London.
5. ibid.

6. Todd, op. cit., p. 118.
7. ibid., p. 118.
8. ibid., p. 122.
9. ibid., p. 130.
10. ibid., p. 131.
11. ibid., p. 130.
12. ibid., p. 134.
13. ibid., p. 136.
14. ibid., p. 150.
15. ibid., p. 152.
16. ibid., p. 157.

4

A change of direction

Sophia and her travelling companion, Isabel Bain, spent their first few days in America becoming accustomed to the humidity of a Boston summer, and to the strangely different customs and manners of the New World. It was barely two months since the Civil War had ended, so emotions were easily stirred by any discussion of the issues over which the war had been fought. The newcomers were warmly received, but they sensed the hostility many Americans felt towards Britain.

Although Britain's attitude had officially been one of neutrality, it was no secret that the Prime Minister, Lord Palmerston, had favoured the idea of a permanently divided American nation. The war had cost thousands of British workers their jobs in the cotton mills, because the North's blockade of Southern ports had cut off the supply of raw cotton. Gladstone was troubled by the suffering of the unemployed; in a moment of indiscretion, when the war was at its height, he had spoken publicly in support of the South. Then there was the matter of the *Alabama* and several other Confederate warships, which had inflicted enormous damage on Union shipping. These warships had been repaired and refitted in British dockyards, a breach of neutrality that the citizens of Boston could not easily overlook.

Sophia first became aware of this feeling when she was a guest in the home of Ralph Waldo Emerson, to whom she had brought a letter of introduction. She records the trend of the conversation, and for once she seems to have acted with commendable restraint:

> Oh, dear, How they turned on the tap, and talked right on end when they got near politics, only pausing to wonder at our 'ignorance' in England (that being, of course, the only source of difference of opinion with them). Finally, after listening with the utmost patience indefinitely – only devoutly wishing to kick over the table – I got mentally collared by Miss Peabody with an accusation of being 'still incredulous', to which I replied very frankly, that 'certainly till I heard both sides I could form no definite opinion'. Emerson was refreshing after the rest, inasmuch as, after speaking, he would allow you to answer.[1]

Emerson must have found Sophia's attitude acceptable, since he took an interest in her proposed tour of schools and colleges and gave her much helpful advice.

A few days later Sophia met Dr Lucy Sewall who, at the age of twenty-eight, had already made a name for herself as one of her country's pioneer women doctors. Sophia and Lucy Sewall quickly became friends. As they talked of their common interest in careers for women Sophia learned of the difficulties encountered by American women with medical ambitions. There was no national register of qualified medical practitioners, but the American Medical Association, at its foundation in 1847, had defined the standards of training necessary to qualify for its membership. Women doctors were not permitted to join the Association, but unless their training met the same rigorous standards the public would group them with the health faddists, religious cult practitioners and even the abortionists.

The two leading medical schools, those of Harvard and Cornell, were closed to women. Other reputable schools occasionally admitted a woman student, but their attitudes changed unpredictably. Elizabeth Blackwell, the first woman in the English-speaking world to obtain a medical degree, applied unsuccessfully to twenty-nine American medical colleges before she was accepted by Geneva College in New York State. Elizabeth obtained her MD in 1849, but when her sister Emily applied to Geneva three years later the College had changed its policy and refused to admit another woman. Emily was eventually accepted by the Cleveland Medical College, from which she graduated in 1854.

Even if they managed to gain entry to medical schools, female students were denied practical training in hospitals, and after graduating they could not obtain appointments as hospital internes. Dr Elizabeth Blackwell corrected this deficiency in her experience by working for six months as a student midwife in Paris. Then she went to London, where she was allowed to visit the wards of St Bartholomew's Hospital. In 1850 a woman doctor, especially one who was shortly to return to America, seemed a harmless novelty and there were no serious objections to her presence at the Hospital. Fifteen years later it would have caused an uproar. Emily Blackwell was also obliged to go to Britain and Europe for her practical training. The experience of the Blackwell sisters demonstrated that if American women were to be assured of entry to the profession, they needed to have their own medical schools and unrestricted access to hospital training in their own country.

In 1853 Elizabeth Blackwell established in New York her own out-patient dispensary for destitute women. Although such a service was desperately needed, many women were afraid to trust a woman doctor, and at first the dispensary attracted very few patients. But when it was seen to be providing an excellent service, its work expanded rapidly. In 1856 Elizabeth was joined by her sister and by Dr Marie Zakrzewska, a young European migrant who had recently obtained an MD at Cleveland Medical College. The following

Illustration 7. Dr Lucy Sewall (1837–1890), the young American whose enthusiasm for medicine as a vocation caused Sophia to review her own plans. (Reproduced by permission of the Sophia Smith Collection, Northampton, Massachusetts.)

year the three women were able to open the New York Infirmary for Women, the first in-patient hospital to be conducted by women doctors. Dr Blackwell intended that the Infirmary would not only provide medical assistance that even the poorest woman could afford, but that it would also be the first centre for the practical training of women doctors and nurses.

In 1856 a medical school for women was founded in Boston; it was called the New England Female Medical College, and had developed from an earlier school of midwifery and nursing. The man responsible for the project was Mr Samuel Gregory, a somewhat eccentric reformer who was not himself a doctor. Gregory won the support of many liberal-minded citizens of Massachusetts for his plan to train women to be doctors. The original teaching faculty of the New England Female Medical College consisted of six men and one woman, but Gregory was eager to recruit women teachers. In 1859 he persuaded Dr Zakrzewska to come to Boston as Professor of Obstetrics at the College.

'Dr Zak', as she was known to her friends, soon found that she could not work under Gregory's direction. Despite his lack of medical training, he tried to dictate the curriculum and was opposed to spending money, even for such basic equipment as a microscope. Dr Zak resigned from the College, but remained in Boston, having decided to devote herself to the founding of a women's hospital in that city. It was largely as the result of her efforts that the New England Hospital for Women and Children, with ten beds and an out-patient clinic, was opened in 1862. This was also the year in which Lucy Sewall graduated from the Female Medical College. After spending a year in gaining further training in Europe, Dr Sewall returned to become the resident physician at the Hospital, where she worked under the direction of Dr Zakrzewska, and had the assistance of two resident women students. The Hospital was so successful that only two years after it opened its doors, it had to be moved to larger premises. The skill and dedication of the resident physician were significant factors in this success.

Lucy Sewall came from an influential Boston family. Her father, Judge Samuel Sewall, had been a campaigner for the abolition of slavery and was also a supporter of the women's movement. Lucy was earnestly dedicated to her profession, but she was also feminine in manner and appearance. Thus, she was a source of reassurance to those who feared that women could only succeed in a 'masculine' profession at the expense of their womanliness.

Sophia and Isabel were given a friendly welcome by the young women doctors at the New England Hospital. Sophia wrote to her mother:

> You don't know what an immense thing it is for us to have got free admission to the Women's Hospital here, – we are always doing something jolly together with the students and doctors, – all women, by the way.
>
> Dr Sewall is resident Physician, and is always asking us to spend jolly evenings there, – or to join them in going to theatres, etc. Yesterday we

Illustration 8. The New England Hospital for Women and Children, Boston, where Sophia began her medical training. (Reproduced by permission of the Sophia Smith Collection, Northampton, Massachusetts.)

made an expedition in the evening to a famous place for ice-cream, 8 of us there were – 4 M.D.s (one of whom is a splendid surgeon, – the first female surgeon I have heard of) two students and we two. After the ices we went back to the Hospital, and played a most ridiculous game of cards called 'Muggins', keeping us in roars of laughter half the time. Then Dr Tyng (the surgeon) sang, and, among other things gave us a specimen of the 'Shaker' singing – with its very peculiar religious dance, – have you heard about the Shakers? I hope to see them and then I will tell you.

But can't you understand how refreshing it is to slip into the bright life of all these working people – working hard all day, and then so ready for fun when work's over? It reminds me of the full colour and life of the old London times when all we working women were together.[2]

Sophia also observed Dr Sewall at work:

Sat for a couple of hours in Dr Sewall's dispensary this morning. Some 36 cases heard and helped more or less. Some coming with bright faces, – 'So much better, Doctor,' – some in pain enough, poor souls. Dr Sewall with such a kindly ready sympathy, and such clear firm treatment for them all. Certainly the right woman in the right place, except in as far as she herself gets to look sadly fagged and tired sometimes.[3]

Sophia met other women whose achievements in different fields were no less remarkable. The astronomer Maria Mitchell was about to take up her appointment as Professor of Astronomy at Vassar College. Sophia found her 'a very nice woman – grand and able and strong and kindly'. Of another she wrote:

We saw Miss Crocker the other day, – late Mathematical professor at Antioch, – and she impressed me extremely with her quiet dignity and wisdom, and her tremendous Mathematics, – I *should* so like to study under her some day. I feel like an uppish dwarf beside some strong quiet giant.[4]

These Americans were demonstrating that women were capable of filling senior academic positions of distinction any man would envy.

Meanwhile, with the help of Dr Hill, the President of Harvard, Sophia had completed the arrangements for her tour. The observant Dr Sewall noticed that she was looking tired, and persuaded her to take a short holiday in the cool New Hampshire mountains before starting her arduous project. Sophia and Isabel stayed with friends of Lucy Sewall, and thoroughly enjoyed a taste of the carefree outdoor life. Sophia described it in a letter to her mother:

I don't think I shall be able to write by the next mail, as we are going for a few days' excursion round the mountains, so I must send you off now as long a letter as I can manage, telling you what we have been doing just lately.

First and foremost, I have been coming in useful as 'teamster', in Yankee parlance, having been chiefly employed in driving my neighbours all about the country lately. You would have laughed, I think, had you seen my 'span' (pair of horses) the other day, – one brown, pretty high, – the other mouse-coloured and some three inches lower, the most delightful variety prevailing in the harnessing and general appearance of the two. Behind these beauties came six of us in a big rough country 'wagon', all of painted wood, – two big seats fixed in a sort of open cart. We went through *such* a ford, – the Penningewassett River, and (when the horses didn't bite each other) we got on grandly. . . . You haven't the least idea what that word 'woods' means, – in England there are just a few acres of carefully preserved trees and 'no trespassers allowed'. Here you plunge into a vast forest, miles and miles every way, – lucky if you can find a path at all, else guiding yourself by sun and stream and taking hours and hours to get a mile or two, – yet all through so grand, so green, and so delicious! If you could just have been with us yesterday! Every few minutes we found some great tree fallen across our path, or some black bog of decayed cedar or pine, – oh, the scents of those! – perfectly delicious; – and then round we had to go, creeping, jumping or gliding round the obstruction. Then we would come to some little clearing, and catch such views of the mountains we were shut in with, – then on again and hardly see daylight through the dense trees. And such mosses, such ferns, such berries!

Then over the river somehow from rock to rock, and such a scramble up among the cascades which came leaping down like liquid silver in the sunlight, and such pools we did so want to bathe in and had to refrain for lack of time and towels! They called the distance 2½ or 3 miles, but we took just 3 hours to get there, – and then coming back pretty sharply in about half the time. The only grief to me was – what perhaps you will hardly sympathize in – that we didn't come across any bears. There are a good many left in the woods and one hears every now and then of their being met, but they are getting few, and they are proportionately timid and modest, running off full speed if they see you. Wouldn't it have been fun to see one?

I think hardly anything strikes an Englisher more than the no-value of wood here. Over the water it's half high treason to hurt a tree; – here, if you want a napkin-ring, you strip the bark off the first birch you come to and make a lot; or, if you take it into your head, set fire to the woods anywhere and have a bonfire of a dozen trees, and no one says a word. We have seen woods on fire over and over again, and no one says more than, – 'Oh, somebody's fired the wood'; and the odd thing is it doesn't seem to spread as one would expect.[5]

Their holiday over, Sophia and Isabel set off on their tour. Their first stop was to be at Oberlin College, some 34 miles west of Cleveland; their route took them through Concord, where they were again guests of the Emersons. Then they allowed themselves a short detour in order to visit Niagara Falls. The spectacle far exceeded Sophia's expectations. From Niagara she wrote to Lucy Unwin:

> I congratulate you with all my heart on the birth of your little son! I think by this time you will have forgotten all doubts and difficulties, and all but pleasant feelings of responsibility, in your great content, have you not? God very seldom sends us either duties or blessings without showing us how to fulfil and enjoy and use them, and I do not doubt but you will have found in your own case all sorts of new powers and instincts develop with the need of them, and will have by this time a pretty definite idea 'What to do with a baby' – Is it not so? . . .
> I wish there existed a visual telegraph (if such a phrase may be coined) and that I could give you a glimpse of the scene I have in front of me, and which is continually stealing my eyes from my paper. No less than Niagara in its full glory! – and what that glory is I don't think any *but* eyes can tell. I have seen a good deal of beauty and grandeur in my life, in Great Britain, Italy, Switzerland, etc., but I think never anything so wonderfully, bewitchingly, grandly beautiful as this. People talk of being disappointed in Niagara, but I think it can only be because, for the first moment, the enormous width of the Falls (900 feet in one case, 2000 in the other, – separated by an island) prevents their recognizing their height as well, or else they have not got the right natures to admire with! (and I think that last is oftener the case than people think).[6]

The long journey to Oberlin gave Sophia and Isabel the opportunity to enjoy the comforts provided for train travellers in America.

> The 'cars' on American railways are always long saloon carriages, with an aisle down the centre leading to doors at the ends, and down each side a row of seats each containing two persons, and commanding a separate window. These seats are cleverly made with reversible backs, so that the passengers can sit with either back or face to the engine; almost all choosing the latter alternative, except when parties of three or four sit facing each other 'sociable' fashion.
> Starting by an evening train, we forthwith secured sleeping berths by payment of an extra dollar, and were initiated into the ingenious plan for their construction. Down came the backs of two opposite seats, which

fitted exactly across the space between, and formed a solid couch, on which was laid a good mattress, a brown rug, and some pillows, a curtain separating off the passage-way. My friend and I secured two opposite berths, and, with windows partly open on each side, soon slept the sleep of the just, disturbed only by the conductor's anxiety to shut up our windows, lest we should, as he said, 'freeze to death *and* be burnt up with sparks from the engine!' Having so good a bed, the regular motion on the broad gauge was really rather lulling than otherwise.[7]

At Oberlin they discovered that the College was not a single building, but rather a collection of houses and offices scattered in different parts of the town. The town had grown up with the College, which was founded in 1833 by the Reverend John Shipherd, a Presbyterian Pastor. The visitors were made welcome by staff and students alike, and were free to observe and to question their hosts. During the ten days that they spent at Oberlin, Sophia saw much to admire, but some aspects of its collegiate life she thought could be improved.

Oberlin is the oldest co-educational college in America. From the time of its foundation it admitted men and women as students and as teachers, and also made no distinctions based on colour. In 1865 there were 900 students enrolled. Sophia noted:

> The two sexes are about equally represented among the students, though the full College course is taken by a smaller number of women than of men. 'Coloured' students – varying widely as to hue – form about a third of the whole number, and I suppose there is hardly any community in America where the coloured and white races meet on so real and genuine a footing of equality as at Oberlin.[8]

The fees charged were remarkably low, only $9 per year for tuition and $3 per week for board. This enabled students from very poor homes to enjoy the advantages of college education. But it also had an adverse effect – with such a small income the College could pay only very meagre salaries to its staff. Some excellent teachers managed to support themselves and their families, and remained at the College for many years, but others left for better-paid positions. Consequently, there were at the College some less able teachers who merely supervised their students' study of the prescribed textbooks.

Life at the College was austere, and a high moral tone prevailed. Although the girls and young men attended the same classes they did not sit together, nor were they supposed to mingle socially at other times. Games of chance were not permitted; even chess was outlawed. Not only alcohol, but also tea and coffee were prohibited. Students were encouraged to perform some manual work each day, to assist in the running of the College, but there were no facilities for games and sports. Sophia could not help contrasting these students with those she knew at home; English students studied less seriously, were much more interested in sport, and appeared to be more healthy. It was a prayer meeting that drew Sophia's attention to the lack of physical and mental fitness of the young people at Oberlin.

> A theological student presided, and the proceedings having been opened by prayer and a hymn, he invited everyone to speak as he or she felt able, requesting each to be 'as brief as possible,' as he felt that God was among them, and that many ought to speak that evening. . . .
>
> In so far as revivals depend on a morbid state of spiritual excitement, and that again on imperfectly developed bodily health, there seemed at Oberlin every facility for their advent. A less robust set of students I have seldom seen, with manners gentle and kind, but more subdued than seemed suited to their age had they been in full mental and physical health. The place impressed me as flat, and not very healthy (though the contrary is asserted) and the water had to be filtered for drinking. From what I saw I imagine that no adequate system of cleansing or drainage prevails; and, though violent epidemics may be rare I think the effects may be seen in the general under-baked look of the whole number of students and Professors.[9]

From Oberlin the travellers went on to Hillsdale College in Michigan, 90 miles west of Detroit. Here they remained for a week, and were again received with great kindness.

> At Hillsdale, one large and handsome brick building, consisting of three portions distinct from roof to basement, contains the College proper and two boarding halls. In the central division, recitation and lecture rooms, with the library and a handsome room for the President, occupy two lower floors; while a good-sized chapel fills the whole of the second storey, is of good height, and has a small organ-gallery at one end. . . .
>
> The whole left wing of the building, with the exception of some ground-floor rooms, is assigned to the female students, and the young men are similarly lodged in the right wing. A large but low dining-hall occupies most of the basement on the left side, and in this all the students resident in the hall meet for meals, the Lady Superintendent and those teachers who lodge in the building being always present, and some of the Professors occasionally. There is no regular order with regard to seats, and the students disperse themselves much as they please, usually retaining the same place during the term – generally two or three girls sitting together, then two or three men, and so forth. The whole arrangements of the College are thoroughly patriarchal and refreshingly simple.[10]

Coloured students were welcome at Hillsdale, but there were not so many there as at Oberlin. Of the 600 students, slightly less than half were females. The tuition fees were $30 per year – higher than at Oberlin, but still modest by the standards of the time. Sophia thought that the teachers at Hillsdale were highly competent and the academic standards excellent. The students seemed to be physically fit and cheerful, although again there were no organized games.

After spending a week at Hillsdale, Sophia and Isabel began the 500-mile journey to their next destination: St Louis, Missouri. Their route lay through Chicago.

We left Hillsdale at about 5.30 a.m. on the morning of October 6th, before daybreak, but by the light of a brilliant moon, that lit up the hoar-frost under our feet, in our rapid walk to the station. The thermometer stood at about 48 degrees and we saw the effects of sharp frost as we proceeded on the railroad, in the brilliant colours of the autumn leaves, some tree-tops being literally crimson and scarlet. But on arriving at Chicago we found it again tolerably warm, and almost regretted that we had on winter clothing, which we were later forced to relinquish altogether, on reaching the still hot summer of St Louis.

In entering Chicago we had again to observe the curious fashion of carrying railroads straight up the principal streets, our line passing by rows of houses and pavements (or rather plank walks) with foot-passengers, and carriages to boot, on each side, all seeming in imminent danger of getting under the engine-wheels, only somehow they did not. Chicago is one of the very rapidly-grown Western cities, and shares their general 'shoddy' character of great magnificence in some parts, and great incompleteness in others. The station at which we alighted was the most disgracefully shabby and dirty of sheds, but the hotel to which we went for dinner was paved with marble, and in all respects, perhaps more finished and more luxuriously well appointed than any we had seen in America.[11]

After enjoying a leisurely dinner Sophia and Isabel left Chicago by train. Again they had comfortable sleeping berths. From time to time Sophia woke and glimpsed, by brilliant moonlight, vast expanses of pasture and cornfields, 'unbroken for miles around by wall, or tree, or shrub'. When they reached the eastern bank of the Mississippi the travellers were transferred to a large horse-drawn omnibus, which was driven down a steep slope on to a ferry boat. The climb up on the other side was even steeper. They were now in Missouri, the first of the former slave states Sophia and Isabel were to visit.

They had come to St Louis to see the Mary Institute, an educational estab-lishment where only women were admitted as students. The Institute, which was under the aegis of Washington University, was administered by two professors who were brother and sister. It was smaller than Oberlin and Hillsdale, having only 132 students, all of whom were white. 'The managers of the school regret extremely that popular prejudice is so strong as to forbid the admission of coloured students', Sophia noted. But she approved of the religious tolerance she saw there; students of the Roman Catholic and Jewish faiths joined with the Protestants in a common form of worship that all found acceptable.

There was no hall of residence for students; those whose homes were far away had to make their own arrangements for board in St Louis. The fees charged for tuition ranged from $80 to $100 per year, depending on the classes taken. Many of the teachers at the Mary Institute were women, and Sophia thought that the standard of teaching here was the best she had seen on her tour so far. Students who had completed satisfactory courses could take degree examinations at Washington University, under the same conditions that applied to men.

The public school system was another aspect of American education that Sophia investigated. She visited several schools in St Louis and some more in Cincinnati, but deferred a more detailed study until she returned to Massachusetts, where the system was most advanced.

From Cincinnati Sophia and Isabel went on to Antioch College, near Springfield, Ohio. They already knew something of the history of this College, which had been founded in 1853 by the members of a small religious sect who called themselves, simply, 'Christians'. The founders and the first President, Horace Mann, pledged themselves to provide the best possible educational facilities at low cost to students; furthermore, no student would be denied admission because of his or her sex, race or religion.

For the first few years the College barely survived its financial difficulties. An ambitious building programme, and the alienation of some potential contributors who disapproved of its policy of racial equality, were chiefly to blame. Horace Mann died in 1859. He was succeeded as President by Dr Hill, who remained at Antioch for three years before being appointed President of Harvard. In 1865, when Sophia visited the College, it was emerging from its difficulties. A mood of optimism prevailed, and several additional teachers had recently been appointed. Sophia was interested to learn that the women teachers were generally acknowledged to be among the best on the staff. She hoped she would be able to make another visit to Antioch before long, to see what changes had taken place.

Before leaving Ohio, Sophia and Isabel made an interesting short excursion outside the world of formal education. They had noticed that sorghum molasses appeared on the table at every meal, and were curious about this unfamiliar substance. They learned that sorghum is a cereal that has thick, juicy stalks. The juice, when extracted and concentrated, makes a delicious syrup. They were taken to a mill to see the sorghum being crushed; the juice was then filtered, and their guide showed them how it was repeatedly boiled down, until it reached the required consistency and was a clear, amber colour.

Sophia's observations in the four colleges, in all of which women were taught exactly as men were, confirmed her belief that a woman's intelligence was fully equal to that of a man. None of the teachers she met disagreed with this view. Some of them were doubtful that the average woman student had enough physical and mental stamina to complete a long degree course. Others were uneasy about the moral dangers of teaching men and women in mixed classes. But Sophia observed that these reservations disappeared as teachers became more accustomed to mixed schools. The most experienced usually said that there was no inherent weakness in the female student, and that both men and women gained from being taught together.

In Ohio, and back in Massachusetts, Sophia was able to visit a number of schools. She found that the American public school system encompassed primary, grammar, and high schools, the last being able to prepare students for entry to college. She noted:

> Public education in America is reduced to an organized system which has no parallel in England, schools for both sexes being provided by the State, supported by general taxation, and opened to all classes alike.
> It is compulsory on parents to provide for the education of their children, and the police have authority to place at school any boys or girls found in the streets.
> At the public schools the large majority of Americans receive at least part of their education, and it is very common to see the children of Members of Congress etc., side by side with those of labourers and artisans, when the quarter of the city for which the school is established embraces the residences of both classes.[12]

In Sophia's view this egalitarian policy would be an advantage if the refined speech and manners of the more fortunate children were adopted as the standard for all; the risk was that the uncouthness of the labourers' children would prevail. She noticed, however, that Americans attached far less import-ance to the social graces than Europeans did.

> I found myself constantly misled . . . when I first came to America, hearing the most barbarous English and the most deplorable pronuncia-tion from many whom I found afterwards to be really learned men and women. The same curious defects are apt to run through the tone, the expressions, and in some cases the handwriting of Americans, who thus do themselves great injustice with Europeans by habitual deficiency in those things which we are wont to regard as the signs and seals of polite education; while, in fact the women at least on the Western side of the Atlantic are, as I believe, more thoroughly educated on the whole than those on our own shores. They are certainly far better mathematicians,

and often have studied classics and physical science to an extent that is comparatively rare in England.[13]

When she compared the American educational system with the one she knew in England she noticed a striking difference:

> If we look for the very highest scholarship, which will be exceptional everywhere, I suppose that American Universities can hardly compete with those of England; nor should we probably be willing to exchange the education received by some of our boys and girls for anything we could find across the Atlantic; but if we examine the results attained in the two countries for all classes and both sexes generally, and inquire on which side inclines the balance of average education, we have, I fear, little chance of successful comparison with America, and must be willing, in all honesty, to yield the palm to her system of Public Schools.[14]

When Sophia returned to Boston she was alone; Isabel Bain had decided to become a student at one of the colleges they had visited. Sophia was invited to spend some time at Nassau with an old school friend who had gone to live there after her marriage, but she felt herself being drawn back to the New England Hospital for Women and Children. When Lucy Sewall suggested that she should share the residence at the Hospital, in return for helping with the work, she accepted with alacrity.

With her training in accountancy Sophia was able to take over the clerical work of the Hospital and soon had the neglected account books in good order. She helped with making up the simpler prescriptions when the dispensary attendant had to leave at short notice, as well as assisting the hard-pressed staff in many other ways.

Contact with the patients made Sophia aware of the brutalizing effects of poverty. In a letter to her mother she told how two of the babies born at the Hospital were found abandoned in the streets the day after they and their mothers had been discharged; there was very little sentiment about motherhood among the really poor women of the city. Sophia offered to act as chaplain, visiting patients who had no friends or relations, and conducting a service on Sundays. But in this she was less successful than she was with her practical work. After three months as chaplain she wrote:

> I have given up my Sunday service, or at least have resigned it into the hands of a minister who already had a service in the medical wards. I found it very hard to find time to prepare properly for it, and sometimes it tried my nerves very much, and besides it got to be a great weight upon me in the way of responsibility and absolute honesty in *what* I said. Things seem so very un-clear to my own mind that it rather weighs upon

me and worries me to be trying to say much about them to others. Perhaps this state may just pass away again, but in the meantime I like best to 'be true to every honest thought,' and, till I'm sure, to be silent.[15]

As she became more and more absorbed in the life of the Hospital, Sophia found that her ideas about the medical profession were undergoing a profound change. She wrote to her mother:

> I find myself getting desperately in love with medicine as a science and as an art, to an extent I could not have believed possible. I always associated so much that is repulsive and nasty with it in my mind, but I find that one really loses all sense of that in close contact, – that the beauty of nature's arrangements and of art's contrivances absorb one's mind from every- thing less pleasant, and I find myself saying to myself a dozen times a day that, did I not feel my life devoted to another object, I would be a doctor straightway. As it is, I mean to use all the time I have in gaining all I can, by observation (for which one so rarely has such a chance) even more than by study, though I find myself devouring all sorts of medical works too, and am quite amazed to find how far even in this little time I am able to understand to a certain extent all sorts of things going on around me, and how *very* interesting they all become in the new light. . . . Of course one has access to an enormous medical library here, and the junior doctors are all as ready to help or show me all I want as possible. I in my turn do all I can to take extra work which I can do off their hands. Today the hospital note-book was handed over to me, and I went round with the physicians taking down directions for food, medicines, etc., and then making up the latter and taking them to the wards: all of which was very little for me to do, and very interesting, but a great deal saved for the over-worked junior doctor of the wards. I am really a *great* deal stronger and healthier than I have been for a long time. . . .
>
> We get up at 6.30 a.m., – breakfast at 7, then go round the wards with the doctors, then I make up the hospital medicines and see what drugs need to be ordered into the dispensary. The Dispensary opens at 9, or two days in the week at 10, and on Mondays and Thursdays (Dr Sewall's days) I am there all the morning, making up prescriptions as fast as she writes them (two of us generally have our hands full, but sometimes I am alone), and very often we have not got through our work when the dinner-bell rings at 1 p.m. Dr Sewall always has an enormous number of patients – from 60 to 70, and if I go down into the Dispensary waiting-room I get seized on so eagerly, – 'Is Dr Sewall here herself?' as she is occasionally obliged to be absent part of the time.[16]

The women who thronged to the New England Hospital had overcome any doubts as to the trustworthiness of women doctors. The pressure of work made it necessary to have two male doctors as assistants at the Hospital, but their clinics remained small, while patients waited for attention in the crowded clinics conducted by women doctors. Sophia believed that many women who were now receiving treatment at the Hospital would have suffered unaided, rather than be treated by a man.

While Sophia was discovering the appeal of medicine as a vocation, Elizabeth Garrett in London was preparing to go into practice. On 28 September 1865 she passed the examination for the Licence of the Society of Apothecaries. Now she was Elizabeth Garrett LSA, a legally qualified medical practitioner! There was one other woman's name on the British Register – that of Elizabeth Blackwell – but Dr Blackwell had returned to New York in 1859, having conducted only a token practice among her friends during her short visit to England. Elizabeth Garrett was Britain's only woman doctor. She could only guess at her chances of succeeding in practice. Would women consult a woman doctor, now that they had one? Would her male colleagues give her the professional support needed by all doctors, or would she be ostracized, unable to refer her patients to specialists or to call for help when unusual difficulties arose? Only time would provide the answers.

It was unlikely that more women would soon join her. The Society of Apothecaries had made a last-minute attempt to exclude her from their examinations, and only her father's stern threat of legal action had made them yield. Her subsequent success strengthened male opposition. Less than a month after Elizabeth Garrett received her LSA, a young woman named Ellen Colborne attempted to become a student at the medical school of St Bartholomew's Hospital, where Elizabeth Blackwell had received such a gracious welcome in 1850.

Ellen Colborne's story is recorded in the diary of Henry Butlin, who was then a second-year student at the Hospital. Butlin notes that on Monday, 16 October, at the end of his physiology lecture Mr Savory informed the class that a lady had been enrolled as a student 'with certain restrictions'. The men were so incensed that for the rest of the day they could talk of nothing else. That evening Butlin met with five of his friends. They wrote a petition to the school's administrators and stayed up until midnight collecting the signatures of their fellow students. Next day Mr Savory told his class that, in deference to their wishes, the lady probably would not be allowed to join them. The students cheered.

But Ellen Colborne did not give up without a fight. Two weeks later Butlin wrote in his diary:

> Went to Anatomy Lecture, after which went into the Medical Theatre, but had not been there long, before in walked the lady, Miss Colborne, (concerning whom, we had petitioned, that she should not be allowed to enter the School) the theatre soon became crowded w. men, who hooted, screamed, etc., but I walked out as soon as I could make my way to the

door; in consequence of the violent state of feeling of the students, Dr Black did not enter the theatre at the proper time, but sent Thomas, (the marker), to beg the woman to go into the museum and speak with Mr Callender, which she did, and order was restored – Mr Callender had about an hour or two before sent for Thorne and told him that Miss Colborne persisted in coming in spite of all he could say or do to dissuade her, and that, having entered at the Hospital, she refused to take back her fees, and, if not allowed to attend the Lectures, would put the matter in the hands of her solicitor.

Miss Colborne's threat of legal action made her opponents change their tactics. The diary entry for Tuesday, 7 November, reads:

Went to Physiology Lecture, which had not proceeded very far, when Miss Colborne walked in; Mr Savory stopped and considered for a moment, and then said, 'Gentlemen, are you desirous that I should proceed with this lecture?' Loud cries of 'No! No!' from all parts of the theatre; 'Well, then, I will put it to the vote,' which he accordingly did, by show of hands, when two men only were in favour of the continuance of the lecture under such circumstances, one of whom afterwards said that he did not know that the *lady* was in the room, and therefore did not understand what was the reason of the abrupt closing.[17]

Ellen Colborne was outmanœuvred; whenever she appeared at the Hospital the lecture would be cancelled. The male students could easily arrange lectures elsewhere, but she could not. She had to admit defeat and was never heard of again as a medical student. Henry Butlin later had a distinguished career as a surgeon and was honoured with a baronetcy.

Sophia continued her work at the New England Hospital, enjoying it more each day, but still uncertain that medicine could replace education as her life's work. For so many years she had planned to have her own school that the idea was not easily abandoned. Her unhappy experience at Mannheim had not deterred her. The problem of religious instruction seems to have given her more serious concern. It was not resolved at Manchester and now, at the New England Hospital, she confronted it again. She agreed with Dr Arnold of Rugby when he said that the school Principal should also be the school Chaplain. She yearned to take on this responsibility, but had grave doubts as to her capacity to fulfil it. At home she had been something of a renegade from the Anglican Church; in America she lost interest in Unitarianism and returned to the orthodox faith of her parents. But perhaps she would change her mind yet again! A school Chaplain could not vacillate like this and still be an effective religious leader. Sophia noticed that Dr Sewall's fine work for others was not hindered by her lack of interest in theology. She said of Lucy Sewall, 'She calls herself a theist, but it seems to me to run close to practical atheism.' Sophia asked herself if it was possible that medicine attracted her simply because if offered an escape from the dilemma of religion; if so, it would not satisfy her for long. After pondering all these problems she decided to pursue her medical studies for the time being because, even if she continued with her teaching career, the medical knowledge could be put to good use.

In her letters to her parents she discussed all these ideas quite openly. Her father, who had been so shocked at her acceptance of payment for her first teaching appointment, had since greatly modified his views on women's work, and encouraged her to study medicine. He sent his thanks to Dr Sewall for her kindness to his daughter, while hoping that she would soon visit England so that he could have the pleasure of thanking her in person. Early in 1866 Sophia decided to return home briefly during the approaching summer. She would soon have been away for a year, so it was time to be reunited with her family and friends. One of the many friends she had continued to correspond with was Lucy Unwin. Mrs Unwin had recently rescued Sophia's former maidservant, Alice, from an uncongenial position. In March Sophia wrote to Lucy Unwin:

> I hope you are quite prepared to renew your invitation to me for next summer, for I'm beginning to think seriously of my visit home, and I want very much to see you! . . .
> I am so glad to hear that you have got Alice with you, and expect to like her. She is a real friend of mine, and a very true and valuable one. . . . I only hope you will let her take as good care of you as she used to do of me. . . .
> Whenever you feel energetic enough to enjoy a chat by pen and paper, I shall be very pleased to hear of your doings. Pray tell me all about the Baby – of course the most wonderful of his kind – and be sure, dear child, that I shall care very much to hear and know about everything that concerns you.
> Please give the enclosed lines to A. I shall enjoin her to feed you up no end, and whenever we do meet, be sure I shall ask if you let yourself be taken proper and sensible care of. I believe in food and rest as just the best doctors in creation – with all my new medical lights![18]

Sophia returned home as planned. Her visit to Lucy Unwin is not recorded, but she almost certainly made it, since this last letter indicates the concern she was beginning to feel about her friend's health. In retrospect, it seems that Lucy was suffering from tuberculosis, a disease about which very little was then known. From this time onwards her health continued to decline. She was a sensitive young woman who could have been helped through her suffering if there had been a woman doctor near her home in Yorkshire. The plight of Lucy Unwin was probably in the back of Sophia's mind whenever she pondered on the need for women doctors.

Mr and Mrs Jex-Blake were delighted to find Sophia in better health and spirits than she had been for several years. If medical work could do this for their daughter then there was much to be said for it. Most of Sophia's friends also encouraged her, but Elizabeth Garrett told her quite bluntly that she thought her not specially suited to medical work. Elizabeth had at times been irritated by Sophia's tactlessness, but she, too, could be quite insensitive. The remark certainly hurt Sophia, though she did not allow it to influence her; she felt that she knew her capabilities better than Elizabeth did. Elizabeth spoke with the self-confidence of a woman who is beginning to achieve her ambitions. After nearly a year in practice in Upper Berkeley Street she still received a regular allowance from her father, but the steady growth of her practice justified her belief that she would soon be self-supporting. It seemed that a competent woman doctor could make her way in the world.

While she was in England, Sophia approached the publishing firm of Macmillan about the possibility of their accepting a book on her tour of educational institutions in America; she was delighted with their enthusiastic response. So she returned to Boston and the New England Hospital with the writing of this book the first item on her programme. Two months later the manuscript of *A Visit to Some American Schools and Colleges* was despatched to the publishers and Sophia was free to turn her thoughts to other matters.

While working on her book she had come to an important decision: medicine was to be her vocation. She enrolled for the anatomy course at the New England Female Medical College, and began the practical work that has always been the basis of anatomical knowledge – the systematic dissection of cadavers. But within a few weeks Sophia realized that the teaching at the College had become quite unsatisfactory. Samuel Gregory's main purpose was to put an end to the attendance of male doctors on female patients, a practice he considered immoral. So long as he could give some kind of training to women he cared little about their proficiency; in fact, he thought women incapable of assimilating advanced scientific theory. Furthermore, the little New England Hospital, although it had grown considerably during the six years of its existence, still could not provide comprehensive practical training for its students. Sophia decided to aim high. She remembered the kindness of the President of Harvard, Dr Hill, so in company with another student, Miss Susan Dimock, she wrote to the President and Fellows of the University, requesting admission to the University's Medical School.

March 11th 1867

GENTLEMEN,

Finding it impossible to obtain elsewhere in New England a thoroughly competent medical education, we hereby request permission to enter Harvard Medical School on the same terms and under the same conditions as other students, there being, as we understand, no university statute to the contrary.

On applying for tickets for the course, we were informed by the Dean of the Medical Faculty that he and his coadjutors were unable to grant them to us in consequence of some previous action taken by the corporation, to whom now therefore we make request to remove any such existing disability. In full faith in the words recently spoken with reference to the University of Harvard, – 'American colleges are not cloisters for the education of a few persons, but seats of learning whose hospitable doors should be always open to every seeker after knowledge' – we place our petition in your hands and subscribe ourselves,

Your obedient servants,
Sophia Jex-Blake
Susan Dimock[19]

The reply came a month later.

Harvard University
April 8th 1867

MY DEAR MADAM,

After consultation with the faculty of the Medical College, the corporation direct me to inform you and Miss Dimock that there is no provision for the education of women in any department of this university.

Neither the corporation nor the faculty wish to express any opinion as to the right or expediency of the medical education of women, but simply to state the fact that in our school no provision for that purpose has been made, or is at present contemplated.

Very respectfully yours,
Thomas Hill[20]

Both letters appeared in the *Boston Daily Advertiser*, probably having been submitted by Sophia, and were the subject of public comment, most of it favourable to the women's side. Sophia and Susan Dimock then tried appealing to the various lecturers individually. Some of them, including two famous men – Professor Oliver Wendell Holmes and Dr Brown-Sequard – would have welcomed the women to their classes, but the University authorities intervened and forbade any such action by individual faculty members. The women's efforts did, however, achieve one useful result; some of the doctors they canvassed agreed to give them clinical teaching in the wards of the great Massachusetts General Hospital. Thus for eight months, as a special privilege, they were able to enjoy some of the benefits that were readily available to all male students. They had to tread warily, because one or two of the medical staff at the Hospital were strongly opposed to the admission of women and were watching for the least excuse to have these two excluded.

While studying, Sophia continued to live and work at the New England

Hospital for Women. In mid-1867 her book on American schools and colleges was published. It was favourably reviewed in the British press, the reviewers finding it not only a sensible and informative work on an important subject, but also entertainingly written. Such comments were, of course, pleasing to Sophia, but in the few months since she completed the manuscipt her interests had changed completely. The author of *A Visit to Some American Schools and Colleges* now seemed like another person.

In July Sophia and Lucy Sewall took a holiday from the New England Hospital and travelled to Maine. Sophia's letter to her mother shows how resourceful members of the 'weaker sex' could be:

Yesterday we drove (as I told you at the end of my last letter) from Newbury port to Portsmouth, and were uncertain when I wrote whether to stay or go further. It had been a hot day, but, after posting your letter, a violent rainstorm came up, deluging the streets for about 20 minutes about $5\frac{1}{2}$ p.m.

After it was over, everything looked so cool and clear that Dr Sewall was anxious to get on, though I was a little afraid of the heavy roads. So we set out soon after six, and had a most delicious drive at first. Bye-and-bye, however, we came to terribly wet clay roads and could go only at a walk. Our horse got tired and it began to get dark, and we found that the distance to go was even longer than we had been told.

It's hard for you to understand the sort of society in these country places, – no gentry and no peasantry – almost all small farmers doing their own work, and owning house and land, with some education but no polish. We stopped at two or three houses, scattered at wide intervals, – and enquired for lodgings, but with no success till after dark when we got to a house belonging to a widow woman who informed us we could come in and have bed and food, but there was 'no one in the house but her, – no one for the horse.' However, I was perfectly ready to act groom, so in we drove to such a queer loose sort of yard, where I unharnessed by very uncertain lantern light, and then the doctor and I had a tremendous job getting our phaeton into a queer coach-house up a sort of hillock!

Then the lantern led on to the 'barn,' which (here as usual) meant also stable, and soon I found myself plunging in the dark through soft masses which proved to be long wet grass, leading my horse by the halter. Then up among big loose stones, and up a step more than $1\frac{1}{2}$ foot high into a barn so low that my horse all but hit his head. Then over some boards set edgewise to divide off stalls . . . the good woman being amazed at my venturing in 'with the horse'!

Then a queer hunt in the half darkness for a pail of water and wooden box for Indian meal (which, stirred with water, often replaces oats here), and then to bed, tired enough!

This morning I groomed the horse, and, so doing, found a stone in his

foot, fed him, and we between us washed the carriage. You may tell Daddy I had no idea what hard work it was before! We washed a long while at it, and somehow, it wouldn't look *quite* clean at last.
(N.B. Why *will* water dry muddy on to a carriage?)
Then we drove on again some distance and found a place for dinner, – one of the big boarding-houses like what I was in at Compton, – and then on again. Dr Sewall began to get tired when we were still 5 or 6 miles from our next point, Kennebunk, – and seeing a notice on a bye-road, 'Atlantic House ¼ mile' – we drove down, – found a charming inn almost on the sands, close to the Atlantic, – fresh and bright and airy, and settled here for the night. If you only knew what my afflictions are in American country inns, – You may imagine my satisfaction at getting here the best supper I have had yet, – excellent fresh fish, lobsters, etc., and currants, and nice bread, and milk. Altogether the best table we've found yet.
It sounds natural, too, to hear the roar of the Atlantic as I write, – only it seems sometimes to murmur, 'Over the sea!' But then it always makes me feel nearer home to see the actual water which is the only thing between us, – of which you at Brighton see but another part.[21]

Summer holidays were not the only occasions that tested Sophia's ability to manage horses – she was often the driver when Dr Sewall was called out on an urgent case. In winter their conveyance was a sleigh.

I drove the doctor eight or nine miles in a pelting snow storm, partly across open country, long bridges and marshes, etc., the thermometer somewhere about 10° or 15°[F], a good deal of wind, which always makes it feel much colder, and the sharp crystals of snow cutting into our faces and eyes like so many pin points and causing actual pain. Towards the end I found it rather hard to see, – some white things seemed to get in front of my eyes; – what do you think they were? Solid icicles hanging from my eye-lashes on the side exposed to the wind, – frozen together into three or four solid little balls as big as small peas, and partly freezing the lids together! When I got in I called Eliza to see them, – you should have heard her 'Gracious goodness!'
Even sealskin gloves fail one in such stormy cold, – one's hands freeze and have to be thawed out as regards sensation several times in a drive! So we carry hot bottles to do it with, and Dr Sewall laughed at the figure I cut yesterday, driving with one hand, the other grasping a big two-quart bottle upright on my lap, and my head bent on one side like a lapwing's to see out of the one eye that wasn't frozen up!
She herself offered to drive again and again, but speed was my object, and I always make the horse go half as fast again as she does. He did gallantly yesterday, – the roads and streets were clear, and we spun over

the white frozen surface at eight or ten miles an hour. When it is not actually snowing, sleighing is very exhilarating, – the horse has a light load and is generally in good spirits, – sleigh-bells jangling merrily.[22]

If her opponents at Harvard had seen Sophia driving her sleigh across the ice, they might have wondered uneasily how long they could hold out against such women, but they remained unmoved by her calmly reasoned letters, such as the one drafted in January 1868:

GENTLEMEN,
                Having during the past year been granted access to the clinical advantages of the Massachusetts General Hospital, but finding it impossible anywhere in New England to obtain adequate theoretical instruction in Medicine, we now earnestly entreat you to reconsider the subject of the admission of women to the lectures at Harvard Medical School, – such admission being, as we understand, forbidden by no past or present statute of the University.
We do not wish to enter on the vexed question of the capability or non-capability of women for the practice of Medicine, as we believe that time and experience only can furnish its true answer, but we now present our urgent petition that some opportunity may be afforded us for the thorough study of the medical science and art, that we may be granted at least some of the advantages that are not denied to every man, and allowed to show whether we are or are not worthy to make use of them. We are willing, Gentlemen, to submit to any required examination, to qualify ourselves according to any given standard, to furnish any personal references, and to abide by any restrictions and regulations which may seem proper to the Corporation or to the Faculty.
Several of the Professors having expressed their personal willingness to allow us to attend their lectures, we earnestly request that the Corporation will authorize our admission to those classes into which the respective Professors do not object to receive us, and that, in any case where the Professor does so object, we may be allowed to receive private instruction from some medical gentlemen approved by the Faculty, whose lectures shall in our case be held equivalent to those given to the College classes in the same subject.[23]

Sophia would have been surprised to know how much practice she would have in writing letters in this vein.

Although she was so far from home, Sophia's interest in the school at Bettws-y-Coed had not faded. Her interest was shared by her family, especially by her sister Caroline, but it was often Sophia who originated plans for improving the school and its amenities. Perhaps it held a special place in her affections because she first saw it when, as a lonely schoolgirl, she was permitted to join the family holiday party in Wales. After that first visit in 1855 Sophia returned nearly every summer to teach and to give the children a party. In 1868 the Jex-Blakes encouraged the local people to rebuild their school. From Boston Sophia wrote to her mother:

> I am glad to understand that you have bought, not the first bit of ground, but another near it. I hope Carry will soon send me some idea of her plans, though, of course, we can't build for some months. I enclose a very rough sketch of what would be my own idea of a school-room with gallery at one end and with classroom at the other, – and besides the class room a sort of lobby with second entrance and with stairs leading to the rooms above for Anne. The porch to have places to hang hats etc., as also under the gallery (as at Hastings).
>
> I can't remember about dimensions, though I have a sort of idea that, when we spoke of buildings before, we planned our schoolroom at 18 ft by 28, and 10 ft or 11 ft high, the class room to be perhaps 11 ft by 8. Ask Carry to see how that agrees with the standard space for 100 children.[24]

Sophia speaks of buying the site, but Bettws records indicate that part, at least, of the land was the gift of Lord Willoughby de Eresby. The local quarry supplied stone for the building, and farmers volunteered to cart the materials to the building site. The new school was completed in 1869.[25] One of the first teachers to work there was a local girl (probably the 'Anne' of Sophia's letter), whose education had been sponsored by the Jex-Blake family.

Another of her Boston letters tells how Sophia acquired a dog, which she named 'Turk'. Turk was to be her loyal companion for many years.

> A few days ago one of the women who had been confined here was fetched home by her husband, and with him came a rather big dog of the setter or lurcher kind, I think, or rather a cross on one of them. The folks went away, and so did the dog, but in half an hour he was back again, scratch-ing at the Hospital door. He was fetched again by the man and again ran back, no one having, so far as I know, petted or enticed him at all. Then he was refused admission or turned out on the street, and when his master came again for him I believe he found him on the street; but in the evening there came a scratching at *our* hall door – not the Hospital, – and in walked the same dog again! I knew nothing of the previous story, but remembered having seen him with the man who came to our house to see Dr Sewall, so I took him in. From that moment he attached himself to me, so that he follows every step I take, and whines at any door I enter without him. As the man didn't come again for him, I drove to his house this morning, – the dog following close to the sleigh all the way (some two miles), and when he got there the dog greeted his master certainly,

70

but directly I rose to go, up he jumped after me. So, as *his* choice seemed to be made, I offered the man $5 (15s. 6d.) for him, and now am undisputed owner of my loyal friend!

It is rather queer, for I had been wishing for a dog of my own, and, though he is not a great beauty, he has a nice face, is very obedient, clean, and, I think, intelligent, – though Dr Sewall professes to disdain him for being 'so big'! – and then one can't help liking even a dog who so plainly declares 'elective affinity'.[26]

The rejection of her appeals to Harvard University meant that Sophia had to look elsewhere for satisfactory tuition. Much as she disliked the thought of leaving Boston, where she had so many friends, she decided to visit New York and make enquiries about Dr Elizabeth Blackwell's proposed medical school for women. In March 1868 she was welcomed to the New York Infirmary for Women by its founder. This was Sophia's first meeting with the famous woman whose graduation from Geneva Medical College nearly twenty years previously had created such a stir. Sophia learned that despite Dr Blackwell's fragile appearance she had overcome adversity that would have defeated any ordinary woman.

Born in Bristol, England, in 1821, she was one of the nine children of Samuel Blackwell, a prosperous sugar refiner. Her parents had enlightened views on education, and believed that, in this regard, there should be no discrimination between sons and daughters. But while Elizabeth was still a child, her father's business began to fail; then a disastrous fire burnt down his refinery. In 1832 the Blackwell family migrated to the United States and settled in New Jersey, where they remained for six years. Still plagued with financial difficulties, Samuel Blackwell then decided to move to Cincinnati, where he became the proprietor of a beet sugar refinery, probably very much like the one for sorghum that Sophia visited during her tour. But before his business was soundly established, Samuel Blackwell died.

The resourcefulness of Elizabeth and two of her sisters enabled the family to survive the crisis. They conducted a school for girls, from which they earned enough to help keep their mother and the younger children. By the time Elizabeth was 23 her responsibility for the family had diminished, but she continued to teach, saving her earnings so that she could later study for some other vocation. She sought more than a means to a livelihood; the profession she chose had to be one to which she could devote her life, because she thought it unlikely that she would every marry. Medicine met her needs, and she was prepared to battle against ignorance and prejudice to achieve her aim.

For three years she obtained intermittent private tuition from the few medical men who were prepared to help her, before she at last gained admission to Geneva Medical College. When she graduated, only eighteen months later, she still needed practical training and more advanced tuition, neither of which was then available to a woman in America. A more liberal attitude was said to prevail in Europe, so Elizabeth went to Paris. But even here she was turned away from the leading medical schools and general hospitals. Eventually she was accepted as a student midwife at La Maternité, a large obstetrical hospital. Her fellow pupils were mostly poorly educated peasant girls who would return to their villages to work as midwives to the farming community.

Elizabeth had been at La Maternité for six months when she had a serious accident. While bathing the eyes of a newborn baby infected with gonorrhoea she splashed her own face with some of the purulent fluid. One of her eyes became so severely inflamed that its sight was rapidly destroyed. A few months later the eye had to be removed in order to prevent complications that could have led to total blindness. From the age of 29, Elizabeth Blackwell wore a glass eye.

Determined not to be crushed by this misfortune she went to England, where she was warmly received as a visiting student at St Bartholomew's Hospital.[27] While in Britain she became friendly with the leaders of that nation's emerging feminist movement. After returning to New York in 1851 her efforts to establish a practice were at first hindered by popular prejudice; the term 'female physician' was regarded by many as a euphemism for 'abortionist', and Elizabeth was ostracized socially as well as professionally. To overcome her loneliness she adopted a little orphan girl, Kitty Barry. Kitty was about 7 years old when she came to live with Elizabeth Blackwell. She thrived in her new home and became devoted to 'the Doctor', as she always called her foster mother. In 1868, when Sophia first met her, Kitty was a young woman in her early twenties, but Dr Blackwell still enjoyed telling friends of an amusing remark she had made as a little girl:

[Kitty] had always been accustomed to call me 'Doctor'. On one occasion she was present during the visit of a friendly physician. After he was gone, she came to me with a very puzzled face, exclaiming, 'Doctor, how very odd it is to hear a *man* called 'Doctor'!'[28]

In 1858, with the New York Infirmary for Women soundly established, Elizabeth was able to leave it in the hands of her capable sister, Dr Emily Blackwell, while she made another visit to England. She was just in time to have her name entered in the first British Register of medical practitioners; after 1858 a foreign degree such as hers would not have been accepted. It was also during this visit that Elizabeth Blackwell met Elizabeth Garrett and inspired her to take up the study of medicine.

During the American Civil War the Infirmary became a centre for the training of nurses, who were needed in large numbers to care for battle casualties. Not until the war was over could Elizabeth continue with her work for the training of women doctors. She realized that the public would tend to regard a school that was only for women as an inferior institution. To prevent this she set standards that were obviously at least as high as those of the best schools for male students. An unusually comprehensive course would be conducted by teachers who were aknowledged leaders in their fields. Examinations would be in the hands of a panel of external examiners, so that there could be no suspicion of 'easy passes for women students'. Students would be accepted for enrolment only after they had passed an entrance examination. Most other medical schools did not hold entrance examinations until some ten years later.

When Sophia arrived in March 1868, six months' preparation had yet to be completed before the College could be officially opened. Nevertheless several young women were already attending the New York Infirmary as students. Sophia's academic record ensured that she was readily admitted to the group. Each afternoon she attended lectures at the Infirmary; her mornings were spent dissecting, and studying anatomy at the Bellevue Hospital. This teaching was vastly superior to that being offered at Samuel Gregory's school in Boston, so Sophia seriously considered undertaking the three-year course in New York. But the expense would be greater than if she had stayed in Boston, as she explained in a letter to her mother:

Living in New York is neither easy nor cheap, you see, . . . I hardly know how I shall manage if I go to a medical college this winter, and have to pay all lecture expenses, etc., besides living, – for women have to incur extra expenses in all sorts of ways, because they can't share the arrangements of some sorts made for men. . . . While studying, Miss Garrett had, I know, to spend lots of money, – paying £50 for a single course of lectures which the men got (in class) for £5 each.[29]

Her parents reassured her that they would gladly increase her allowance if she wished to study in New York. Her only regret then was that she would miss the companionship of the medical women at the New England Hospital. In bantering mood she wrote to Lucy Sewall:

I am glad that you find out (as I told you you would) that I did do one or two little things while you wondered how I spent my time. I wish, however, that you had someone to do them now, – I am afraid you will get so tired. I shall ask Eliza if you eat properly. Tell her that I mean to write to her next time.
The little book of your bills is on my shelf in my secretary, – a small account book. Don't muddle the things in looking for it. Be sure and put down in it all the bills you send out. Can't you get Miss Call to write them for you? She really can *write* (unusual in the N.E.H.) . . .
Tell me if Eliza does nicely, – tell her I asked after her and her house-keeping and Robert.
I am glad that my son Turk behaves better as he grows older. Give him an extra bone with my blessing.[30]

Such light-hearted exchanges did not take place at the New York Infirmary, which was dominated by the personality of the middle-aged Elizabeth Blackwell. Years of adversity had intensified Elizabeth's natural seriousness and made it impossible for her to shed her cares.

Sophia's plans were becoming more clearly defined. She had not quite given up hope of being admitted to Harvard, but it was now certain that, either in Boston or New York, a three-year course of study lay ahead of her. With this accomplished, she would work as Dr Lucy Sewall's assistant for a year or two, before returning to London to open her own practice. The question of registration in Britain does not seem to have concerned her. Perhaps she assumed that, by then, women with good foreign degrees would be granted registration; on the other hand, she may have been prepared to work as an unregistered practitioner, on the assumption that her American training would be acceptable to patients and colleagues.

After spending two months in New York, Sophia prepared to take her summer holiday. On this occasion Lucy Sewall had agreed to come to England with her. Sophia's family and friends, who were eager to meet the American woman doctor, arranged numerous engagements for the two travellers. One of their first commitments was to visit Mrs Unwin, who was grateful for the opportunity to consult a woman doctor. Back in London Sophia attended a lecture on education, given by her former teacher, the Reverend Denison Maurice. To her delight, Maurice referred to her book on American schools and colleges as a valuable contribution to the subject. Sophia also noted in her diary, 'After the lecture he *thanked* me for my book. I'm cock a hoop now!'

Doubtless Sophia also renewed her acquaintance with Elizabeth Garrett. She would certainly have heard that Dr Garrett's practice was now quite large, and among her patients were several ladies who were leaders of London society. The eminent surgeon James Paget (later Sir James Paget) had recently acted as Elizabeth's consultant on a difficult case. He was one of the most respected members of the profession, so it was likely that other consultants would follow his example and come to her aid when requested. In addition to her private practice she had opened an outpatient clinic – St Mary's Dispensary for Women and Children – where poor women were treated for a charge of only one penny per visit. Patients flocked to the Dispensary, its success further enhancing Dr Garrett's professional reputation.

But although one woman was succeeding handsomely, the prospects for others were actually becoming worse. Sophia's arrival in London almost coincided with the announcement that the Society of Apothecaries had altered its constitution. In future, candidates for examination would have to produce certificates to show that *all* their training had been obtained in the Society's classes. Since women were not admitted to some of these classes, all women candidates were now effectively excluded. The portal through which Elizabeth Garrett had entered the profession was closed.

The holiday passed quickly. Sophia's parents were so pleased with their daughter's friend that they made her a generous gift; on her return to the New England Infirmary Lucy Sewall would find herself the owner of a new carriage that was small and ideally suited to her needs.

Sophia went back to Boston with Lucy Sewall, in order to make a last appeal to Harvard. When this was refused, she went on to New York, where the opening of Dr Blackwell's school was imminent. Sophia's parents did all they could to help. Alice, the capable maid who had accompanied Sophia to Edinburgh, now came to housekeep for her in New York. Sophia found lodgings at 222 East Tenth Street: 'two back parlours and two above, – gas and all $55'. In a letter to her mother written a week later she described how these rooms now made a comfortable home for three – Sophia, Alice and dog Turk.

> The term begins tomorrow, and I am glad to say that Alice and I have just succeeded in getting things into some sort of order in time. Besides laying down carpets, buying a stove and kitchen pots and pans, bed-steads and chairs, etc., I have been providing winter stores in American fashion, and yesterday bought two barrels of potatoes, 30 lbs. of butter, etc., etc., to say nothing of flour and wine. My money is running terribly low, – I have only about £20 left when this month's rent is paid; but then most of my things are bought now, and besides I can borrow from Dr Sewall if needful. Besides the Hospital owes me about £10 or £11 for duties paid, so I can probably get on till my next quarter comes.[31]

On 2 November 1868 there was a ceremony to mark the opening of the Women's Medical College of the New York Infirmary. Sophia was in the audience and made notes on Elizabeth Blackwell's address:

> It has required fifteen years of patient working by faith (for the way has been very dark) to lay the foundation of a college. We have been facing these two perpendicular cliffs, lack of money and lack of skill, and have been striving in every possible way to climb them. Little by little, however, we have laid one stone upon another, until we have a foundation sufficient to stand on. It is small, certainly, but solid. . . .
> Medicine is a learned and confidential profession and should draw to its ranks the most highly educated, the most irreproachable in character. This most noble profession, like all high things, is susceptible of the worst abuse. The good which women may accomplish in medical practice is also the measure of the evil they may do. Education, long and careful, should be the safeguard of society in this matter. From many causes, women are peculiarly exposed to the great temptation of practising ignorantly and superficially. The College should foresee this danger and provide the long and careful training which alone can discriminate between the worthy and unworthy candidate. . . . The College must be

an honest and earnest attempt to give women the very highest education that modern science will afford. . . .

Let us give all due weight to sympathy, and never dispense with it in the true physician, but it is knowledge, not sympathy, which can administer the right medicine. It is observation and comprehension, not sympathy, which will discover the kind of disease; and though warm sympathetic natures, with knowledge, would make the best of all physicians – without sound knowledge, they would be most unreliable and dangerous guides.[32]

Next day, work at the College began in earnest. Sophia was pleased with the standard of the teaching. The opportunities for learning in New York more than compensated for the loss of the companionship of her Boston friends.

My daily routine is pretty regular throughout the week. I go to the dissecting room at 9 a.m. and work till about 11.15. At 11.30 comes a lecture on Anatomy and Physiology on alternate days, – and I get home to lunch a little before one. Alice always has things ready and nice for me, and I rest for about half an hour after lunch, before going to the afternoon lectures which begin at 2 p.m. and continue (except on Saturday) till 5, – three lectures of an hour each. I have just put in a petition to Dr Emily Blackwell (who manages everything and is very nice) for five minutes space between each two lectures, for opening windows and a walk up and down the corridors, – to which she instantly assented as desirable.

Pleasant as it was to live with the Doctor, and extremely grateful as I feel for the very great good she has done me, I confess now to rather enjoy-ing a completely independent nest once more, – for a while at least. You see it was inevitable that at Boston everything had to be shaped to suit Hospital work, and that was sometimes a nuisance.

I can study and write and read in a much more thoroughly undisturbed way here than I could there, – in fact it would have been simply impos-sible while living there to work as I am doing now, – there were so very many inevitable interruptions.[33]

Sophia's satisfaction was short-lived. A week later she received an urgent message from home that her father was critically ill. She rushed back to England with all possible speed, but was too late. Thomas Jex-Blake was already dead.

Although for some time Sophia had been aware of her father's declining strength, she had not expected the end to come so soon. She felt his loss keenly, but was even more concerned for her mother, who would now be much more reliant on her children. Sophia's brother Thomas had his own family and a busy professional life, having recently been appointed headmaster of

Cheltenham College. Her sister Caroline was still unmarried, and should have been the ideal companion for her mother, whose views on all important subjects concurred with her own; but their unruffled relationship gave them little emotional satisfaction. Mrs Jex-Blake felt much closer to her tempestuous younger daughter, with whom she had so often been at loggerheads. Without hesitation Sophia renounced her plans for studying in New York. She sent Alice instructions to dispose of the stores and furniture so recently acquired, and to return home.

Notes

1. M. Todd, *The Life of Sophia Jex-Blake*, London: Macmillan, 1918, p. 161.
2. ibid., p. 165.
3. ibid., p. 163.
4. ibid., p. 163.
5. ibid., p. 164.
6. ibid., p. 167.
7. S. Jex-Blake, *A Visit to Some American Schools and Colleges*, London: Macmillan, 1867, pp. 1–3.
8. ibid., p. 17.
9. ibid., pp. 31–3.
10. ibid., pp. 69–70.
11. ibid., pp. 102–3.
12. ibid., p. 155.
13. ibid., pp. 224–5.
14. ibid., p. 225.
15. M. Todd, op. cit., p. 176.
16. ibid., p. 173.
17. A. Franklin, *St. Bartholomew's Hospital Medical Journal*, November 1931.
18. Todd, op. cit., p. 184.
19. ibid., p. 190.
20. ibid., p. 190.
21. ibid., p. 193.
22. ibid., p. 197.
23. ibid., p. 195.
24. ibid., p. 198.
25. I.W. Jones, *Betws-y-Coed: The Mountain Resort*, Glasgow: Hay, Nisbett and Miller, 1974–5. In 1950 the Urban Council approved the change of spelling from Bettws to Betws.
26. Todd, op. cit., p. 197.
27. Elizabeth Blackwell, 'A reminiscence of forty years ago', *St. Bartholomew's Hospital Medical Journal*, September 1894.
28. E. Blackwell, *Pioneer Work in Opening the Medical Profession to Women*, London: Longman, Green & Co., 1895.
29. Todd, op. cit., p. 200.
30. ibid., p. 199.
31. ibid., p. 204.
32. I. Ross, *Child of Destiny*, New York: Harper, 1949.
33. Todd, op. cit., p. 206.

5

The Edinburgh campaign begins

The anguish of her newly widowed mother made Sophia feel that, by comparison, her own ambitions were of little importance. She was quite prepared to forego her planned career in order to be her mother's constant companion. But those who knew them well could have predicted that such an arrangement would not suit either mother or daughter for long. Within a few weeks Sophia was writing to Lucy Sewall:

> You can fancy what this house is now, – so silent and mourning, – and so much cut off even from outside, and at any rate no people or work or occupation of any interest outside ourselves.
> M[other] and C[aroline] have their regular ways and plans, I suppose, but it is so long since I have been at home except for a visit, that it's hard for me to fit in anywhere, and of course everybody's feeling more or less sad and pained doesn't make matters smoother. Just at present I am getting my books and drawers etc., to rights, and after that is done I mean to try and read some Medicine at least, – perhaps if we stay here all winter I may apply to visit at the Hospital, etc. – only it would be rather disagreeable all alone.[1]

Mrs Jex-Blake took comfort from the knowledge that her younger daughter was permanently back in England. It would please her even more to see her able to resume her studies and thereby regain her good spirits. But another interesting project was soon to keep Sophia fully occupied for several months. At the end of the year she was approached by Macmillan, the publishers of her book on American schools and colleges, with a request that she contribute to a collection of essays on the theme of women's education and their changing role in society.[2] Mr Alexander Macmillan's original intention was that all the essays would be written by women, but later he chose five men and five women for the panel of authors. The editor of the volume, and the writer of the introduction, was to be the noted feminist Mrs Josephine Butler. Sophia liked Mrs Butler and was also friendly with one of the authors, the redoubtable

Frances Power Cobbe, so she was glad to accept the invitation to write on the subject of medicine as a career for women. Elizabeth Garrett, as the only registered woman doctor practising in England, may well have been considered first for the commission, but Mrs Butler would have had a reason for preferring not to deal with her. They did not see eye to eye on an issue dear to Mrs Butler's heart.

Josephine Butler, who was then in her early forties, was the wife of a Liverpool schoolmaster. She was already well known for her work in rehabilitating destitute women and prostitutes, having established a number of homes where these women could take refuge while they tried to obtain respectable employment. While this work continued, Mrs Butler became engrossed in another cause that was to be her dominant interest for nearly twenty years; this was the campaign for the repeal of the Contagious Diseases Acts of 1864, 1866 and 1869.

The Acts provided for the legalization of brothels in eleven towns where there were army garrisons or naval stations. Prostitutes working in the brothels had to be licensed and were required to undergo six-monthly medical examinations to ensure that they were not spreading venereal disease. The law also empowered special police in the specified towns to arrest any woman suspected of being an unlicensed prostitute, and to compel her to undergo a medical examination. Mrs Butler believed that the Contagious Diseases Acts not only failed to prevent the spread of disease, but that they actually promoted prostitution. Furthermore, because of the Acts innocent women were being humiliated and assaulted. In 1869 she founded the Ladies' National Association to fight for the repeal of the Acts. Florence Nightingale was one of her many influential supporters. But there was also a strong body of opinion in favour not only of retaining the Acts, but of extending their provisions to the whole nation, rather than just a few garrison towns. The British Medical Association supported this view. Elizabeth Garrett's work at the St Mary's Dispensary had impressed her with the magnitude of the problem of venereal disease; she favoured the retention of the Acts, regarding them as the lesser of two evils. Mrs Butler deeply regretted that Dr Garrett was one of her opponents, especially as her support could have been so valuable.

Now that she was back in England Sophia was able to observe Elizabeth Garrett's progress more closely. She knew that Elizabeth had not been satisfied with the LSA as her only medical qualification. More recently Elizabeth became aware of a move to have women admitted to the MD examination of the Sorbonne, so she wrote to Lord Lyons, the British Ambassador in Paris, asking him to submit an application on her behalf. The application was successful, and in February 1869 Elizabeth was notified that she could take the first examination within a few weeks. A series of difficult examinations would follow at intervals of several months, and even if she passed all of these, it would be more than a year before she could take the final examination. Nevertheless, the news that an Englishwoman was to be the first female candidate for the MD Paris stimulated a great deal of public interest both in Britain and in France. While mentioning it in a letter to Lucy Sewall, Sophia also told her American friend how the Princess Louise, the Queen's second-youngest daughter, had paid Elizabeth an impromptu visit to wish her success.

Meanwhile, Sophia had spent many hours in the Library of the British Museum gathering material to use in her essay, which she began with a brief review of women's place in medical history. She argued that natural instinct leads women to concern themselves with the care of the sick. In medieval times nunneries, as well as monasteries, were centres for healing and education. But in the seventeenth and eighteenth centuries progress was made in medicine as a science, while at the same time the education of girls was restricted to the domestic crafts. Hence, women generally could not compete with men as medical practitioners, although a few who had the good fortune to be well educated were able to show that women were still capable of performing outstanding work in this field: in the seventeenth century Lady Ann Halket and Mrs Elizabeth Bury were famous for their skill as physicians. In more recent times Italian universities had appointed women to several of the highest positions in their medical faculties. Sophia acknowledged that these successful women were exceptional and proved nothing about the capabilities of women in general. But neither was there any objective proof of women's intellectual inferiority to men. She said that the matter could easily be tested by granting women 'a fair field and no favours' – teaching them as men were taught and subjecting them to exactly the same examinations.

Sophia then dealt with some of the other arguments that were often brought against the proposal of medical training for women: the degrading of women's 'purity', the lack of demand for women doctors, their exclusion from practice by the Medical Act of 1858, and the difficulty of providing adequate medical schools for women. All the problems implied by these arguments were either imaginary or readily solved, Sophia claimed. The one great danger was that women eager to enter practice might accept inferior training, thereby endangering their patients and bringing discredit on all women doctors. While writing this warning, she could probably hear in her mind the voice of Elizabeth Blackwell delivering her address at the opening of the Women's Medical College in New York. She concluded her essay with an appeal to the British universities to open their degree examinations to women:

> Is there not one of the English, Scottish or Irish Medical Schools or Universities that will win future laurels by now taking the lead generously and announcing its willingness to cease, at least, its policy of arbitrary exclusion? Let the authorities, if they please, admit women to study in the ordinary Classes, with or without any special restrictions (and it is hard to believe that at least the greater part of the lectures could not be attended in common); or let them allow the women to matriculate, and then, if they think needful, bid them make their own arrangements, and

gather their knowledge as they can; with this promise only, that, when acquired, such knowledge shall be duly tested, and, if found worthy, shall receive the regular Medical Degree.

Surely this is not too much to ask, and no more is absolutely essential. If indeed the assertions so often made about the incapacity of women are true, the result of such examinations (which may be both theoretical and practical, scientific and clinical) will triumphantly prove the point. If the examinations are left in the hands of competent men, we may be very sure that all unqualified women will be summarily rejected, as indeed we desire that they should be.

If, on the contrary, some women, however few, can under all existing disadvantages successfully pass the ordeal, and go forth with the full authority of the degree of Doctor of Medicine, surely all will be glad to welcome their perhaps unexpected success and bid every such woman, as she sets forth on her mission of healing, a hearty God-speed![3]

By the time Sophia had completed a draft of her essay and sent copies of it to several friends for their comments, her mother was well enough to undertake a lengthy visit to Cheltenham, where she would be near her son and his family. This left Sophia free to pursue her own interests. She later explained how she came to set her sights on Edinburgh University:

> I first applied to the University of London, of whose liberality one heard so much, and was told by the Registrar that the existing Charter had been purposely so worded as to exclude the possibility of examining women for medical degrees, and that under that Charter nothing whatever could be done in their favour. Knowing that at Oxford and Cambridge the whole question was complicated with regulations respecting residence, while, indeed, neither of these Universities furnished a complete medical education, my thoughts naturally turned to Scotland, to which so much credit is always given for its enlightened views respecting education, and where the Universities boast of their freedom from ecclesiastical and other trammels. In March 1869, therefore, I made my first application to the University of Edinburgh.[4]

Edinburgh University had special attractions for Sophia. Its medical faculty had for many years been acknowledged as one of the best in the nation, with teachers such as Syme, Simpson and Christison attracting large numbers of appreciative students. Furthermore, Sophia already had friends in that city, and her campaign on behalf of Elizabeth Garrett had introduced her to many influential people at Edinburgh University. But the most important consideration of all was that when they turned Elizabeth away seven years previously, the University authorities had implied that their decision was not irrevocable, and could be reversed at some future time. Perhaps that time had arrived.

In March 1869 Sophia went to Edinburgh, where she was the guest of her friends Mr and Mrs Burn Murdoch. Other old friendships were renewed, but she also made the acquaintance of two men who were to give her invaluable support in the difficult times ahead. One of these was Professor David Masson, the other Mr Alexander Russel. Although they came from dissimilar backgrounds and were unalike in their personalities, both men believed in the importance to society of improved educational facilities for girls and women.

David Masson, who was then in his forties, had been Professor of English Literature at University College, London, for twelve years before being appointed to the Chair of Rhetoric and English Literature at Edinburgh University in 1865. He was the author of many scholarly works on literature, the most notable of which was his biography of John Milton. Masson was convinced that women should be allowed to share the advantages of university education, but his enthusiasm was tempered with tact and discretion, qualities that made him an effective proponent of the women's cause at Edinburgh University.

Alexander Russel, who was 50 years old, was the editor of the daily newspaper the *Scotsman*. His widowed mother had given him the best education she could afford, but most of his learning was acquired through reading and private study. He was a man of liberal, humanitarian views. These he expressed in his newspaper, through which he exerted considerable political influence. He was liked and respected by his journalist colleagues, one of whom once wrote of him:

> Russel of the *Scotsman*, . . . who looked like three Dickens characters rolled into one – with the bald benevolent head and spectacles of Pickwick, the shrewd expression of Sam Weller, and the abrupt enunciation of Alfred Jingle; who told innumerable good stories and of whom innumerable good stories were told.[5]

Although she had these friends to help her, it was always Sophia who took the initiative in efforts to achieve her ambitions. She never was, or wished to be, carried along by others. Four days after arriving in Edinburgh she wrote to the Dean of the Faculty of Medicine, Professor J.H. Balfour:

SIR,

As I understand that the statutes of the University of Edinburgh do not in any way prohibit the admission of women, and as the Universities of Paris and Zurich have already been thrown open to them, I venture earnestly to request from you and the other gentlemen of the Medical Faculty permission to attend the lectures in your Medical School during the ensuing session.

I beg to signify my willingness to accede to any such conditions, or agree to any such reservations as may seem desirable to you, and indeed to withdraw my application altogether if, after due and sufficient trial, it should be found impracticable to grant me a continuance of the favour which I now request. You, Sir, must be well aware of the almost insuperable difficulty of pursuing the study of Medicine under any conditions but those which can be commanded by large colleges only; and, in view of the increasing demand for the medical service of women among their own sex, I am sure that you will concede the great importance of providing for the adequate instruction of such as desire thoroughly to qualify themselves to fulfil the duties of the medical profession.

Earnestly commending my request to the favourable consideration of yourself and your colleagues,

I am, Sir,

Yours obediently,

Sophia Jex-Blake[6]

It was a modest request; she asked only for permission to attend the medical lectures during the next summer session, reasoning that if she sought admission to the complete four-year course and to the examinations for the degree in medicine, those members of the Faculty who were nervous about admitting women would probably vote against her. A minor request was more likely to succeed. If she could then show her opponents that a woman's presence at the lectures need not offend or inconvenience anyone, she would probably be allowed to continue for the rest of the course.

In her methodical way, Sophia made herself familiar with the structure of the University's administration, so that she knew exactly how her application would be handled. She later recorded the information:

> For the sake of clearness, let me first explain, in few words, who constitute the different bodies that take a share in the government of Edinburgh University, taken in the order in which my application was considered by them. The *Medical Faculty* of course consists of Medical Professors only; the *Senatus* comprises all the professors of every faculty, and also the Principal; the *University Court* is composed of the Rector, the Principal, and the Lord Provost of Edinburgh; with five others appointed respectively by the Chancellor, the Rector, the Senatus, the Town Council of Edinburgh, and the General Council of the University; and, lastly, the *General Council* of the University consists of all those graduates of Edinburgh who have registered their names as members. Each of these bodies had to be consulted, as also the Chancellor, before any important change could be made.[7]

In the days leading up to the Faculty meeting, Sophia visited most of the members, seeking their support. The attitudes she encountered were varied.

Sir James Young Simpson, the eminent obstetrician, was one she knew would be helpful; in 1854 he had ignored criticism by some of his colleagues when he employed Emily Blackwell as his assistant, giving her the practical training she could not obtain in America. Sir James and his wife were kind to Sophia. On several occasions they invited her to breakfast, so that she could discuss the progress of her campaign with the doctor before he began his busy day's work.

Professor Syme, who was shortly to retire from the Chair of Surgery, was guarded in his response; he thought that if women were prepared to limit their practices to obstetrics and gynaecology, there would probably be no opposition to them. Robert Christison, Professor of Materia Medica and Therapeutics, was polite, but told Sophia quite unequivocally that he would vote against her.

Sophia's application would be referred to the Senatus of the University even if the Faculty approved it, but she had been told that the Faculty represented the greater obstacle. If the medical staff accepted her, it was unlikely that there would be any opposition from the non-medical staff. When she reviewed her two days of canvassing she calculated that four members of the Faculty would vote in her favour, three would vote against her and three were doubtful.

She was not kept in suspense for long. On 23 March a majority of Faculty members voted in her favour! Sophia was overjoyed:

> Surely I shall have to institute a festival for March 23rd. I wonder who's the saint. It will be very odd if any other day in my life will be (if all goes well) as vital an epoch as today. . . .
> I feel as if everybody was my peer today, for I want everybody to shake hands with me. I am so glad.[8]

But nothing could be taken for granted. Three more days of canvassing the non-medical members of the Senatus followed. There was a worrying rumour that Professor Christison intended to move that the decision of the Senatus be postponed while a legal opinion was obtained. But on Saturday 27 March the Senatus also voted in her favour.

For several days Sophia was the toast of the town, invited to dine at some of the 'best' homes, and showered with congratulations. She was aware that Professor Muirhead, who had not previously seemed hostile, had appealed to the University Court to have the decision of the Senatus reviewed because of its far-reaching implications. There was also a rumour that a group of students had signed a petition to the Court, claiming that the presence of a woman in their classes would prevent the lecturers from dealing adequately with topics of a 'delicate' nature. Nevertheless, Sophia was reassured by her friends that the decision of the Senatus was unlikely to be overturned, so she returned home to Brighton to prepare for the forthcoming term of study.

Three weeks later she was informed by letter that the University Court had met and had overruled the decision made in her favour by the Senatus. The Court's verdict was quoted in the letter:

The Court, considering the difficulties at present standing in the way of carrying out the resolution of the Senatus, as a temporary arrangement in the interests of one lady, and not being prepared to adjudicate finally on the question whether women should be educated in the medical classes of the University, sustains the appeals and recalls the resolution of the Senatus.[9]

Sophia's friend Professor Masson, who had represented her interests at the hearing, wrote giving an account of the proceedings. He thought that an appeal from nearly two hundred students had been the deciding factor; the Court was afraid to risk a public protest by a large body of students. Nevertheless, Masson thought, all was not lost. While the Court would not consent to mixed classes in all medical subjects, and was not prepared to make special arrangements for only one woman, it might give its approval to separate classes being held for a group of women, say half a dozen.

So the battle, instead of being over, was beginning again, with the enemy having won the first skirmish. In her letter to Lucy Sewall, Sophia admitted to feeling tired and disappointed, but she also had some good news. She was rewriting her essay on medicine as a career for women, incorporating some new material, and she had made a new friend. Miss Ursula Du Pre was a highly intelligent young woman who also yearned to study medicine, but was prevented from seeking a career because her invalid mother depended on her care. Ursula Du Pre's common sense and good humour were to make her one of Sophia's most valued friends.

While expressions of goodwill were heartening, Sophia's urgent need was to find a group of women who shared her ambitions, were well educated, and were able to stay in Edinburgh for the four years of a medical course. She had missed the summer term, but could she gather together a class in time for the winter term? In the event, this problem was solved with surprising ease. The controversy over the admission of women to Edinburgh University was widely publicized in the *Scotsman* and other newspapers. Within a short time Sophia received letters from two women who were interested in joining a class, and one of them knew of several others.

The first to write was Isabel Thorne. Mrs Thorne, who was 34 years old, was the mother of four children, the youngest only a few months old. She was a Londoner by birth, but her husband's business had dictated that the early years of their marriage were spent in China. She believed that the death of one of her babies in that country could have been prevented if skilled medical treatment had been available. This sad experience made her wish that there were well-trained women doctors able to provide a better medical service for women and children, both at home and abroad. When the family returned to England, Joseph Thorne encouraged his wife to take up the study of medicine herself; he offered practical help with the care of their children, as well as his moral support. So family responsibilities would not prevent Isabel from embarking on a four-year course of study.

The second letter came from Miss Edith Pechey, a young school teacher who had become dissatisfied with teaching as a career and was strongly attracted to medicine. She wrote:

> Before deciding finally to enter the medical profession, I should like to feel sure of success – not on my own account, but I feel that failure now would do harm to the cause, and that it is well that at least the first few women who offer themselves as candidates should stand above the average of men in their examinations.
>
> Do you think anything more is requisite to ensure success than moderate abilities and a good share of perseverance? I believe I may lay claim to these, together with a real love of the subjects of study, but as regards any thorough knowledge of these subjects at present, I fear I am deficient in most. I am afraid I should not without a good deal of previous study be able to pass the preliminary exam. you mention, as my knowledge of Latin is small and of Euclid still less. Still, if no very extensive knowledge of these is required (and doctors generally seem to know very little of them) I could perhaps be ready by the next exam., and the study of Carpenter at the same time would be a relaxation. Could you give me any idea when the next matriculation exam. will be held, and whether candidates are examined in *all* the books of Euclid. If I thought I could prepare myself in time for this, I think I could arrange pecuniary and other matters so as to enter in October as you advise; and, though for some reasons I should prefer to wait another year, yet, as I am nearly 24, it will perhaps be better to lose no time.[10]

Edith's modest letter did not do justice to her intellectual ability. She was the daughter of a Baptist minister who had himself been an outstanding student at Edinburgh University; her mother, too, was quite a scholar. Thus, she had grown up in an environment that had developed her mental faculties and equipped her to undertake a demanding course of study.

Soon two more intending students joined the group. They were Mrs Helen Evans (the young widow of a cavalry officer) and Miss Matilda Chaplin; they were both women of excellent character and ability. Sophia returned to Edinburgh to prepare another application, and to begin again the routine of personal appeals and letter-writing. This application, however, would be much more ambitious than the last. Now the women were seeking not just admission to one term's lectures, but matriculation and all that that implied – the right to attend all the classes and examinations required for a degree in medicine.

The application was considered in turn by the Medical Faculty, the Senatus and the University Court. Although there was considerable opposition at each stage, by 23 July all three bodies had granted their approval. The General Council and the Chancellor still had to be consulted, but success was now almost certain. The matriculation examination was due to be held in October, ten days before the next meeting of the Council, but the women were given permission to take the examination in anticipation of the Council's approval.

Sophia could not pause to celebrate. First, she had to find her own accommodation in Edinburgh, since she could not go on accepting the hospitality of the Burn Murdochs. The house she found was close to the University, comfortable, and with more room than she needed. Edith Pechey, who impressed Sophia as being 'as good an ally and companion as could well be had', decided to share with her. Their home at 15 Buccleuch Place became the headquarters of the women students. Isabel Thorne settled her family in Edinburgh, and Helen Evans and Matilda Chaplin also found lodgings nearby.

The matriculation examination was now only a few weeks away, and it was vital that all the women should pass. The examination was in two parts. English, Latin and mathematics were compulsory subjects; in addition, each candidate had to choose two subjects from a group that included Greek, French, German, higher mathematics, natural philosophy, logic and moral philosophy. While brushing up on her own knowledge, Sophia acted as mathematics tutor to the others.

The results of the examination, which was held on 19 October, were gratifying. In all, there were 152 candidates, five of them women. The women all passed and four of them appeared in the first seven places. On 2 November 1869 they signed the matriculation roll. Edinburgh University, the first British university to open its doors to women, now had five female undergraduates!

Among the many congratulatory messages Sophia received was one from Dr Elizabeth Blackwell. It was a pleasing coincidence that the signing of the roll in Edinburgh took place on the anniversary of the opening ceremony of the Women's Medical College of the New York Infirmary. The College was thriving, although it was no longer under Elizabeth Blackwell's direction. A few months after the opening ceremony she had returned to England to live, leaving behind her the fruits of twenty years' work.

Elizabeth's explanation for this astonishing move was that she was no longer needed in America; with her sister Emily in charge both the College and the Infirmary were in capable hands, and now she was free to devote herself to the medical women's campaign in Britain. It is true that Elizabeth was by nature more of an explorer than a settler, but it is difficult to accept her statement as the whole explanation. Having become an American citizen she was, in many ways, more American than British in her outlook, and there was still important work she could have done in America. Furthermore, on her return to Britain she seems to have been content to play a relatively minor role in the medical women's movement. A personal conflict, such as a rift with her sister Emily, could have precipitated Elizabeth's decision, but neither of the sisters ever admitted that they had had a serious disagreement. It may have been simply that Elizabeth suddenly tired of the burden she had carried for so many years,

N. *628*

UNIVERSITY OF EDINBURGH.

Form to be filled up by every Student on First Application for a Matriculation Ticket.

This Form should be duly filled up, and handed to the Registrar prior to payment of the Matriculation Fee, and Signature in the Album.

1. Name in full, ...	*Sophia Louisa Jex Blake*
2. Birthplace, ...	*Hastings —*
3. Age last Birthday, ...	*29.*
4. Faculty or Faculties in which the Applicant proposes to Study, . .	*Medical*
5. *School Education*—School or Schools attended by the Applicant, with the period of attendance at each, . .	*Boarding School. 9 years —*
6. *Previous Medical Education,*— (*a*) Medical School or Schools, (*b*) Number of years thereat, . (*c*) License or Licenses, . . .	*In N. E. Hospital for Women & Children &c — Boston . U.S.*
7. *Previous University Education,*— (*a*) University or Universities, . (*b*) Years thereat, ... (*c*) Faculty or Faculties, ... (*d*) Degree or Degrees, . . .	

Illustration 9. Sophia's application to matriculate at Edinburgh University, 1869. (Reproduced by permission of Edinburgh University Library.)

and a move to Britain offered her an escape. Her recent personal crisis did not, however, diminish Elizabeth Blackwell's delight at the success of the five women who were now students of medicine at Edinburgh University.

Notes

1. M. Todd, *The Life of Sophia Jex-Blake*, London: Macmillan, 1918, p. 214.
2. J. Butler (ed.) *Woman's Work and Woman's Culture*, London: Macmillan, 1869.
3. S. Jex-Blake, 'Medicine as a Profession for Women', in J. Butler (ed.) *Woman's Work and Woman's Culture*, London: Macmillan, 1869.
4. S. Jex-Blake, *Medical Women*, Edinburgh and London: Macmillan, 1886, p. 70.
5. The *Spectator*, 22 July 1876.
6. Todd, op. cit., p. 235.
7. S. Jex-Blake, *Medical Women*, p. 71.
8. Todd, op. cit., p. 238.
9. S. Jex-Blake, *Medical Women*, p. 75.
10. Todd, op. cit., p. 254.

6

A disputed prize and a students' riot

If Sophia's opponents at Edinburgh University thought that their decision against making 'a temporary arrangement in the interests of one lady' would discourage her, they were mistaken. She had always believed that she was acting on behalf of all women who shared her ambitions; the University had, in effect, strengthened her position. The group who joined her in Edinburgh readily accepted her as their leader and were content to leave the planning of their campaign in her hands. For Sophia, as with many born leaders, there was no distinction between serving and leading. She could serve the cause best by leading it. The task soon absorbed her so completely that she had almost no separate personal life. Thus, the story of her life between 1869 and 1877 is an account of the medical women's campaign.

One of the historic documents in this story is the Edinburgh University Calendar for 1870. It contained a new section, which appeared under the heading *Regulations for the Education of Women in Medicine in the University*. One paragraph of notes and seven *Regulations* defined the status of women students. They would receive all their tuition in classes separate from those for men. Because their classes would be small, they must expect to pay higher fees; just how much higher could not be determined immediately, because the University proposed to admit to some of the lectures other women who were taking only one or two subjects and were not candidates for degrees. Apart from the separate classes and high fees, the women would be treated exactly as the men were, 'subject to all the regulations now or at any future time in force in the University as to the matriculation of students, their attendance on classes, examination, or otherwise.'[1]

A careful reading of the *Regulations* revealed one potential difficulty: the professors of the various faculties were *permitted*, but not *required*, to conduct classes for women. Male students who signed the matriculation roll were certain of being admitted to classes, whereas female students were dependent on the goodwill of the lecturers. Sophia was reassured by the helpfulness of the lecturers in physiology and chemistry, who were the first she approached. They readily agreed to conduct separate courses for the women during the winter term that was about to begin.

One of Sophia's letters to Lucy Sewall reports the progress of her plans:

> Everything is just as we would have it, but that Professors are not com-
> pelled to lecture to us. We have already arranged for two courses for this
> winter, – 5 lectures a week each, – Physiology and Chemistry; and we
> are now arranging for Anatomy, both in lectures and dissecting.
>
> As we have to make entirely separate arrangements, the Anatomy will
> be very expensive, – about £100 probably for us five, – and of this I shall
> pay about one-third, as two of the students are not at all rich.
>
> Still it is worth any money to get the thing done, and I am only thankful
> that I *can* spend the money. Of course I borrow it from my Mother. My
> fees for this year will be about £55 or £60, – about $400, – for the
> 6 months.
>
> I have made up my mind to spend if needful £1000 on this business. I feel
> sure that one does more good in thus concentrating one's energies and
> one's funds to get one thing done thoroughly, than in frittering away lots
> of small sums in charity, – Don't you think so? It *is* a grand thing to enter
> the very first British University ever opened to women, isn't it?
>
> My darling, you *must* come and see us this summer, for, as I tell the
> other students here, the whole thing is due to *you* primarily; – when they
> say that they feel grateful to me for having worked for this, I say, 'Thank
> Dr Sewall, – she made me care for Medicine, and resolve that a *thorough*
> education should be open to Englishwomen.' So I told Dr Blackwell too
> when she said something pretty to me. She is *very* pleased about
> Edinburgh.
>
> Well, dear child, I have settled down now for the winter in my new little
> house. It amuses me to hear of your expenses in furnishing. The whole I
> have spent is under £35, – about $200, – and yet we are very comfortable!
> Miss Pechey is very nice and very clever, – you will like her very much,
> and she is excellent company. . . . Our classes begin on Nov. 3rd. I am
> *very* busy till then.[2]

Sophia kept an accurate record of the money she borrowed from her mother to
help her fellow students; in due course she repaid it all, almost certainly from
her own pocket.

That first winter term was a happy one. The five could hardly believe their
good fortune in being able to pursue their studies in an academic environment
never before accessible to women. Sophia, especially, was in her element.
Hard work, with a worthy goal in sight, suited her personality. Gone were the
irritable outbursts that sometimes alienated acquaintances and tested the
loyalty of her friends. Alice Hughes, the maid who had been with her in New
York, came to housekeep for her in Edinburgh, bringing with her their
faithful dog Turk. The house at 15 Buccleuch Place was a comfortable and
cheerful meeting place for the women students. The few exchanges they had

with their male colleagues were polite and cordial. Time passed quickly and soon the students were all preparing for the examinations that were held in March, at the end of the winter term. The women were anxious to acquit themselves well. Little did they think that academic success could create new difficulties for them.

When the results were announced, the women discovered that not only had they all passed, but four of them had obtained honours in both subjects. In chemistry their results were particularly gratifying. Sophia's name appeared in tenth place on the list of 231 candidates; Edith Pechey had done even better, being listed third. Edith had indeed won first place among the candidates who were taking the course for the first time.

Some forty years previously, Professor Hope, the then Professor of Chemistry, had instituted annual awards known as the Hope Scholarships. The four students who achieved the highest marks at the first-term examination in chemistry were to be granted free use of the facilities of the University laboratory during the next term. On this occasion the two men whose names were listed in first and second places were ineligible because they were taking the course for the second time. Edith Pechey had first claim on a Hope Scholarship. But Edith Pechey was a woman!

Dr Crum Brown, the Professor of Chemistry, was in a quandary. At first he had been pleased to help the women students, but as the term progressed he had observed that some of his most respected colleagues in the Medical Faculty resented the presence of women in the University. Many of the male students also turned hostile when they saw that the women were capable of outstripping them in competitive examinations. Professor Crum Brown feared that the award of a prize to a woman now would be an affront to some of his friends, and a provocation to the male students. So he awarded the Hope Scholarships to men whose names were all lower on the list than Miss Pechey's, and justified this by saying that she was ineligible for a prize because she had been taught in a special class. Yet the Professor himself had said on more than one occasion that he gave the women the same lectures as he gave the men; furthermore, the men and the women had taken the same examinations at the same time, although they sat in different rooms to write their answers.

The loss of the Hope Scholarship was not a serious blow to Edith Pechey. She and Sophia had improvised their own little chemistry laboratory at 15 Buccleuch Place, so the women students were not entirely without facilities for practical work. But the Professor had placed himself in an awkward position. Having exploited the matter of the separate classes, he now felt unable to issue the women the usual certificates of attendance at his chemistry classes. Instead, he gave them credit for attending a ' "ladies" class in the University'. But only the standard certificates met the Faculty's requirements for the medical degree; the Professor's 'strawberry jam labels', as Sophia called them, were valueless.

In desperation, the women appealed to the Senatus. Edith Pechey stated her claim to a scholarship, and the five asked that they be granted the standard certificates for their chemistry classes. The Senatus met on 9 April 1870. After some debate on the subject of the certificates, a motion in favour of granting the women's request was carried by a majority of one. The vote on the Hope Scholarship was equally close. Professor Christison, seconded by Professor Sanders, moved:

> that the authorities of the University have not passed any Resolution extending to females the right of competing for those University Prizes which have hitherto been competed for by, and were originally destined for, male students of the University, and
> that Dr Crum Brown appears to have acted in conformity with the law and practice of the University in assigning the Hope prizes to the students of his male class of Chemistry.[3]

This also was carried with a majority of one. So it was established that the women could not be prize winners at their University, no matter how well they performed, but a barrier to their graduation had been removed.

The episode of the Hope Scholarship, although minor in itself, had an important consequence. The publicity it was given in newspapers throughout Britain drew the attention of the public to the difficulties being encountered by a small group of women who were studying medicine at Edinburgh University. Almost all of the accounts were favourable to the women's cause. *The Times* said:

> [Miss Pechey] has done her sex a service, not only by vindicating their intellectual ability in an open competition with men, but still more by the temper and courtesy with which she meets her disappointments. Under any view of the main question, her case is a hard one, for it is clear both she and the other lady students were led to attend the classes under the misapprehension of the privileges to which they were admissable. If the University intended to exclude ladies from the pecuniary advantages usually attached to successful study, the intention should have been clearly announced.[4]

The *Spectator* was satirical:

> To make women attend a separate class, for which they have to pay, we believe, much higher fees than usual, and then argue that they are out of the pale of competition because they do so, is, indeed, too like the captious schoolmaster who first sent a boy into the corner and then whipped him for not being in his seat.[5]

93

Even the *British Medical Journal*, usually unsympathetic to the medical women's cause, was critical of the University's treatment of Miss Pechey.[6]

Sophia was learning that publicity could be a powerful weapon, though it had a tendency to drift away from the main target. The attendance certificates were far more important to the women students than their eligibility for prizes, but because the story of the Hope Scholarship was more dramatic, it was on this that the journalists chose to write.

When her four colleagues left Edinburgh for the spring vacation, Sophia remained at her post, trying to complete arrangements for the next term's lectures. For each subject she had to find a teacher who was willing to conduct a separate course for the women; then there were the fees to be negotiated. Already she was having difficulties. The debate over the Hope Scholarship had deepened the divisions between supporters and opponents of the women students. The situation was complicated by other factional differences between members of the University staff – men who were not interested in the women's cause had to align themselves with colleagues whose support they needed in some unrelated dispute. Consequently, some of the professors who previously seemed co-operative now told Sophia that they were too busy to teach women students. The important subject of anatomy, which she thought had been settled, became a problem when Professor Turner changed his mind about conducting a course for women.

Professor Masson was in favour of taking bold action on the women's behalf. When the General Council of the University met later in April he proposed that henceforth the women students should be admitted to the ordinary classes along with the men, except for a few lectures, which could be held separately. Although the motion was seconded by the Dean of Medicine it provoked heated debate, and was lost by 47 to 58 votes. Masson wrote to Sophia:

> No speaking on our side could have changed the vote, those present were all predetermined. . . . People today are consoling me – for I was really downcast – by saying the result was a success in its kind, and an omen of final success when the thing comes up again, as it must. All very well; but how shall I console *you*? What are *you* to do this year? . . . Time – a year or two – will rectify the thing generally, here and elsewhere; but how you are to get on with us is the question. Christison . . . seems determined to get rid of you, and trusts to effecting this by mere continuance of the present arrangement. Whether you can wriggle on with us by any ingenuity in the hope of beating him is for your consideration. Would it might be so![7]

The Times of 25 April 1870 commented on the debate in the Edinburgh University Council on Professor Masson's motion.[8] While unconvinced by Masson's arguments in support of combined classes for men and women, the writer was even more critical of statements made by two of his opponents. Professor Laycock had said that some women seeking medical training could be 'basely inclined', meaning that they intended to become nothing more than abortionists; unless careful enquiries were made into the characters of women applicants, teachers could be harbouring 'Magdalenes' in their classes. *The Times* naturally wondered who Laycock was not equally concerned about the characters of his male students. Christison was quoted as saying that male students were sometimes charged with being 'a little irregular' in their behaviour, and he thought it unlikely that they would improve in the presence of ladies of their own age. In other words, women students' manners and morals must be impeccable, but men could be as base as they pleased. *The Times* commented, 'It is the strongest argument against the admission of young ladies to the Edinburgh medical classes that they would attend the lectures of Professors who are capable of talking in this strain.'

While dismissing Christison's contribution to the General Council's debate as trivial, *The Times* did not report the more significant part of his speech. He had argued that it was illogical to propose radical changes to the organization of the medical school simply because five ladies in their first term had obtained good marks for their chemistry and physiology papers. There were no indications that large numbers of women wished to take up the study of medicine, nor was there any proof that there was a strong public demand for women doctors. His own enquiries led him to believe that such a demand did not exist. Mixed classes for the study of medicine were unacceptable, and the academic staff of the University certainly could not find the time to conduct two separate courses, one for men and one for a mere handful of women. Finally, Christison gave the women the unwelcome advice they so often received from their enemies, 'Become midwives, not doctors!'[9]

Events were to prove Masson right in thinking that Robert Christison was the women students' most dangerous opponent. Why was Christison so resolutely opposed to women as doctors? The medical men who feared them as competitors were mostly the younger ones who were struggling to rise up from the lower ranks of the profession. Christison, on the other hand, was now over 70 years old, and coming to the end of a brilliantly successful career. His opposition was at first simply an expression of loyalty to his profession. He seems to have shared the view of many of his contemporaries that Nature intended women to be mothers and housekeepers, so she did not endow them with the intellectual ability and stamina of men. Consequently, if they were to enter any learned profession in significant numbers they would inevitably lower its standards. Christison's estimate of women's ability is suggested by an anecdote that he enjoyed and recorded in his private journal:

I heard a strange story of a certain maternity hospital the other day: it seems to be in a deplorable condition for medical attendance, good food, bedclothes, and cleanliness. The filthiness especially is excessive, and there is no getting the better of it. Lately a determined effort was made to improve matters, and a committee of ladies was appointed to undertake the cleaning department. They held many meetings, differed much with one another as to the means, failed utterly with such measures as they tried, discussed and fought the question again, could arrive at no definite conclusion, and finally gave up in despair the cleansing of the patients; whereupon one of the ladies wound up the controversy with the comforting reflection: 'After all, what does it signify whether they are clean or not, if they go to heaven!'[10]

Christison was able to harbour this distorted view of women because he lived in a masculine world. He had been a widower for twenty years; he had three sons, but no daughters and no sisters. He worked with men, and his hobbies of mountaineering and commanding the University Rifles kept him in the company of men in his leisure time. He had seen the medical profession and Edinburgh University well served by three generations of men, some of them members of his own family.

Christison's father had been Professor of Humanity at Edinburgh University for fourteen years. Robert and his twin brother Alexander were born in 1797. Alexander became a clergyman, but Robert, after completing an arts course at the University, took up the study of medicine. His early specialization in analytical chemistry and forensic medicine led to his appointment to the Chair of Medical Jurisprudence when he was only 25 years old. One of his achievements in this post was the establishment of British forensic medicine on a sound scientific basis. He appeared as an expert witness in some of the most famous cases of the period, including the trial of the murderers Burke and Hare in 1829. His evidence was always impartial and incontrovertible.

In 1827 Christison was appointed to the medical staff of the Edinburgh Royal Infirmary. Five years later he resigned from the Chair of Medical Jurisprudence and was appointed to the Chair of Materia Medica and Therapeutics; after this his work became more clinical in character, with the result that he built up a large practice. He wrote prolifically on medical topics and involved himself in the administration of the Royal Infirmary and the University to a truly remarkable degree. He was Physician-in-ordinary to the Queen in Scotland, and President of the Royal Society of Edinburgh.

When Sophia began her campaign in Edinburgh, she soon became aware of Robert Christison's power. He was one of the most widely known and respected men in the public life of the city. Many of his younger colleagues referred to him as 'our Nestor'. With his tall, lean build and shock of white hair, his appearance was as distinguished as his reputation. He spoke in a rich bass voice and with such an air of authority that he had no difficulty in subduing the rowdiest class of students. He naturally assumed the role of leader in the campaign against Edinburgh's women medical students. So Sophia Jex-Blake and Robert Christison were pitted against each other like opposing generals in a war. The differences between them were many and obvious, but they had two important characteristics in common: they were both prepared to fight for their beliefs with a persistence that was almost irrational, and they were both unable to consider, even momentarily, that right may not be entirely on one side.

Largely because of Christison's influence, the University adhered to its policy of restricting the women students to separate classes. Sophia decided that the difficult problem of the anatomy course could be deferred until the winter term of 1870–1. In the mean time she made arrangements for the approaching summer term, when the subjects taken by the women would be botany and natural history (zoology). Professor Balfour, who lectured in botany, was quite willing to hold special classes for the women. Professor Allmann, if he had been free to decide for himself, would have admitted the women to his ordinary classes in natural history, but he refused to conduct a separate class for them. So for their tuition in natural history Sophia was obliged to turn to the extramural schools of Edinburgh.

These schools had a long history.[11] In 1505 the Incorporation of Barber Surgeons begun conducting public lectures in anatomy, thus establishing the custom for doctors of the city to deliver lectures for which they charged fees. The University was founded in 1583, but it did not have a medical faculty until 1726. The schools outside the University, or 'extramural schools' as they came to be known, continued to be well supported, because many of their lecturers were the profession's leading men. The famous surgeons John Lizars (1792–1860) and Sir William Fergusson (1808–77) were both for some years teachers in the extramural schools of Edinburgh.

Until the middle of the nineteenth century the schools were administered very informally, groups of lecturers sharing rented lecture rooms for a few years, and then disbanding, often to form new groups. In the second half of the nineteenth century the Royal Colleges of Physicians and Surgeons of Edinburgh took over the supervision of the extramural schools and recognized their training of examination candidates for College diplomas. One of the leading schools was conducted in a building known as Surgeons' Hall, which adjoined the Royal College of Surgeons. In addition to lecture rooms, the Hall had a well-equipped dissecting room for classes in practical anatomy.

There was a spirit of rivalry between the University Faculty and the extramural schools. The extramural lecturers tended to be more innovative; they were the first to offer courses in special subjects such as diseases of the skin, mental disorders and children's diseases. Sometimes senior appointments at the University were filled by men from the extramural schools. In 1855 the University recognized extramural teaching as fulfilling its degree requirements, and thereafter allowed its students to take up to four of their subjects in the extramural system. So when University lecturers refused to accommodate the women students, there was an alternative source of tuition available.

Sophia approached Dr Alleyne Nicholson, an extramural lecturer in natural history. He proposed admitting the women to his ordinary class, but his friends warned him that he could be stirring up a hornets' nest. Nicholson wrote to Sophia:

> They advise me . . . not to commence abruptly on Monday without any warning, but to give my opening lecture separately, to my ordinary class at one o'clock, and to you at 2 p.m. At the conclusion of the hour I should explain to the students how matters stand, and should ask their permission to make over to you a bench in the general class. This is the advice which is given me, and I have no doubt as to its wisdom.
>
> I am fully aware that this will not be nearly as satisfactory to you as unconditional permission on my part; and I must beg you to believe that it is in many respects far from being so satisfactory to my own feelings in the matter. If I were a thoroughly independent man I can assure you that I should not be deterred from doing what I thought right in this question by any fear of the consequences. As things really stand, however, I do not feel justified in running the risk of losing my ordinary class in whole or in part, as I am assured I should do if I were to attempt to introduce this innovation wholly without warning.[12]

Fortunately, the men were all in favour of inviting the ladies to join them, and Sophia was able to record that 'the first "mixed class" was inaugurated and continued throughout the summer without the slightest inconvenience'. Even that very conservative lady Mrs Jex-Blake had overcome her misgivings, as she told Sophia in a letter:

> I don't now at all object to mixed classes. As the teaching must at present be given *by men*, I don't see why there should not be mixed classes to listen: and I feel confident if you continue to have such a nice set of women, the tone of the young men generally will be greatly raised. If mixed classes answer so well at Zurich and Paris, why not here?[13]

The concern Dr Nicholson felt about the reaction of his male students reflected the power enjoyed by the student body, both in the University and in the extramural schools. A lecturer's status, and certainly his income, depended on his ability to attract and hold classes of students. In many instances the students paid their fees directly to their lecturers and, since they could choose between the University and the extramural schools, they were able to boycott the classes of anyone who seriously displeased them. Joseph Lister was already an eminent surgeon when he applied for the Chair of Surgery at Edinburgh University in 1869, but even he would have been gratified by a letter he received from the medical students of that city. It bore 127 signatures, and assured him that if he came to Edinburgh he would attract 'a large band of attached and devoted followers'.[14]

Although the students wielded power as a group, individually they were highly vulnerable. Many of them were immature young men who were far from home, and had not yet learned self-discipline. There were no tutors or counsellors to guide them. Poverty was a common problem. Edinburgh's reputation for good teaching, low fees and cheap lodgings attracted large numbers of students, but less than half of those who began courses ever succeeded in graduating.

The medical students knew that their problems did not end with graduation, because the profession was overcrowded. If they did not have wealthy parents to help them, they could be faced with years of hardship, perhaps selling soap and perfume to help eke out a living. It is little wonder, then, that they were not at all eager to welcome women to the ranks of the profession. If it were true, as the women's supporters claimed, that female patients would prefer to consult doctors of their own sex, then male doctors could lose large sections of their practices to the newcomers.

While the five were quietly pursuing their studies in Edinburgh, one of their countrywomen won international acclaim in Paris. On 15 June 1870 Elizabeth Garrett presented herself for the final examination for the MD, and passed with distinction. She was showered with letters of congratulation, one of them from Sophia. Changes were occurring in Edinburgh too. The sudden death of Sir James Young Simpson deprived the women of one of their most valued friends. Joseph Lister replaced Syme as Professor of Surgery. Whereas Syme had mildly disapproved of women medical students, his successor was strongly opposed to them. Lister believed that any lowering of the barriers separating the sexes would lead to a decline in moral standards. For a man with his Quaker upbringing there could be no better reason for locking them out, and any further discussion of the matter was a waste of time.

Perhaps Lister should be excused for regarding the question of women's entry into the profession as of minor importance. Three years before he came to Edinburgh he had published in the *Lancet* his historic paper entitled *On a New Method of Treating Compound Fracture, Abscess, etc.* In this he suggested that the fatal complications which so frequently followed injuries and surgical operations could be prevented. Building on the work of Semmelweiss and Pasteur, he developed the theory that wounds became 'poisoned' because they were invaded, not by noxious gases in the atmosphere, but by living micro-organisms that multiplied and spread throughout the victim's body. He outlined an 'antiseptic method' for preventing wound infection. Lister's work was later to transform the practice of surgery and save countless lives, but for a decade after his article was published, he had to contend with sceptics who were either unable or unwilling to follow him.

Not all of the women's opponents had Lister's altruistic motives. In 1870 the *Lancet* published a long letter by an artless gentleman, Dr Henry Bennett. Bennett began by claiming that women were intellectually and physically incapable of being competent doctors. He saw the field of midwifery as their rightful place. Here, they could serve a useful purpose by relieving the busy medical man of that section of his work which was the most burdensome, and also the least lucrative. Bennett then went on to develop the theme of Caucasian male superiority:

> The principal feature which appears to me to characterise the Caucasian race, to raise it immeasurably above all other races, is the power that many of its *male* members have of advancing the horizon of science, of penetrating beyond the existing limits of knowledge – in a word, the power of scientific discovery. I am not aware that the female members of our race participate in this power, in this supreme development of the human mind; at least I know of no great discovery changing the surface of science that owes its existence to a woman of our or of any race. What right then have women to claim mental *equality* with men?[15]

The *Lancet* published Sophia's reply. She easily demolished Bennett's first suggestion:

> After saying that women are 'sexually, constitutionally, and mentally unfitted for hard and incessant toil,' Dr Bennett goes on to propose to make over to them as their sole share of the medical profession what he himself well describes as its 'most arduous, most wearing and most unremunerative duties'. In the last adjective seems to lie the whole suitability of the division of labour according to the writer's view. He evidently thinks that women's capabilities are nicely graduated to fit *half-guinea* or *guinea* midwifery cases, and that all patients paying a larger sum of necessity need the superior powers of the '*male* mind of the Caucasian race.' Let whatever is well paid be left to the man; then chivalrously abandon the 'badly remunerated' work to the women.[16]

Sophia was kinder to her opponent in dealing with his second theme. She ignored the absence of logic in his argument that because a few men had made great scientific discoveries the average male must be superior in intellect to the average female. She herself readily conceded that the success of five women students in their first year at a university was no proof that all women who sought admission to professional education were able to benefit from it. She restated the argument that she had first expounded in her essay on *Medicine as a Profession for Women* – that it was pointless to debate the relative abilities of men and women when the matter could easily be put to the test by giving them equivalent training and subjecting them to the same examinations.

Most readers of the correspondence would have judged Sophia the victor, but Elizabeth Garrett probably regretted that the *Lancet* had published Sophia's reply. In her view a woman's belittling of a medical man would strengthen the hostility to the women's cause of other possessors of the 'superior male Caucasian mind'. Elizabeth preferred to emphasize the achievements of women, rather than the deficiencies of men.

The summer term of 1870 passed without incident. Isabel Thorne recalled, many years later, how the five women enjoyed Dr Nicholson's lectures and the excursion to a dredging site on the Firth of Forth (probably to study fossils).[17] But as the end of the term approached Sophia realized that the appearance of peace was deceptive. Their medical opponents had brought their influence to bear on the uncommitted lecturers, both in the University and in the extramural schools, until most of the younger men were afraid to help the women in case they harmed their own careers. The women had to take the important subjects of anatomy and surgery in the forthcoming winter term, and since the University lecturers certainly would not conduct classes for them, they had to appeal again to the extramural schools. Fortunately, at Surgeons' Hall Sophia found two very highly regarded lecturers who were willing to help – Dr Handyside in anatomy, and Dr Heron Watson in surgery. Both proposed admitting the women students to their ordinary classes, without any of the preliminary consultation with the men that Dr Nicholson had thought necessary. Meanwhile the women's group had acquired two new members – Mary Anderson and Emily Bovell. Henceforth the group was often referred to as the 'Edinburgh Seven'.

The winter term did not begin officially until November, but at Surgeon's Hall those students who wished to do so could start their work in practical anatomy a month earlier. The Seven were glad to avail themselves of this privilege, so they were allotted a corner of the dissecting room and were ushered in on the first day. Sophia had already had experience of practical anatomy classes in Boston and new York; the awesome sight of dismembered human bodies did not shock her. If the other women were disturbed, they gave no external sign of their feelings, and any of the men who expected to see them faint or become hysterical were disappointed. In the following weeks Dr Handyside observed that the women's earnest concentration on their work set the men an example. He was encouraged to hope that this would be one of the best classes he had had for some years.

When the General Council of the University met on 28 October 1870, there was again a motion before it that it should relax some of the restrictions that were forcing the women students to obtain their tuition outside the University. The strongest opposition to the motion came from Professor Christison, who created quite a stir when he said that the Queen herself approved the stand he was taking against the women students. Even with this illustrious support, he managed to have the motion defeated by only the narrowest of margins; there were 46 votes in favour, 47 against.

Attendance at lectures and practical classes constituted only part of the students' training; clinical experience in a hospital was also essential. Only one hospital, the Edinburgh Royal Infirmary, met the requirements of the University, and to this hospital the matriculated students of the University were granted access as a matter of course. But when Sophia applied to the Infirmary on behalf of the Seven, her application was refused. She then prepared a more detailed application, enclosing letters from Drs Handyside and Watson, who recommended the women as excellent students, deserving of assistance and encouragement. There were also letters from three members of the Infirmary's medical staff, who said that they were willing to teach the women students in their wards. At the next meeting of the Managers of the Infirmary the application was discussed and was almost approved, but then an opponent of the women objected that more time was needed to consider it, so voting on the motion was deferred for a week.

The week was one of frantic activity. Although her days were largely filled with lectures and practical classes, Sophia still found time to write letters and make calls to explain the women's case; a twelve-hour working day became her routine. Her opponents were no less active. They made sure that every member of the Infirmary Board who was likely to vote against the women knew the importance of the next meeting. A petition against the admission of women students to the Infirmary was signed by 500 students, although Sophia believed that many of those who signed when the document was pushed in front of them had no clear knowledge of its import. At the subsequent meeting of Infirmary Managers the students' petition was regarded very seriously, and when the vote was taken the application by the women students was rejected by a large majority. It was a severe setback. But Sophia was learning from her opponents; if they could show dogged persistence, so could she. The fight to gain entry to the Infirmary was just beginning.

The disturbing effects of the week of campaigning continued to be felt after the Managers' meeting. Sophia later recalled:

> From that time the behaviour of the students changed. It is not for me to say what means were used, or what strings were pulled, but I know that the result was, that instead of being, as heretofore, silent and inoffensive, a certain proportion of the students with whom we worked became markedly offensive and insolent, and took every opportunity of practising the petty annoyances that occur to thoroughly ill-bred lads, – such as shutting doors in our faces, ostentatiously crowding into the seats we usually occupied, bursting into horse-laughs and howls when we approached, – as if a conspiracy had been formed to make our position as uncomfortable as might be.[18]

Friends of the Seven told them that the crude behaviour of the students could be blamed on some of the professors, who were deliberately inciting them. One professor was reported to have said during a lecture that it was really much to the credit of the men that they had not pelted the ladies away from their classes. After this the Seven took the precaution of walking to Surgeons' Hall together, rather than in ones and twos, but they were not prepared for the disturbance that took place on Friday 18 November.

At four o'clock that afternoon Dr Handyside's anatomy class were to take an examination. As the Seven approached Surgeons' Hall they found the usually busy thoroughfare of Nicholson Street blocked by a noisy mob. The ringleaders of the mob were a dozen or so of the roughest students from Dr Handyside's class. They had been joined by a larger group of students unknown to the women, and by a number of ne'er-do-wells from the local streets. Several hundred curious onlookers watched as the students, many of them drunk, gathered around the gate leading to Surgeons' Hall, awaiting the arrival of the Seven. When the women were seen approaching the outskirts of the crowd they were greeted with shouts of abuse and pelted with refuse, but with grim determination they pushed on. Ignoring the heckling and jostling of the crowd, they made their way to the gate, only to have it slammed in their faces as they reached it. But almost immediately a student who had been watching from inside the Hall rushed to the women's aid. He wrenched the gate open, ushered them through, and accompanied them into the lecture room. Dr Handyside evicted a number of intruders and then began the examination, ignoring the noise of the crowd still gathered outside. Proceedings were interrupted briefly when one of the rioters forced open a back door and pushed a pet sheep into the lecture room. The unruffled lecturer advised his class to take no notice of the animal, saying that it had more sense than those who had sent it in. Despite their gruelling experience, the women all passed in their examination. When it was time to leave, some of their fellow students formed a bodyguard for them, shepherding them through the crowd and seeing them safely to their lodgings. The women's clothes were stained with the mud that had been thrown at them, but they were otherwise unscathed. For several days the bodyguard of friendly students accompanied them to and from their lectures. After that, protection was no longer necessary, although occasionally a fistful of mud or a barrage of insults would be hurled at the women, and insulting anonymous letters arrived in the mail.

The Riot at Surgeons' Hall became a landmark in the history of the medical women's campaign. It attracted widespread publicity and won the women many new friends and sympathizers, but it was to have an even more dramatic sequel.

Notes

1. The Edinburgh University Calendar, 1870–1, p. 166.
2. M. Todd, *The Life of Sophia Jex-Blake*, London: Macmillan, 1918, p. 267.
3. Minutes of the Senatus of Edinburgh University, 9 April 1870.
4. *The Times*, 25 April 1870.
5. The *Spectator*, 9 April 1870.
6. *British Medical Journal*, 16 April 1870.
7. Todd, op. cit., p. 273.

8. See also *Lancet*, 30 April 1870.

9. *Life of Sir Robert Christison, Bart* (edited by his sons), London and Edinburgh: William Blackwood & Sons, vol. II, pp. 46–9.

10. ibid., p. 347. See also p. 50 in the same volume – Christison was also fond of quoting, in the original Latin, one of the Statutes of the Spanish College of the University of Bologna, recorded in 1337:

> And since Woman is the origin of sin, the weapon of the Devil, the expulsion from Paradise and the corruption of ancient law, and because all conversation with her must be carefully avoided, we forbid and expressly prohibit anyone from introducing any woman, however honourable, into the said College. And if he does otherwise, let him be severely published by the Rector.
> (May the action be fortunate and propitious.)

But Sophia could have informed the Professor that the University of Bologna did not then, or later, exclude women from its academic life; indeed, some of its most distinguished scholars were women.

11. D. Guthrie, *Extramural Medical Education in Edinburgh*, London and Edinburgh: E. & S. Livingstone, 1965.

12. Todd, op. cit., p. 276.

13. ibid., p. 279.

14. Sir R.J. Godlee, *Lord Lister*, Oxford: Clarendon Press, 1924, p. 240.

15. *Lancet*, 18 June 1870.

16. ibid., 9 July 1870.

17. I. Thorne, *Sketch of the Foundation and Development of the London School of Medicine for Women*, London: Women's Printing Society, 1915, p. 13.

18. S. Jex-Blake, *Medical Women*, Edinburgh and London: Macmillan, 1886, p. 90.

7

The battle moves to the law courts

When the other women students left Edinburgh to enjoy Christmas with their families, Sophia remained behind. She spent part of Christmas Day at the office of the *Scotsman* arranging for the inclusion of some important notices in the next issue of the paper. If it had not been for the intervention of her friends the Massons, who insisted that she join them for dinner, she could have forgotten that it was Christmas. All this activity was caused by some recent developments at the Royal Infirmary. After December 1870 the Board of Managers would be appointed for one year only, although retiring members could be re-elected. A public meeting of contributors to the Infirmary was to be held on 2 January, and at this meeting the Board for 1871 would be appointed. Since the only contentious issue likely to arise at the meeting was that of the admission of female students, the new Board would almost certainly reflect the view of a majority of the contributors on this matter. Sophia knew that her opponents would be campaigning vigorously, and she would not let them have the field to themselves. Right up until the morning of the meeting she was busy writing letters and making personal calls.

The Annual Meeting of Contributors was usually held in the Edinburgh Council Chambers, but the recent riot at Surgeons' Hall had so captured public interest in the plight of the women students that there was not enough room in the Chambers for all those who wished to attend. After some discussion as to the propriety of using a church for a secular purpose, the meeting was transformed to St Giles Cathedral. Early in the proceedings there were nominations for a Board made up of men who would have been sympathetic to the women, but this was at once challenged by a speaker representing the Infirmary's medical staff, most of whom opposed the teaching of women students. Sophia, as a contributor to the Infirmary, was entitled to be heard. When she rose to her feet some of those present probably recalled the story of the last occasion on which a woman's speaking voice rang through the Cathedral. During the reign of Charles II a spirited lass called Jenny Geddes, who objected to the doctrines of the preacher, interrupted one of his sermons, lending emphasis to her words by throwing her wooden stool at him!

Sophia's performance was only a little less dramatic. Her voice was charged with emotion when she reviewed the events of the women's first year in Edinburgh. All the opposition they had met could, she said, be traced to a small group of men. She continued:

> I want to point out that it was certain of these same men, who had (so to speak) pledged themselves from the first to defeat our hopes of education and render all our efforts abortive – who, sitting in their places on the Infirmary Board, took advantage of the almost irresponsible power with which they were temporarily invested, to thwart and nullify our efforts. I believe that a majority of the managers desired to act justly in this matter; but the presence of those bitter partisans, and the overwhelming influence of every kind brought to bear by them, prevailed to carry the day – to refuse us not only admission on the ordinary terms, but also to refuse us every opportunity which could answer our purpose. I know of the noble protests made against this injury by some of the most respected and most learned members of the Board, but all their efforts were in vain, because strings were pulled and weapons brought into play of which they either did not know or could not expose the character.[1]

When she referred to the riot at Surgeons' Hall she threw caution to the winds and named her chief adversary (who was then present in the Cathedral).

> I will not say that the rioters were acting under orders, but neither can I disbelieve what I was told by indignant gentlemen in the medical class – that this disgraceful scene would never have happened, nor would the petition have been got up at the same time, had it not been clearly understood that our opponents needed a weapon at the Infirmary Board. This I do know, that the riot was not wholly or mainly due to the students at Surgeons' Hall. I know that Dr Christison's class assistant was one of the leading rioters, and the foul language he used could only be excused on the supposition I heard that he was intoxicated. I do not say that Dr Christison knew of or sanctioned his presence, but I do say that I think he would not have been there, had he thought the doctor would have strongly objected to his presence.[2]

At this point Professor Christison interrupted, appealing to the chairman to censure the speaker. At Christison's insistence Sophia was instructed to withdraw the word 'intoxicated'. She did so, but still had the last word: 'If Dr Christison prefers that I should say he used the language when sober, I will withdraw the other supposition.'

Despite Sophia's efforts, the meeting re-elected the members of the retiring Board, so for at least another year the women students had no prospect of being admitted to the wards of the Infirmary. Sophia later noted that this was the first occasion on which women contributors to the Infirmary exercised their right to vote. Sixteen of them did so, and all voted for candidates who would have admitted the women students. She also observed that of the thirty doctors who voted, there were five who supported the women students' side. For some time it had been apparent that among both the students and the qualified members of the medical profession there was a small but important minority who were in favour of opening the profession to women, and were prepared to help to achieve this.

The dispute that once concerned only the women students and the University administrators was now being taken up by the general public. Two weeks after the Infirmary elections another public meeting was called to consider the case of the women students. It attracted a large crowd that represented both sides in the dispute. A petition signed by 956 Edinburgh women was presented. It expressed the signatories' 'earnest hope that full facilities for Hospital study will be afforded by the Managers to all women who desire to enter the Medical Profession'. Mrs Nichol, a frail elderly lady, captured the attention of the audience when she said that she represented more than 1,300 women from all levels of Edinburgh society. These women were anxious to know what kind of men were to be the sole medical attendants of the next generation, if women doctors were not allowed. Mrs Nichol continued:

> If the students studying at present in the Infirmary cannot contemplate with equanimity the presence of ladies as fellow students, how is it possible that they can possess either the scientific spirit, or the personal purity of mind, which alone would justify their presence in the female wards during the most delicate operations on, and examinations of, female patients?[3]

This pertinent question was applauded by some of the audience, but a group of rowdy male students laughed and hissed.

Sophia had not intended to speak on this occasion, but she could not let pass unchallenged a remark made by one of her opponents. He said that Miss Jex-Blake herself had told him that she could not continue with her studies in America because the character of female medical students in that country had so deteriorated as to be quite intolerable. When Sophia rose to object the male students shouted in derision and pelted her with peas, but she was not intimidated. She denied emphatically that she had ever made such a comment. She said that, on the contrary, it was her observations of the noble work being done by medical women in America that inspired her to devote her life to the cause of medical education for women in Britain. The American women doctors who were her friends had few equals, and certainly no superiors. The previous speaker made a half-hearted apology, saying that he could have misunderstood remarks Miss Blake made during a conversation they had held two years previously.

The battle moves to the law courts

The meeting concluded without achieving anything more than additional publicity, most of it favourable, for the women's cause. Another meeting called a few days later by Mr William Law, the Lord Provost of Edinburgh, had a much more tangible result. At this meeting a committee was formed to help with the planning of the women's campaign, and to raise money for it. The Committee for Securing a Medical Education to the Women of Edinburgh was founded in a mood of goodwill and enthusiasm, and had a membership of three hundred of the city's most respected citizens. As the purpose of the Committee became more widely known, it recruited to its membership men and women who were at the forefront of the nation's various social reform movements. They included the Bishop of Exeter; the Rt. Hon. Russell Gurney, Recorder of London; Miss Frances Power Cobbe; Professor Fawcett, MP; Charles Darwin; Lady Anna Gore Langton; and Miss Harriet Martineau.

But Sophia was never allowed to enjoy success for long. The Committee was barely formed when she received an unpleasant surprise, in the form of a defamation writ. The writ was issued in the name of Mr Craig, a medical student who was also employed as Professor Christison's classroom assistant. This was the man she had accused of leading the riot at Surgeons' Hall. The amount sought in compensation was the formidable sum of £1,000. Sophia's family and friends rallied to her support. Her mother, who once would have been reduced to nervous prostration by such an event, remained calm and helpful. Her brother wrote an excellent letter as soon as he heard the news.

The Athenaeum
Jan. 23, 1871

My Dear Sophy,

I will gladly pay half expenses of your action for libel brought by Dr Christison's assistant.

I think it vital that you should have the best legal assistance, and win. Be careful, and don't let them 'draw' you into indiscretions that are most forgiveable morally, but damaging to the cause practically.

I don't the least want to lecture you or assume the Mentor. I only want you to win all along the line.

Your aff. brother,
T.W. J-B.[4]

This was a generous gesture on Thomas's part. As the Principal of Cheltenham College he was now a prominent figure in the conservative realm of Church education; having his sister involved in a highly publicized lawsuit could have caused him embarrassment.

Previously, Sophia had welcomed publicity because it had been centred on the women's campaign and not on herself personally. But this case would be very different. It was Sophia Jex-Blake's character that would be vindicated or besmirched; the women's campaign would be affected only secondarily. She also knew that her real opponent in the lawsuit was not young Craig, but his employer, Christison, who hoped that by this means he would discredit her as the women's leader. The case was not to be heard until the end of May, so for four months she had to try to push it to the back of her mind while she continued her studies.

In March, as the winter term ended, the students all took examinations, and again the women were very successful. It was the custom for the Presidents of the Royal Colleges of Physicians and Surgeons to attend the end-of-term ceremony of the extramural schools to present the prizes. On this occasion both gentlemen cancelled their engagement because women students were among the prize winners, and it was against their principles to bestow academic awards on women. No ceremony was held that term, the prizes being distributed by mail, much to the astonishment of the interested citizens of Edinburgh. But the class lists were, as usual, published in the newspapers, with the women's names shown in their correct positions. The incident provoked much amused discussion. The presidents had exposed themselves to ridicule, and helped, rather than hindered, the women's cause.

In April Sophia received an invitation to speak at a meeting of supporters of women's suffrage, to be held in London at the end of the month. She wondered whether it would be wise to associate herself publicly with another feminist cause, but was reassured on this score by Professor Masson and other friends in Edinburgh. She attended the meeting and gave an excellent address. Also at the meeting at the Langham Hotel was Elizabeth Garrett, who had recently married, and was now Mrs Garrett Anderson. Her husband, James Skelton Anderson, was a partner in a prosperous shipping firm that was the forerunner of the Orient Line. He admired his wife's achievements, and thoroughly approved of her continuing with her work. Elizabeth's career was to be enhanced by her marriage, certainly not ended by it.

Sophia's views on marriage changed as she matured. At eighteen she had expected to marry, as nearly every other young woman did. Now, at thirty, she thought it more likely that she would always remain single. She realized that her independent nature was not well fitted to the exacting partnership of marriage, but perhaps a more important reason was her commitment to the feminist cause. Helping other women to gain their rightful place in society absorbed all her mental and emotional resources. Even so, Sophia must have felt a twinge of envy when she compared her lot with Elizabeth's. Elizabeth was enjoying professional success and personal happiness, while she herself was committed to a bitter struggle, with no certainty as to its duration or outcome.

The defamation case was heard at the end of May, and lasted for two days. The courtroom was packed on both days. Christison was known to be a skilled, unshakeable witness, with vast experience of courtroom procedure. Sophia Jex-Blake was a novice by comparison, although she had shown that she could be a fiery and effective speaker. Most of the spectators probably expected the women students to be gauche and strident, but easily vanquished by their astute male opponents. There was considerable surprise when Sophia, Edith Pechey and Isabel Thorne were each called to the witness box – their demeanour was ladylike, their appearance pleasingly conventional. When cross-questioned they answered with quiet confidence. By contrast, Professor Christison for once appeared nervous and indecisive. But the outcome of the case was determined more by the complexities of the law than by the calibre of the witnesses.

Sophia's barrister, Mr Young, had advised her that she should not herself attempt to prove the truth of her accusations against Craig. Instead, evidence obtained by cross-questioning Craig and his friends would be used to justify her statement that he had been one of the leaders of the riot and had behaved like a ruffian. But Mr Shand, the barrister appearing for Craig, appealed to the Judge, Lord Mure, to disallow such questioning of his client. The appeal was granted. Craig could not even be made to admit that he was at the scene of the riot. Sophia was thus left without a defence.

In his final address to the jury, Shand asked for a significant sum of money to recompense his client. 'A nominal sum . . . would be an injury instead of an assistance', he said. This remark may have had the reverse effect from the one he intended. When the jury delivered its verdict they found in favour of the claimant, but awarded him damages of one farthing! The verdict was a popular one. Sophia's spirited defence in the witness box was in marked contrast to her opponent's avoidance of giving any account of his actions. A leading article in the *Glasgow Herald* probably expressed the views of many of its readers when the writer commented:

> Miss Jex-Blake has completely vindicated the title of her sex to aspire to the highest honours not merely in medicine but in law. She has shown herself a perfect mistress of the art of self defence. In no cricket field this season have there been so many dangerous balls admirably stopped, and so many badly bowled ones dexterously played.[5]

However, the episode was not quite over. Several weeks later the Court announced its decision on the apportioning of legal expenses. Sophia was to pay the costs of both parties, a total sum of £916! One of the jurymen wrote to the *Scotsman* protesting that this had not been the jury's intention. He said that during their deliberations they considered the matter of legal expenses, and asked the Clerk of Courts for guidance. They were told that their proposed verdict would not require the defendant to pay the costs of both sides; evidently this advice was incorrect. He added:

> It seems a very illogical result to affirm that the pursuer had suffered no damage by the alleged slander, or, at least damage of only one farthing, and at the same time to compel the defender to pay a large sum for

expenses, especially when the origin of the whole matter was a riot in which the ladies were so badly used.[6]

Sophia could have appealed against the Court's decision, but was advised that the outcome of such an action was most uncertain, and that she might only incur additional costs. In any case, her anxiety over the large debt was quickly relieved. Not only did her brother's cheque for half the sum arrive promptly but, better still, the Education Committee opened a public appeal to raise the money. Contributions and letters of support poured in. They came from distinguished and wealthy members of society, and from working men and women who thought the Court's decision outrageously unjust. Within a short time the appeal was fully subscribed. The Education Committee insisted that Thomas Jex-Blake's cheque be returned to him, and still there was a surplus of £112 after all the expenses had been paid. This was added to a fund that had been established so that at some future date a hospital for women, *staffed by women doctors*, could be founded in Edinburgh.

Sophia was discovering that each setback she experienced resulted in a surge of popular sympathy for the medical women's cause. Public opinion was becoming her greatest source of strength. The power of her opponent, Professor Christison, was of a more private kind. It sprang from his numerous professional appointments and his close associations with influential people. He was a member of every one of the University's administrative bodies that controlled the teaching of medicine – the Medical Faculty, the Senatus, the Court and the General Council. In addition, he sat on the Board of the Edinburgh Royal Infirmary, and was a Crown representative on the General Medical Council, which controlled the registration of medical practitioners for the whole of Britain. He was generally thought to have the ear of the Queen herself, and at the other end of the social scale he commanded the loyalty of most of the students who crowded into his lectures.[7] For several decades his wisdom and integrity had earned him the veneration of his colleagues. 'What right', they would have said in 1869, 'has a brash young woman to defy such a gentleman, especially as he is old enough to be her grandfather?'

But the episodes of the Hope Scholarship, the riot at Surgeons' Hall and the defamation case against Sophia shed a different light on events. The women students were now seen to be asking for nothing more than fair treatment, which was constantly being denied them. The newspapers and journals were often critical of the conduct of the women's opponents and sometimes mentioned Christison by name. His handling of this affair seemed to be the one regrettable action in his long career. Criticism affected his judgement adversely. He strayed from his usual path of dignity and honour, to indulge in vindictive counter-moves against the women students. For several years these moves succeeded in stopping the women's progress but, in retrospect, it appears that Christison was unwittingly serving their cause.

The house at 15 Buccleuch Place was livelier than ever, having recently become the home of Isabel Thorne and her four children, as well as Sophia and Edith Pechey. Four women joined the group attending extramural medical lectures, and these, too, used Buccleuch Place as their headquarters. Sophia was rather like a headmistress, watching over the younger students, as well as arranging their admission to courses. One of them later said that she would have preferred more freedom to make her own mistakes, but that was not Sophia's way. Her help, given unstintingly, could sometimes overwhelm the recipient. But despite the inevitable minor disagreements, the women who met at Buccleuch Place were a happy, friendly group who stood by each other through their shared adversity.

One of the most frequent callers was Miss Agnes McLaren, the daughter of Edinburgh's Parliamentary representative. She was such a tireless worker for women's suffrage, and so well liked for her tact and good humour, that the women students affectionately dubbed her 'St Agnes'. The lawsuit was barely over when Sophia received a letter from Miss McLaren, who said that she and several members of her family were about to make a holiday visit to Germany, and would be away for three weeks. On 7 June Sophia replied:

> Though we all miss you here almost daily, I am unselfish enough to be heartily glad that you are going to Germany. I am sure the change of air and scene must do you good, and the chestnut trees at Heidelberg must be simply lovely now.
>
> When you get to the top and sit and look down at the valley of the Neckar, you may picture me (as a lonely English teacher at Mannheim) going over there on Sundays to church, and climbing to that brow to enjoy the setting sun and the infinite peacefulness and beauty of the whole scene.
>
> I only *wish* I could be there with you! If you stay at all at Mannheim, do go and see my old school, the 'Grossherzogliches Institut' – I think they still remember my name there, – and I should like so much to hear news of them. They would be electrified to hear of me as a doctor.
>
> I finished up by having scarlet fever there, and shocked them all by refusing to submit to the stupid old German regimen of starvation and shut windows! . . .
>
> I do most heartily wish you a pleasant journey and great rest and refreshment in it. Do you know that when I got your letter such a longing came over me to see the Rhine again that for a moment I almost thought of asking you if you would take me with you, but five minutes reflection showed me how wrong and foolish it would be for me to leave home just now in the midst of term, and with these 'appeals' still undecided, and with my petition to the Senatus coming on! But it *was* a huge temptation all the same![8]

Sophia's friends must have argued very persuasively that she should take a holiday, because only a day after writing this letter she joined Agnes

McLaren's party. But instead of enjoying a nostalgic visit to Germany, she was to observe the aftermath of a tragic event in French history.

When the travellers arrived in Paris on 13 June 1871 they found the city in turmoil. In January the Franco-Prussian War had come to an end, with France capitulating and victorious German troops marching through Paris. The Emperor Napoleon III and the Empress Eugenie were exiles in England. The Assembly that was elected in February had failed to win popular support, and there were frequent clashes between the various political factions. At the end of May intermittent fighting had culminated in a bloody street battle in which many lives were lost. By the time the McLarens' party arrived hostilities had ceased, but there were bodies still lying in the streets, and damaged buildings marked the sites of the most severe encounters. Finding it impossible to continue their journey to Germany, the party returned home.

As soon as Sophia arrived back in Edinburgh she began a new approach to the University on the difficult problem of the women's lectures. There had been no relaxation of the University's rule that the women must receive all their tuition in separate classes, and most of the professors still refused to make these special arrangements for them. Some excellent lecturers in the extramural schools were still prepared to help, and not all of them demanded high fees to compensate for the small size of the women's classes. But University regulations permitted candidates for the medical degree to take lectures in the extramural system in only four subjects; for the other subjects, attendance at University classes was compulsory. Having used their allowance of four extramural classes, and being only half-way through the medical course, the women had reached an impasse.

On 26 June Sophia wrote to the Senatus pointing out the problem and suggesting two possible solutions. First, the University could appoint additional lecturers to teach the women, with the cost to be borne by the women students. Second, the University could permit women students to take a greater number of extramural classes. The Senatus sought a legal opinion, which was presented at its meeting a month later:

> In the original foundation of the College, now the University of Edinburgh, the objects of the Founders are expressed in very general terms, and nothing occurs to indicate the sex of the youth for whom its benefits were designed. But from the tenor of the Statutes and Ordinances which have from time to time been enacted for its internal regulations, as well as by the light afforded by immemorial usage, we are satisfied that the University has all along been and must still be regarded as an institution devoted exclusively to the education of male students. The result of this view, in our opinion, is that males alone have any right to demand, and on complying with the regulations of the University to obtain, admission to the privilege of Studentship.
>
> We are further of opinion that the only persons legally entitled to the

character of Students of the University are those who can gain admission as a matter of right, there being a corresponding obligation in law on the part of the University to teach them.

We do not think that the Senatus Academicus, whether acting alone or in concert with the other governing bodies of the University, has power to admit ex gratia to the full privileges of students a person or class of persons who by the Constitution of the University are disqualified from enforcing their own admission. It may be that the Senatus or other authorities can give permission to the Professors of the University to teach persons not legally entitled to demand admission as students; but we do not think that persons who have attended lectures by virtue of such privileges have, even when permitted to matriculate, any right to claim the position or privileges of students.[9]

The women's opponents in the Senatus were delighted to hear this confirmation of their view that the University had no obligations whatsoever to its women students. Professor Masson failed to win support for a motion that steps be taken to ensure that 'the ladies who had matriculated and completed part of the course be enabled to complete their studies'. A motion that Miss Jex-Blake be informed that the Senatus was unable to comply with either of her proposals was carried by a majority of one. The minutes record that this motion was seconded by Professor Lister.

Sophia and her friends detected an additional threat in the legal opinion given to the Senatus; there could be an attempt to exclude women from the examinations leading to the medical degree. Four such tests, known as the Professional Examinations, had to be taken during the four-year course. The First Professional, in chemistry, botany and natural history, could be taken at the end of the second year, or deferred until the third or fourth year. The five original students would be eligible to enter for the First Professional Examination to be held in October 1871, as they had met all the University's requirements in these subjects. They decided to obtain a legal opinion on the University's obligation to admit them to examinations, as well as to provide them with tuition. This involved Sophia in a great deal of work, as she alone could supply a detailed and accurate record of all that had occurred since her first application to the University in March 1869.

There was yet another vexing incident, in July 1871. The Presidents of the Royal Colleges of Physicians and Surgeons had made a symbolic gesture by refusing to distribute prizes to women students; now they took a more positive action. They notified the extramural lecturers who held their classes in Surgeons' Hall that after the end of the summer term of 1871 women students would not be allowed to enter the Hall if they were studying for medical qualifications. Student midwives would, however, be admitted as before! Once again the presidents were derided in a number of newspapers for an action that seemed to indicate very clearly that they feared the competition of women doctors. For Sophia the change meant more difficulty and inconvenience in arranging the women's extramural lectures.

Sophia was beginning to feel desperately in need of a holiday, so she was delighted when Lucy Sewall wrote from Boston that she would be visiting Britain in September. Sophia replied:

My Darling,
                    I am so sorry for your loss of poor little Scamper, – I have got a splendid big 'Collie' for you here, – the handsomest I ever saw, – if you can take him back with you. If, that is, you *must* go back; but, oh, Lucy, I do *so* wish you would stay with us here for a few years.
People are getting wild for women doctors here, – and you might make almost any income, and do quite incalculable good by living here for the next five years.
We have eleven women studying here now, and absolutely no one to give them adequate uterine teaching!
This morning I had a quite spontaneous offer of £200 to help found a Women's Hospital here, and I believe that in a week I could get ten times that amount promised.
You should organize everything exactly as you liked, and, republican wretch as you are, you would be a sort of Queen among us, – and, what you would care for much more, would do quite infinite good to everybody concerned, – ladies, poor women, students, and all.
However, you shan't be bothered or worried. I think the strongest argument of all will be when you see for yourself how sorely we need you.
I shall not make any definite plans for you till after you come. If you like to stay quietly in Scotland all the time, we will do so, or I will go with you to Zurich or Paris or anywhere you like. . . . Send me early word of the steamer by which you expect to come, and, if at all possible, I will meet you at Liverpool. . . .
I send you another copy of my Suffrage speech, and hope you have received the newspapers about the trial.
                                        Your very aff.
                                        S.L.J-B
Turk has put on mourning for Scamper, – crape round his left arm, as they do in the army. He evidently quite understands, for he doesn't try to get it off.[10]

Leaving Isabel Thorne in charge at Buccleuch Place, Sophia went to Liverpool to meet Lucy's ship. The two friends then journeyed to Shipley, in Yorkshire, to see Mrs Unwin, whom they had last visited together in 1868. Since then Mrs Unwin's health had declined still further, and she was pathetically eager to consult the woman doctor again. Neither Lucy Sewall nor

Sophia recorded the nature of her illness, but by 1871 it must have been apparent that she was suffering from advanced tuberculosis. Dr Sewall was grieved to have to report to Mr Unwin that his wife did not have long to live.

After this sad beginning Sophia and Lucy had a quiet, but enjoyable, holiday. They attended a meeting of the British Association for the Advancement of Science, and then travelled to Perthshire, where they were joined by Ursula Du Pre. The three friends stayed at a farmhouse that provided them with simple comfort and wholesome food. Another of the amenities it boasted was its own ghost! The three visitors later claimed to have heard some ghostly sounds, but they never caught sight of their ethereal fellow lodger. They spent their days taking long walks, or driving in the country, as Sophia and Lucy had done in Maine four years previously. Their evenings passed in conversation, reading and letter-writing. Lucy and Sophia again discussed the idea of their becoming partners in a medical practice, once Sophia had qualified; they came to the same conclusion as they had previously – each felt bound by duty and personal inclination to work in her own country. Soon it was time for Lucy to return home. Sophia accompanied her to Liverpool, and on the way they paid a last visit to Mrs Unwin.

When Sophia returned to Edinburgh at the end of September the legal opinion sought by the women students and their friends of the Education Committee had been supplied. The Lord Advocate and Sheriff Fraser, having considered the question in great detail, concluded that the University Court had acted within its powers when, in 1869, it allowed the five women to matriculate; as matriculated students of the University they must be regarded as having the same rights and privileges as those enjoyed by male students. It was also reassuring that the new University Calendar for 1871–2 again included, unchanged, the *Regulations for the Education of Women in Medicine in the University*. Sophia and her colleagues decided to enter for the First Professional Examination to be held on 24 October. She also encouraged three more women, whose academic records were excellent, to come to Edinburgh to study medicine. They had written asking her advice, and she offered to arrange for them to take the Preliminary Examination for matriculation. This would be held on 17 and 18 October. Her advice does not seem so rash when it is remembered that there was no other British university or recognized medical school prepared to accept applications from women.

Sophia submitted to the University an application and examination fee for every one of the women candidates, and all were accepted. Even so, early in October her friends warned her that there were rumours abroad that an attempt would be made to prevent women from taking either of the examinations. It was not long before the rumours were substantiated. On 14 October each of the women candidates for the First Professional received a letter from the Dean:

116

Madam,

I am instructed by the Medical Faculty to inform you that your name and your fees have been received in error by the Clerk of the University as a candidate for the First Professional Examination during the present month, but that the Faculty cannot receive you for such examination without the sanction of the Senatus Academicus.

I am, Madam,
Your obedient servant,
J.H. Balfour
Dean of the Medical Faculty[11]

The Senatus was not due to meet until 21 October, three days before the examination date. On 16 October Sophia received another even more extraordinary letter:

Madam,

I am desired by the Dean of the Medical Faculty to inform you that he has been interdicted by the Faculty from giving examination papers to ladies on the 17th and 18th curt. Kindly communicate this fact to the ladies whose names you some time ago handed in to me for this examination.

I am, etc.,
Thomas Gilbert[12]

But the ladies had already arrived in Edinburgh for the Preliminary Examination, which was to be held the following day!

Sophia spent the rest of the day of 16 October scurrying across Edinburgh from one office to another. First, she took the letter to her solicitor, who suggested that they seek the opinion of the advocate Mr Fraser. Fortunately, Fraser was able to see them at once. He had no hesitation in stating that this action of the Dean was illegal. The solicitor then wrote a strongly worded reply to the Dean:

Dear Sir,

We have been instructed to obtain the opinion of counsel with reference to the legality of your refusal to admit ladies to the Preliminary Examination in Arts, which will take place tomorrow.

We beg now to enclose the memorial submitted, and the opinion given thereon by Mr Patrick Fraser, for your perusal, and request that you will, at your earliest convenience, return them to us.

We beg to point out that you are individually responsible if the refusal is persisted in, and that we have been instructed, in that case, to raise actions for damages against you at the instance of each of the memorialists. You will also observe that the instructions of the Medical Faculty, being in themselves illegal, will be no defence against such actions.

117

We trust that you will, in these circumstances, reconsider the matter, and see fit to retract the refusal, and prevent the necessity of further proceedings.

We are etc.,
Millar, Allardice, & Robson, W.S.[13]

This letter was delivered by hand (probably by Sophia herself); it produced the desired effect. The Dean issued new instructions that the women were to be admitted to the examinations, but his note to Sophia ended with a warning, 'I must inform you that I admit them provisionally until the matter is decided by the proper authorities, and without prejudice as regards myself.'

Next day the Misses Dahms, Miller and Mundy took the Preliminary Examination, which they all passed easily. But when they applied for their matriculation tickets, they were told by a clerk that Professor Christison had instructed him not to issue tickets to women. On this occasion the Senatus overruled Christison, so the three new students at last succeeded in matriculating.

The First Professional Examination was now imminent, and Sophia still did not know whether her group would be allowed to take it. Then, at the Senatus meeting on 21 October a decision in their favour was obtained. The women candidates who presented themselves three days later all passed, but Sophia was not one of them. Exhausted by the work and anxiety of the last few weeks, she thought it wiser to defer her attempt until the following year. Some of the women's friends privately expressed the view that their opponents at the University had deliberately timed their actions to achieve just this effect.

Sophia was shortly to receive another shock. In the winter of 1871–2 three of the Edinburgh Seven announced that they were giving up their studies in order to be married. Helen Evans, whom Sophia had coached in arithmetic so that she could pass her matriculation examination, had proved an excellent student. Now she was to become the wife of Mr Alexander Russel, the editor of the *Scotsman*. Matilda Chaplin was to marry Professor Ayrton of Edinburgh University, and Mary Anderson would become Mrs Marshall. Sophia knew that she would miss the companionship of these able young women. She also knew that her opponents would use them as examples to support the claim that higher education is wasted on women because they marry and make no practical use of their knowledge. This argument was still being used well into the twentieth century, although it is based on a very narrow view of the purpose and benefits of education. Sophia would have been happier if she could have known then that two of the three would later return to their medical studies and complete them. In any case, in 1872 there were still seven women studying for the degree in medicine of the University of Edinburgh; the defectors had been replaced by the three newcomers. There were also six or seven women attending the extramural lectures without having matriculated at the University. They probably intended to obtain Swiss or French degrees and to practise in Britain without being registered. Some of these held scholarships, which had been generously donated by Dr Garrett Anderson and several of her friends.

One of Professor Christison's strongest arguments against the admission of female medical students to the University was that the lecturers in the Medical Faculty would be intolerably overworked if they had to conduct classes for women, as well as those for men. The Committee of friends of the women students did not dispute this dubious claim. Instead, they offered to pay for additional lecturers to teach the women. The Committee was also willing to provide suitable lecture rooms if the University could not accommodate the extra classes. The offer was discussed at a Senatus meeting that was dominated by Professor Christison. Not only was the Committee's offer declined, but the meeting resolved to recommend to the University Court that it rescind the *Regulations* of 1870–1 admitting female students. The Court did not act on this recommendation; indeed, it confirmed the existing *Regulations*. The incident demonstrated that Christison's opposition was no longer based on principles or logic. He would not rest until the women were shut out of the University.

Sophia's group, who had now completed two years of study, sought some assurance that they would be allowed to complete the course and graduate. Dr Alexander Wood tried to gain them this assurance at a meeting of the University Council held at the end of October 1871. He moved that the University was bound in honour and justice to ensure that those women who had already completed part of the course were granted the facilities to complete it. He did not ask the University to commit itself to accepting all women who might in the future seek to enter its portals, but merely to keep faith with those it had already accepted.

A petition to the Council in support of Dr Wood's motion bore the signatures of nine thousand women. It had been organized by Mrs Henry Kingsley, a staunch friend of the women students, who had witnessed the riot at Surgeons' Hall. Mrs Kingsley later said that with more time and more helpers she could have collected ten times as many signatures. Even the *Lancet* said in its editorial that the University should honour its obligations to its women students.

At the meeting Dr Wood was given a sympathetic hearing. Then it was the turn of the opposition, which was led as usual by Professor Christison. But it was Christison's ally, Professor Turner, who scored the most effective blow. He quoted from Sophia's original application to the University, in which she had said:

I beg to signify my willingness to accede to any such conditions, or agree to any such reservations as may seem desirable to you, and indeed to withdraw my application altogether if, after due and sufficient trial, it should be found impracticable to grant me a continuance of the favour which I now request.[14]

In now asking for so much more, Sophia appeared to be guilty of gross inconsistency. This was a telling argument. When the vote was taken there were 97 votes in favour of Dr Wood's motion, 107 against. The matter was referred back to the Senatus and the University Court, thus ensuring that the old game of move and counter-move would continue with unabated intensity.

Sophia was not entitled to speak at a meeting of the Council, so she could not point out that the letter quoted to such effect was the one that had accompanied her first application to the University, to attend lectures for one term. This application had been unsuccessful. Later, when the five women were accepted as students, the agreement was quite different, as the relevant section in the University Calendar testified. The *Scotsman* printed Sophia's forthright letter in which she corrected Professor Turner; she then went on to show that the experience of the defamation suit had not made her afraid to speak her mind:

> I will venture to say, that, instead of the daily trials of the past two years and the apparent deadlock at which we have now arrived, we should have found nothing but smooth paths for our feet, and no difficulties from either students or professors, had Professor Christison but kept to the promise he voluntarily made to me at the close of my single interview – of two minutes – with him two years ago – 'I shall vote against you, but I shall take no measures to oppose you.'[15]

The *Lancet* was highly critical of the Council's decision:

> The Edinburgh school has come badly out of its imbroglio with the lady students. The motion of Dr Alexander Wood, to which we made reference last week, was negatived by a majority of ten. As we then pointed out, the issue before the General Council was neither more nor less than this, – to keep faith with the female students whom the University had allowed to proceed two years in their medical curriculum. The Council was not asked to commit itself in the slightest degree to any opinion, favourable or unfavourable, to the admission of ladies to a medical career. It had only to concede, in common courtesy, not to say common fairness, the right to which the best legal advice had shown the female students to be entitled, – the right to carry on the studies they had been allowed to prosecute half way towards graduation.[16]

The *Lancet*'s criticism was unlikely to weigh heavily on Professor Christison's spirits at this time, for he was quietly rejoicing in a piece of personal good fortune that would soon become generally known. His diary contained the following entry for 10 October 1871:

The Prime Minister, on his way south from Balmoral, called on me this evening, and informed me in the kindest and most gracious manner, that if it was agreeable to me he would recommend her Majesty to confer upon me a baronetcy, as a compliment to myself, to the medical profession in Scotland, and to the University of Edinburgh.[17]

Four days later Christison wrote to Gladstone accepting the honour.

As the end of the year approached, Sophia and her friends had to prepare for the next annual meeting of the contributors to the Edinburgh Royal Infirmary. At that meeting the Board of Managers for 1872 would be elected, and again proceedings would be dominated by the debate on the admission of women students. One of the arguments would be that the resources of the Infirmary were already strained in providing teaching facilities for the six hundred or so male students; if several wards were to be allocated to less than a dozen women students, the men would be unfairly deprived. This argument depended on the assumption that it would be quite improper to teach male and female students in the same wards, even though ordinarily the men were taught in the presence of female nurses. The women's opponents seized upon such minor difficulties and magnified them, as a means of warding off a fundamental change in their profession. With a little tact and goodwill on their part most of these difficulties could have been easily overcome, but they were not prepared to face a future in which familiar social patterns were swept away.

Sophia had enthusiastic and capable supporters, but she still felt personally responsible for the campaign and its outcome. In the weeks leading up to the Infirmary meeting she spared no effort. Her diary for the last few days records the following notes:

Home after 10 p.m. Then to write leader for Monday. Done about 12.15 p.m. Then to relight fire and get warm, – then bed!
Sunday, Dec. 31st. Wrote paragraphs and finished article. Went down to *Scotsman* office. . . .
Oh, dear, I hope the things will be in right tomorrow, – and oh, *how* I hope we may win!
We have 296 votes more or less promised. *We ought.*[18]

The meeting proved to be no less dramatic than that of the year before. Again two panels of Managers were nominated, one favourable to the women, the other opposed. The favourable party was elected with a small majority – 177 votes for, 168 against. Then Professor Masson moved that all registered students of medicine should be admitted to the educational advantages of the Infirmary, without distinction of sex. This motion was greeted with so much enthusiasm that it appeared certain to be carried. At this juncture all the avowed opponents of the women walked out of the meeting in a body! The motion was carried unanimously.

Sophia later recalled that at this moment she almost fainted, from the combined effects of relief and tiredness. As congratulations were showered on them the women students felt that at last the tide had turned in their favour. But how short-lived their victories always were! At the next meeting of contributors a fortnight later the election of Managers was challenged. Among those who had voted were the representatives of a number of Scottish firms that contributed to the Infirmary. Now it was claimed by the women's opponents that voting by firms was unconstitutional. If the firms' votes were deducted from both factions the women's side would lose by one vote. Firms had voted, unchallenged, at many previous elections. Their eligibility was now disputed merely as a means of wresting victory from the women. The *Scotsman* was scathing:

> It mattered nothing that firms had voted since the Infirmary was founded; that contributors qualified only as members of firms had, as has now been ascertained, sat over and over again on the Board of Management, and on the Committee of Contributors. It was of equally slight importance that the firms whom it was now sought to disqualify had been among the most generous benefactors of the charity, and that, with the imminent prospect before them of great pecuniary necessity, it would probably be impossible, without their aid, to carry out even the plans for the new building. The firms had voted in favour of the ladies, and the firms must go, if at least the law would (as it probably will not) bear out the medical men in their reckless endeavour to expel them.[19]

No settlement of the dispute was possible by negotiation, so the next step was to appeal to the courts for a legal decision. The case could not be heard for at least six months; in the mean time the 1871 Board continued to manage the Infirmary and the women students were still denied admission to the wards. Several sympathetic doctors provided some teaching for them at outpatient clinics they conducted for the poor of Edinburgh. Sophia herself often attended midwifery cases under the supervision of one of these men. But none of this could replace the comprehensive instruction the women should have been receiving in the wards of the Infirmary.

Sophia and her friends were becoming convinced that they should undertake yet another lawsuit, despite the expense involved and the risk of defeat. The University's refusal to grant the women students normal access to lectures and degree examinations seemed to be unshakeable by less drastic means. She mentioned this proposal in letters to her brother. Tom's replies sounded a note of caution.

> I do not think you can gain anything by sueing the Professors or by going to Law with the University in any other shape. It may be too late now to persuade, but it would be at all times hopeless to compel, a great University to open its doors to ladies. . . .

You can make better use of your time by getting University instruction elsewhere, than by throwing legal pebbles at the University gates of Auld Reekie: and life being short you had better gather up the net result of your Scotch experience, and go to Zurich or Paris, or wherever your own knowledge and judgment lead you.[20]

Sophia must have been disappointed by her brother's failure to appreciate the importance of a British qualification for the women students. She explained it to him in her next letter, but he still advised against the proposed lawsuit.

There is more to be said for legal action than I knew of: for I thought Paris or Zurich degree was legal qualification in England: though of course to go abroad for degree is objectionable in several ways, and the language must slightly increase the difficulties.

Still there is nothing to be said for legal action unless it is likely to succeed: and of that your Scotch lawyers are the best judges: though their expectations hitherto have been more sanguine than accurate in your case.

I am sorry I cannot be of much use, and very sorry the Trades Union is so strong and so well organized.

It must be very annoying, and is certainly a horrible waste of time: but half of most people's time is spent in untying the foolish knots of blind opponents. . . .

It seems hardly possible that you should get on with your own Medical education while there is so much polemical business on hand; but if you carry the point for all women, it will be cheaply bought at the sacrifice of two or three years of individual training in books and bones.[21]

Sophia did not overlook the possibility that at another university hostility to women students had diminished. It was now almost seven years since Elizabeth Garrett was rebuffed by St Andrews, so it seemed appropriate to make discreet enquiries again there. Perhaps a separate medical school for women could be established at St Andrews. Unfortunately nothing had changed in seven years. One or two of the Professors were friendly, but the majority were still resolutely opposed to opening the doors of the University to women. It was safer to stay on in Edinburgh, where she had many loyal and able friends. If necessary she would carry the battle into the law courts, and she would do her best to win.

Notes

1. The *Scotsman*, 3 January 1871.
2. ibid.
3. M. Todd, *The Life of Sophia Jex-Blake*, London: Macmillan, 1918, p. 300.

4. ibid., p. 307.

5. The *Glasgow Herald*, 2 June 1871.

6. The *Scotsman*, 12 July 1871.

7. O.D. Edwards, *The Quest for Sherlock Holmes*, Edinburgh: Mainstream Publishing Co., 1983, p. 193. The author of this biography of Arthur Conan Doyle makes some interesting comments on Robert Christison. Conan Doyle was a medical student at Edinburgh University during Christison's last year as a Professor. Years later, when creating the character of Sherlock Holmes, Conan Doyle drew on his memories of the academic expert in forensic medicine. Edwards suggests, however, that Christison contributed even more to another of Conan Doyle's characters – the arch-villain Professor Moriarty. Moriarty is described as wielding his power through a vast network of agents whom he controlled 'like a spider in the centre of its web'.

8. Todd, op. cit., p. 324.

9. Minutes of the Senatus of Edinburgh University, 28 July 1871.

10. Todd, op. cit., p. 327.

11. ibid., p. 333.

12. ibid., p. 333.

13. ibid., p. 334.

14. ibid., p. 235.

15. ibid., p. 337.

16. *Lancet*, 4 November 1871.

17. *Life of Sir Robert Christison, Bart* (edited by his sons), Edinburgh and London: Blackwood & Sons, 1885–6, Vol II, p. 431.

18. Todd, op. cit., p. 345.

19. The *Scotsman*, 29 January 1872.

20. Todd, op. cit., p. 353.

21. ibid., p. 353.

8

The end of the Edinburgh campaign

The hearing of the dispute over the Infirmary election was postponed until July so, regardless of its outcome, the women students would be deprived of hospital training for more than half of 1872. The University authorities were also as intransigent as ever. In January Sophia again appealed to the University Court to provide the women with tuition and to admit them to degree examinations. This time her letter was accompanied by a copy of the statement prepared by the Lord Advocate and Sheriff Fraser, in which these gentlemen declared that there was no legal barrier to the University's complying with the women's request.

At its meeting on 8 January the University Court considered Sophia's letter and decided that the question had been 'complicated by the introduction of the subject of graduation, which is not essential to the completion of a medical or other education'. The Court suggested that the ladies should accept, instead of degrees, 'certificates of proficiency'. If they would agree to this the Court would do what it could to meet their needs with regard to instruction.

Of course 'certificates of proficiency' would not entitle the women to be registered as qualified medical practitioners. As a temporary solution to the impasse Sophia then suggested that the matter of graduation could be left in abeyance, provided that meanwhile the women could receive instruction. The University Court agreed to this, and it seemed that a considerable advance had been made. However, when Sophia asked for assurance that the instruction given under this agreement would conform with the requirements for graduation, she was told that no such assurance was given or implied. The Court would make no further concession beyond its certificates of proficiency, and proposed to do nothing more to help the women complete their training.

It seemed to Sophia and her closest advisers that there was now no alternative to seeking legal redress. In recording these events Sophia later wrote:

We had no less authority than that of the Lord Advocate of Scotland for believing that we were absolutely entitled to what we had so humbly solicited, and that a Court of law would quietly award to us what seemed unattainable by any other means; we had the very widely spread and daily increasing sympathy of the community at large, and received constant offers of help from friends of every kind, who were none the less inclined to befriend us because our opponents stood in high places, and were utterly relentless in their aims and reckless in their means. Under these circumstances, we did the one thing that remained for us to do, we brought an action of declarator against the Senatus of the University, – praying to have it declared that the Senatus was bound, in some way or other, to enable us to complete our education, and to proceed to the medical degree which would entitle us to take place on the Medical Register among the legally-qualified practitioners of medicine.[1]

Some of her more distant friends thought, as her brother did, that the action was ill-advised. Dr Blackwell was one who wrote in this vein, but Sophia tried to reassure her:

Dear Dr Blackwell,

I suppose rumour very seldom does report things correctly, so I do not wonder that you have been misinformed about the action which we are on the point of bringing against the Senatus. It is not one for breach of promise (what fun Punch would make of it if it were!) but simply an Action of Declarator whereby we pray one of the Judges of Session to declare that the Senatus is bound to complete our education, according to the decided opinion given by the Lord Advocate of Scotland.

In the brief space of a letter it would be impossible for me to submit to you all the facts and grounds on which our intention is based, tho' I should be glad to explain them in detail if you were on the spot, but you will be glad to hear that not only are the whole of the students here of the same mind as myself on this point, but our determination is strengthened by the advice and concurrence of some of the wisest heads in Edinburgh, including those of friendly Professors. I hope therefore that you will believe that, though you find a difficulty at a distance from the field of action in concurring in our present step, you would probably do so if all the facts of the case were as thoroughly before you as they are before us and our counsellors.

It is just because I find that London friends are so little au courant of the facts that I am hoping to give an explanatory lecture when in town next month, and I need not say how doubly glad I shall be to give every explanation and information to you to whom all of us medical women owe so much gratitude and respect as our pioneer and forerunner.

Believe me,
Yours truly,
S. Jex-Blake[2]

The 'explanatory lecture' that Sophia referred to in her letter was one she had agreed to give at a public meeting to be held in London in April. She was to speak on the Edinburgh campaign for medical education for women. In the mean time she was involved in the drafting of the women's case against the University. Sheriff Fraser asked her to supply him with notes on the history of the attendance of women at European universities. Sophia had already exhausted British sources of information on the subject, so she decided that for this project she would employ a researcher to visit Italy. The young woman who accepted the task was given a list of instructions that shows just how methodical (and demanding) Sophia could be:

1. At each University get access, if possible, to the official archives and lists of students, and make a complete list of every woman who studied there, with date, Faculty, and other particulars.
2. If you cannot get access yourself, get the lists made by some official, and, if possible, compare it with originals or other authorities.
3. If possible get the Secretary or Librarian, or some Professor to attest the list with his signature, as truly extracted from the records.
4. Pay any necessary fees, having as far as possible arranged for these beforehand.
5. Make copies in one book of every list obtained, of name and address of each person making or attesting such lists, and of all additional information likely to be of value.
6. Send off attested lists to me in registered letters as soon as obtained, marking in your M.S. book the exact duplicate in case of loss and sending a separate letter to Miss P. to announce dispatch.
7. Do not let your own M.S. book out of your hands for any purpose.
8. Send all lists on foolscap and not on foreign paper.[3]

Preparation of the women's case evidently was carried out as efficiently as Sophia could wish, since by 27 March the Senatus had been served notice of the action and was meeting to consider its response. There was some discussion of a motion that the University should not contest the women's claims, but the motion was soundly defeated. Six professors placed on record their protest against the decision to contest; it was significant that only one of the six, Dr Hughes Bennett, was a member of the Medical Faculty.

When the winter term ended, most of the women students decided to take a short holiday and then to seek informal teaching elsewhere for the duration of the summer term. There were no grounds for hoping that worthwhile lectures could be arranged in Edinburgh with the court case pending. Two went to Paris to study, two went to Dr Lucy Sewall's hospital in Boston and Edith Pechey worked as an assistant in a Liverpool maternity hospital. In mid-April Sophia left Edinburgh to spend a few days in the country, preparing her London lecture. Edith wrote to her:

Did you advertise your lecture in the *Lancet*? I expect you will have a lot of blackguardly doctors there in consequence. Don't have any libel cases, and don't be hard on the students. They're very bad, but they're not so bad as the Professors. I know you are very busy writing and so on, and that there would be plenty of copying for me to do if only I were at hand. Don't you want me to bully and be bullied by?

How I wish I could be in the gallery to make faces at you and throw peas![4]

Sophia arrived in London on 25 April. She was met by her friends Ursula Du Pre and Agnes McLaren who, that evening, listened to her reading her lecture notes and offered last-minute suggestions. Next day Sophia spoke to a large audience at St George's Hall. The chairman was the Earl of Shaftesbury; Drs Blackwell and Garrett Anderson were among the distinguished group on the platform, and there were many of Sophia's old friends from Queen's College in the audience. A group of medical students came, not to jeer, but to act as stewards, a gesture that she greatly appreciated.

Some of the audience were a little disappointed that the fire they had come to expect from Sophia Jex-Blake was lacking on this occasion. Perhaps she was tired, or perhaps she needed the stimulus of a hostile audience to rouse her fighting spirit. If a few were disappointed, others thought so highly of her address that she was urged to undertake a lecture tour of the provincial cities, but with her commitments in Edinburgh such a tour was out of the question. Instead, her lecture was published in book form, along with the essay she had contributed to Mrs Butler's volume *Women's Work and Women's Culture* (1869). Sophia's book, which bears the simple title *Medical Women*, is a valuable record of this section of feminist history.

Her friendship with Josephine Butler was severely strained at about this time. Sophia now agreed with Elizabeth Garrett Anderson that the repeal of the Contagious Diseases Acts could be detrimental to public health, so she, too, declined to support Mrs Butler's campaign. When Edith Pechey wrote to Mrs Butler inviting her to join the Education Committee, she received a reply that conveyed the depth of Mrs Butler's disappointment in the medical women.

My dear Miss Pechey,

        You are welcome to use my own and my husband's names if you think they will do your cause *any good*. We cannot conceive that they would, and, on that ground alone, we should be as glad that you should not use them. It had better be left to Miss Jex-Blake's judgment.

All the world knows that we are on opposite sides on one of the most vital questions of the day, and that the Medical ladies have no sympathy with the efforts being made to get rid of the scandal of a great State system of legalised Prostitution, and therefore it appears to Mr Butler and me an inconsistency that our names should appear in any such adverse connexion, deeply as we desire the prosperity and success of the medical woman movement.[5]

Sophia wrote to her old friend:

Dear Mrs Butler,

As Miss Pechey tells me that you leave me to decide whether or no to place on our Committee your name and Mr Butler's, I write to say that I shall most gladly avail myself of your permission so to use your names.

I am glad to say that our Committee is made up of over a thousand friends who not only differ widely on the point to which you refer, but among whom differences no doubt exist on almost every other question, social, political and religious.

As we cannot hope that even the most conscientious among us will always agree on matters of judgment, I am sure that the only wise rule is to keep each question distinct by itself, and to welcome for it the support of all who care for its success, whether or no they agree on other points. With kind regards to Mr Butler, believe me,

Yours truly,

S. Jex-Blake[6]

Sophia's letter was brilliant, but Mrs Butler responded coolly. She could not bring herself to 'agree to disagree' on a subject about which she felt so deeply.

In June Sophia had just finished work on the manuscript of *Medical Women* when she received a telegraph that her mother was seriously ill. Mrs Jex-Blake was then staying with relations in Norfolk. Less than an hour after the telegraph arrived Sophia was on her way, with a sixteen-hour journey by train and coach ahead of her. Her mother, who was then 71 years old, had a stone in one of her kidneys. This caused her to suffer from episodes of kidney infection, which were sometimes life-threatening. Devoted care enabled her to recover, though a permanent cure was not possible. On this occasion Sophia spent nearly three weeks with her mother. Then, confident that her patient was out of danger and in good hands, she returned to Edinburgh, where preparation for the lawsuit against the University was in its last stages.

The case began on 17 July 1872. It was purely a matter of legal interpretation of the constitution of the University, so no witnesses were called. Counsel for the two parties presented their arguments to the Lord Ordinary, Lord Gifford, and awaited his decision. This came some eight days later. A few lines in the long statement contained the decision the women had so desperately sought:

[The Lord Ordinary] finds that, according to the existing constitution and regulations of the said University of Edinburgh, the pursuers are entitled to be admitted to the study of medicine in the said University, and that they are entitled to all the rights and privileges of lawful students in the said University, subject only to the conditions specified and contained in the said regulations of 12 November 1869: Finds that the pursuers, on completing the prescribed studies, and on compliance with all the existing regulations of the University preliminary to degrees, are entitled to proceed to examination for degrees in manner prescribed by the regulations of the University of Edinburgh.[7]

In his supporting statement the Lord Ordinary refuted the main arguments of the University's counsel. He could find no justification for the claim that the University had been founded exclusively for males; like other Scottish universities it was modelled on those of Italy, which admitted women students and even had women on the academic staffs. The male noun and pronoun were used in the charter simply for the sake of brevity. While it was true that no woman had yet taken a degree in Scotland, women had not lost the right to university education. The Lord Ordinary also found that the regulations of 1869, under which the present women medical students matriculated, had been properly drawn up and had received the approval of every governing body in the University. There were no grounds for claiming that the regulations were irregular or invalid.

Lord Gifford said that he could not direct the Professors to admit women to the ordinary classes at the University, but the University Court undoubtedly had the power to recognize extra-academical teachers, thus making it possible for the women students to receive tuition that would prepare them for degrees. He hoped that this solution would end the unfortunate dispute.

Throughout the three years of struggle Sophia had been helped by wise and distinguished friends, but all agreed that this victory was truly hers. It had been won at the expense of her own studies, however, and she was likely to go on making this sacrifice. With the winter term about to begin, she must at once find lecturers willing to teach the women students. There was little hope that the University would accommodate them, and as they were now debarred from Surgeons' Hall she would need to rent a house to provide them with lecture rooms. The publicity given the women's campaign by the newspaper reports of the Lord Ordinary's judgment, and by the publication of her book *Medical Women*, brought her additional work. Donations were received from well-wishers; these had to be acknowledged and recorded. She was also asked to write articles for journals, a request she rarely refused because of the need to win and hold the interest of the public. With all these distractions it was not surprising that Sophia neglected her own career. At the end of the summer term she had been feeling rather despondent when she wrote to Lucy Sewall, 'I am getting more and more doubtful whether I myself shall ever finish my education. I think when once the fight is won I shall creep away into some wood and lie and sleep for a year.'

This mood did not last for long. In October the First Professional Examination in natural history, botany and chemistry would again be held, and Sophia was determined that this time she would be a candidate. She was reasonably confident that five weeks of study, without any serious interruptions, was all the preparation she needed; surely she could manage this. Then a new development suddenly made these plans seem unimportant. The University decided to appeal to a higher court against the Lord Ordinary's judgment.

Sophia was not surprised that her opponents in the Medical Faculty were unwilling to accept defeat. Even while rejoicing, she had wondered what their next move would be. Now it seemed that the hearing of the appeal could coincide with the date of the First Professional Examination. For several weeks her studies took second place to conferences with friends and legal advisers on planning the women students' defence. About a week before the examination the appeal was deferred; indeed, another eight months were to elapse before it eventually came to court. Sophia tried to return to her studies, but then another disaster occurred. A close friend who lived at Falkirk, some twenty miles from Edinburgh, became seriously ill. Sophia made several hurried trips to Falkirk to give whatever help she could. A brief entry in her diary records the events of the first day of the examination, 22 October, 'Did good paper in Nat., – fair in Chemistry, poor in Botany. Went down to Falkirk to sleep.' Next day she came back to Edinburgh for the examination in practical chemistry, and was met by a solicitor asking for papers needed for the preparation of the defence against the appeal.

Sophia was so anxious about her performance in the examinations that she kept copies of her answers to all the questions. On reviewing these she thought that she had probably done well enough to pass. When the results were announced she had failed in all three subjects. Sophia was mortified, her friends were embarrassed. One of the chief arguments of her opponents had always been that women were intellectually inferior to men, but until now the results obtained by the women students at Edinburgh had been better than those of the average male student.

Sophia could not help but wonder if her answers had been assessed without bias. There was no anonymity for candidates; their names appeared on each of their papers. Edith Pechey suggested that they should seek the opinion of Professor Huxley of London University. Huxley was not only a renowned scientist, he was also a man who could be trusted to give an unbiased opinion. After reading Sophia's copy of her natural history paper, Huxley said that he did not regard it as good enough to have earned a pass. This was the paper she had thought her best.

Sophia well knew that her preparation had been deficient. Immediately after the examination she was dissatisfied with her performance, but later she seems to have become convinced that she should have passed. Huxley's verdict she thought could be explained by his being unfamiliar with the standard required for this particular examination at Edinburgh University. Failed candidates often do not perceive their own shortcomings, and in Sophia's case there were unusual circumstances that could foster a sense of injury. She discussed her suspicions with her brother; Thomas advised her to try to forget the episode, since it would be impossible to prove that the examiners had acted unfairly.

Her recovery from the wound to her pride was helped by the quickening pace of the campaign. The publicity given to the plight of the women students in Edinburgh had captured the interest of several parliamentarians, who thought that the solution lay in legislative action. In August 1872 Sir David Wedderburn spoke in Parliament of the injustices inflicted on the women. He moved that the grant to the Scottish universities be reduced by an amount equivalent to the salaries of the medical professors at Edinburgh University! However, the Lord Ordinary's judgment had been delivered only a few days previously, and it seemed that in future the University would be obliged to meet its obligations to women students. Sir David therefore was prepared, having drawn the matter to the attention of the House, to let it rest.

In 1871 James Stansfeld, MP for Halifax, heard Sophia speak at the public meeting on women's suffrage and subsequently became interested in her battle for women's medical education. Stansfeld was a man of liberal outlook whom Gladstone had appointed to preside over the Poor Law Board and the Local Government Board. In his youth he supported the Chartist movement and was a friend of Mazzini. He also knew Professor Masson, and from him learned more of the opposition Sophia was meeting at Edinburgh University. He was sufficiently impressed to invite her to come to London to meet a number of people who could help the cause. Sophia's ability to state her case effectively inspired confidence in potential supporters. She, in turn, was encouraged by their willingness to embark on a political campaign if Edinburgh University won its appeal against the Lord Ordinary's decision.

It was now almost a year since the Royal Infirmary Managers for 1872 were elected and then prevented from taking office. The legal appeal made by the women's opponents (most of them doctors on the staff of the Infirmary) was decided in favour of the women's supporters on 23 July. But their opponents appealed again, and the hearing of this appeal was repeatedly deferred, while the women were still denied admission to the Infirmary.

On 30 October 1872 the Infirmary Secretary, Mr Peter Bell, wrote to members of the medical staff, asking if they thought it practicable to admit female students on exactly the same terms as male students; if they did not think this advisable they were asked to suggest some other scheme that would enable women to obtain a qualifying course of instruction at the Infirmary. Professor Joseph Lister submitted a lengthy reply. It was his custom with professional correspondence to write drafts of his letters, which were then rewritten for him by his wife. Mrs Lister must have taken a special interest in this letter, in which her husband expounded his belief that the presence of women students would quite disrupt the work of the Infirmary.

Sir,

To the two queries of the Managers' Committee transmitted by you I beg to reply as follows.

First. I do not "consider it practicable to admit female students to the Hospital on exactly the same terms & at the same hour as the male students." The reasons which are generally held to make it inexpedient for ladies to attend lectures on medical subjects along with male students in the college class-rooms apply with tenfold force against such mixed attendance in the wards of an hospital, where the treatment of the living human body takes the place of theoretical discussion and inanimate illustration, & the students instead of being placed under the eye of the teacher are necessarily crowded together & withdrawn more or less from his control.

Secondly. I am unable to "suggest any scheme to enable female students to obtain a qualifying course of instruction at the Infirmary."

Proceeding on the assumption that mixed attendance is inadmissable, it seems to me highly improbable that any of our Physicians or Surgeons would willingly sacrifice entirely their opportunities of teaching male students in order to devote themselves to the instruction of a few ladies. At the same time considering the very large numbers of young men who study medicine in Edinburgh, for whom the means of clinical instruction in the Infirmary are already too limited, it would be a very serious thing to deny them access to the eighty beds which would be necessary in order to satisfy the regulations to the examining boards. Even if the hospital were sufficiently large to justify the creation of additional physiciancies and surgeoncies on the condition that those appointed to them should restrict their teaching to ladies, it is not likely that the Managers would on such terms secure the services of those best fitted for the treatment of patients.

On the other hand no physician or surgeon in extensive private practice could afford time to make a second visit in the day in order to teach the ladies; while such a plan would have the obvious objection that in surgical cases an operation or daily dressing once done could not be repeated.

There is another arrangement that may at first sight suggest itself, viz. that each physician or surgeon might have some of his beds devoted to the teaching of men & the rest in another part of the building restricted to the instruction of women; & that he might divide his visit between those different parts of the institution.

But independently of the great inconvenience that would be involved in having the services of the medical officers so scattered, it will be obvious to the medical Managers that such a scheme would prove quite unworkable in consequence of the uncertain duration of the hospital visits. Sometimes the state of the patients may be such that a few minutes may suffice for the purpose, while at other times unforeseen occurrences may make the visit extremely protracted.

There are some other difficulties attendant on this question to which, as my opinion has been asked, I feel it needful to allude. One is that if ladies are admitted as students they must also be allowed to hold hospital offices, without which no studentship can be regarded as complete, while at the same time without female junior officials the avoidance of mixed attendance would be an impossibility. Thus we should have not only female Dressers & Clerks, but female House-Surgeons & House Physicians, on whom would devolve the charge of the patients in the absence of their superior officers. And it must be a matter of serious consideration for the Managers whether they would be prepared to entrust to young ladies duties which often tax to the utmost the energies of men.

Again any regulations for the admission of women to study in the Infirmary must apply not only to the exceptionally high class of ladies whom the present exceptional circumstances have brought forward, but to ordinary specimens of students, good, bad, & indifferent, such as are met with in the male sex. Such persons when appointed to the junior hospital offices of Dressers & Clerks would claim as an essential part of their privileges admission at all times of the day to the Infirmary where they could not be prevented from mixing with young men in similar positions. And in the case of the female House Surgeons and House Physicians, the fact of these young people residing under the same roof with the corresponding officers of the other sex, & being thrown into intimate association with them for consultation & aid in professional emergencies, would, I fear, lead in the long run to great inconvenience & scandal.

Hence it seems to me clear that if women are to be taught to practise medicine, it must be done in entirely separate institutions.

Lastly, I would remark that even if hospitals be formed for the exclusive education of ladies, I believe it can never be right for young women to study in male wards; and the Managers would, in my opinion, incur a very grave responsibility if they were to introduce such a practice into the Royal Infirmary of Edinburgh.

I am, Sir,

Yours truly,

Joseph Lister[8]

In December 1872 the final appeal against the counting of votes at the previous election of Infirmary Managers was heard. Voting by firms was declared to be valid, so the Board of Managers elected in January finally took office, only two weeks before its term expired. This short-lived Board's most notable achievement was the admission of women students to the Infirmary. Two conditions were imposed – the women were to be taught separately from the male students, and they were to be restricted to a small number of wards, about one-sixth of the hospital. To Sophia and her colleagues the conditions were of minor importance; what really mattered was that at last they had access to the clinical training which is a vital part of the medical course.

The Board of Managers elected in January 1973 was opposed to women students. Although the gains the women had so recently made could hardly be taken away from them, it was obvious that nothing more would be done to improve their conditions at the Infirmary. Fortunately, two of the senior members of the medical staff strove to give the women adequate teaching. Dr George Balfour, a physician, conducted three special ward rounds for them each week, and at times arranged additional ward teaching. Dr Heron Watson, a busy surgeon, gave up his Sunday mornings to conduct a class for them. He also tried to arrange for them to be present in the operating theatre when he had some instructive cases for them to see. He offered to have the women screened from the view of the male students who would also be present, but even so his request was refused, despite the fact that nurses regularly attended such operations without any objections being raised.

Less than two months after they began their visits to the Infirmary wards, one of the women's opponents complained that Dr Heron Watson's use of Sunday mornings for his teaching was an offence against the observance of the Sabbath. The Lord Provost (Mr James Cowan) attended one of the Sunday classes himself to see if it did indeed offend against religious principles. He declared it to be 'a truly Sabbatic work of healing', and the protest was dropped.

Generations of medical students, both before and since Sophia's time, have retained vivid memories of their first ward rounds. The lessons learned in the classroom, library and laboratory suddenly took on new meaning when they saw this knowledge being put to practical use in the care of the sick. The bedside teaching given by wise and experienced practitioners justifies the claim that medicine is both a science and an art. The women students were doubly appreciative of their ward teaching because they had had such a long and bitter struggle to obtain it. But when Isabel Thorne recalled these times many years later, she realized that they had had only a small share of what was regularly available to the men:

[For us] there were no attendances on casualties or out-patients, no pathological demonstrations, no surgical dresserships, no special departments of any kind; we had to be content with what our kind friends could give, which was limited to teaching on patients in their own wards, and we were allowed to take notes on a few cases in Dr Balfour's wards.

Very grateful were we for the facilities thus afforded us, and for our teachers' goodness in bestowing on us so much of their valuable time.[9]

The women students were still jeered at sometimes as they went about their work, or were pelted with refuse as they walked to or from their classes. When Sir Robert Christison wrote of his own student days in Edinburgh he described a very different way of life:

> I doubt whether any other medical school offers such a union of advantages as our resident Infirmary officers enjoy – ample materials for study; able superiors, engaged in teaching, and ever on a level with the times; a confidential position of much trust; companions from the ablest students of a populous University; museums and libraries freely open; professors and others, to whom it is a labour of love to foster diligence and talent; a city abounding with all sorts of rational amusement; and good society, easy of access.[10]

When the winter term of 1872–3 ended, the women had to find lecturers for the following term. With the future at Edinburgh still so uncertain, Sophia decided to approach some of the other universities again. She and her friend Agnes McLaren were visiting Newcastle University, and finding that nothing had changed there, when Edith Pechey wrote from Edinburgh with the news that the hearing of the appeal against the Lord Ordinary's judgment was imminent. Sophia and Agnes hurried back.

The hearing, which was very brief, took place a few days later. The Lord Ordinary's verdict that women were entitled to the same rights and privileges as those enjoyed by male students of Edinburgh University was overturned. Seven of the judges decided against the women's claim, while five supported it. The crux of the argument was the validity of the University Court's decision in 1869 to allow the five women to matriculate. The majority of the judges found that the University Court had acted illegally, since the University was not empowered to teach or examine women. The women students were ordered to pay the costs of the case, which amounted to £850. An appeal to the House of Lords was possible, but Sophia was advised not to take this action. So the Edinburgh campaign was over. The first British university to open its doors to women had closed them again after less than four years.

Some observers thought that the medical women's cause was finally defeated, but they were mistaken. Although the judges' decision was a severe setback, Sophia knew that the years of work in Edinburgh were not wasted. She and her friends had clearly demonstrated women's ability to meet the demands of medical training, even under the most unfavourable conditions. Having thus refuted one of the favourite arguments of their opponents, she was already planning the next stage of the campaign.

Sophia and her fellow students stayed on in Edinburgh for another nine months. Although graduation had been denied them, there were still some valuable opportunities for continuing their training at the Infirmary and in the extramural schools. Sophia later wrote:

> In the following winter we attended, in the Extra-mural School, courses of Clinical Medicine, Midwifery, Materia Medica, and Pathology. . . . Our work at the Infirmary also went on as before both in the medical and surgical wards, thanks to the unfailing kindness of Dr Watson and Dr Balfour.
>
> By the end of the winter session 1873–4, we senior students had taken all the classes available in Edinburgh, and had also had two years of Hospital instruction; so that, as graduation was hopeless, for the time at least, it was useless for us to remain longer, and, at the end of March 1874, the medical classes in Edinburgh were given up, – I will not say finally, but for the time being.
>
> On March 2nd, 1874, was held the last great meeting of the Committee for Medical Education of Women in Edinburgh, to consider the position of affairs consequent on the decision of the Court of Session and the termination of our studies in Edinburgh.[11]

By then the women students and their advisers had decided that the next phase of the battle would be a political one, and that it would be fought in London.

Notes

1. S. Jex-Blake, *Medical Women*, Edinburgh and London: Macmillan, 1886, p. 141.
2. M. Todd, *The Life of Sophia Jex-Blake*, London: Macmillan, 1918, p. 356.
3. ibid., p. 359.
4. ibid., p. 362.
5. ibid., p. 364.
6. ibid., p. 365.
7. Extract from the Judgment of the Lord Ordinary, as reproduced in Jex-Blake's *Medical Women*, Narrative Section, p. 19.
8. Archives of the Edinburgh Royal Infirmary, Medical Archive Centre Lothian Health Board.
9. I. Thorne, *Sketch of the Foundation and Development of the London School of Medicine for Women*, London: Women's Printing Society, 1915, p. 18.
10. *Life of Sir Robert Christison* (edited by his sons), Edinburgh and London: Blackwood and Sons, 1885–6, vol. I, p. 66.
11. Jex-Blake, *Medical Women*, p. 152.

9

'The time for a reform has come'

During those last weeks in Edinburgh Sophia managed to combine her studies and the canvassing of political support in London. By making overnight rail journeys between the two cities she was able to meet with influential people who could help the cause, and yet not miss many of her lectures. Her efforts soon bore fruit. Only a month after the University had won its lawsuit, Sir David Wedderburn again spoke in the House of Commons on the subject of the medical women's campaign. He gave notice of his intention to bring in, during the next session, a bill to grant to the Scottish universities the power to award medical degrees to women. The purpose of the bill was to prevent other institutions from using the Edinburgh verdict as a legal precedent justifying their own exclusion of women.

Elizabeth Garrett Anderson disapproved of this latest development. She regarded Sophia's Edinburgh campaign as a disastrous failure, which was about to be repeated in London. On 5 August 1873 *The Times* published a letter from Dr Garrett Anderson, in which she argued that the women led by Sophia Jex-Blake were wrong to persist in their efforts to gain access to a British university.

> The real solution of the difficulty will, I believe, be found in English-women seeking abroad that which is at present denied to them in their own country. By going to Paris, female students can get, without further difficulty or contention, at a very small cost, a first-class medical education, a choice of all the best hospital teachers of the place, a succession of stimulating and searching examinations, and a diploma of recognized value. The one serious drawback to the plan is, that the Paris degree, in spite of its acknowledged worth, does not entitle its holder to registration as a medical practitioner in this country.[1]

Dr Garrett Anderson then described how, in her opinion, each of the disabilities associated with being unregistered could be overcome. Her letter ended with a statement of the creed that governed her own professional life:

138

'Nothing succeeds like success'; and if we could point to a considerable number of medical women quietly making for themselves the reputation of being trustworthy and valuable members of the profession, the various forms which present opposition now takes would insensibly disappear, and arrangements would be made for providing female medical students with the advantages which it appears hopeless to look for at present in this country.[2]

On 23 August *The Times* published Sophia's reply. She began by denying that the cause was lost in Britain. In recent years women had gained access to the excellent medical classes of the extramural schools of Edinburgh, and had been taught in that city's Royal Infirmary. They must continue the fight for registration if they were ever to gain their rightful place in the profession:

We live under English law, and to English law we must conform, so far as lies in our power; if we are arbitrarily precluded from such compliance, it is to the English Government that we must look for a remedy. I can imagine few things that would please our opponents better than to see one Englishwoman after another driven out of her own country to obtain medical education abroad, both because they know that, on her return after years of labour, she can claim no legal recognition whatever, and because they are equally certain that, so long as no means of education are provided at home, only a very small number of women will ever seek admission to the profession. I do not say that a woman may not be justified in going abroad for education if her circumstances make it imperative that she should as soon as possible enter upon medical practice; but I do say, and I most firmly believe, that every woman who consents to be thus exiled does more harm than can easily be calculated to the general cause of medical women in this country, and postpones indefinitely, so far as in her lies, the final and satisfactory solution of the whole question.
It is no easy thing to remember at all times that – 'They also serve who only stand and wait'; but I do believe profoundly that at this moment the very best service we can do to the cause in which we are all interested, is to make use of every opportunity open to us in this country to qualify ourselves as thoroughly as possible for the profession we have chosen, and then (refusing resolutely to be driven into byways or unauthorized measures) to demand, quietly but firmly, that provision for our ultimate recognition as medical practitioners which we have a right to expect at the hands of the Legislature.[3]

One of the politicians who supported Sophia's approach was the Home Secretary, Mr Robert Lowe. Mr Lowe, whose electorate was the University of London, was impressed by a petition he received from 471 graduates (about one-third of the total number) of that university. The petitioners requested legislation to ensure that *all* the universities of Britain had the power to grant degrees to women. Sophia and her friends were delighted that this petition had been organized by a medical graduate, Dr Alfred Shewen, and that sixty of those who signed it were also medical men.

Just when it seemed that some headway was being made, there was an unexpected turn of events. On 26 January 1874 Mr Gladstone dissolved Parliament and called an election. The Liberals were defeated and the Conservative Party, led by Mr Disraeli, took office. Sir David Wedderburn, who had been so willing to help the women's cause, did not stand for re-election. However, members from both sides of the new House supported Mr Cowper Temple (Liberal) and Mr Russell Gurney (Conservative) when, together, they brought in a 'Bill to Remove Doubt as to the Powers of the Universities of Scotland to Admit Women as Students and to Grant Degrees to Women'.

This seemed quite innocuous, since it would merely grant additional powers to the universities, without compelling their use. But at Edinburgh the group led by Sir Robert Christison saw the bill as a dire threat. Their victory of the previous year rested on the argument that Edinburgh University's charter did not enable it to admit women. If the bill became law, Sir Robert and his friends would be disarmed. So a strange phenomenon was then observed – a group of gentlemen striving desperately to ward off an increase in their own powers!

In a letter to the Lord Advocate Christison made a vehement attack on the bill:

Its very preamble is a misrepresentation – 'Whereas doubts have arisen as to the powers of the Universities of Scotland to admit women as students, and to grant degrees to women.' There are no such doubts. It has been declared by a decision of the whole Bench of the Court of Session that the admission of women to study or graduate is contrary to their charters. Nearly a year has passed since this decision; it has not been appealed against, and never will be. But not only are there no doubts to be removed; the Bill introduces new and most serious doubts. It proposes that grave and difficult questions, which the Legislature itself ought to settle, shall be decided by the University Courts and Senates, in which notoriously great dissensions have arisen as to those very plans and questions. . . . Suppose a University Court accepts the power offered, and issues a regulation for admitting women to medical study. Professors may resist – nay, will. Can the Court compel? Is there not a violation of private rights? Hence quarrels in the Court – quarrels in the Senate – University feuds – lawsuits for the removal of doubts. Or have the women got rights by the move? The right of compulsion to teach them, for example? It is not easy to compel a man to do that which he hates, or force him to that which he feels may kill him. But some litigious woman will certainly try it on him, backed by a male "Executive Committee", in a transport of universal love and particular male-volence. Or it may be proposed, as was suggested in the late action at law, to thrust a deputy on a recalcitrant professor. Then arise more doubts – in a Bill for removing doubts which have no existence![4]

Petitions against the bill were sent by the University Court, by the Medical Faculty, and by the Senatus of Edinburgh University, but these lost much of their impact when comparison of the documents showed that the same signatures appeared on all three. Petitions against the bill were outnumbered by those in favour. Among the latter was one from thirteen professors of Edinburgh University, and there was another from a group of teachers in the extramural schools who had taught the women students. Even more significant were the petitions in support of the bill sent by the Town Councils of Edinburgh, Aberdeen and Linlithgow, and another signed by 16,000 women pleading that medical training be made available to women.

Sophia had left Edinburgh and was observing these developments from a distance. Her brother had recently) been appointed Headmaster of Rugby School, a position he was to occupy with distinction for thirteen years. Mrs Jex-Blake divided her time between the family home at Brighton and a smaller house she had taken near her son's school. When Sophia left Edinburgh she stayed with her mother at Rugby for several months.

The second reading of the bill, listed for 26 April 1874, was deferred at the request of the Member for Edinburgh, Dr Lyon Playfair, who claimed that more time was needed to consider its implications. Sophia was now quite accustomed to the delaying tactics used by her opponents. Two months later, on 12 June, the first general debate on the bill took place and this event was the indirect cause of Sophia's making a regrettable blunder. In its editorial review of the debate *The Times* censured Edinburgh University for its treat-ment of the women students, but was even more critical of those who, like Mr Cowper Temple, believed that a system of education that had evolved to meet the needs of men was also suitable for women. The writer commented sarcastically, 'It is a little amusing, indeed, that one of the Ladies, who had rendered herself most conspicuous, should, after all, have failed under the test of examination . . . .'.[5]

Sophia did not see the article for several days. By then her friend Isabel Thorne had already rushed to her defence:

Sir, – . . . It is so notorious to whom you refer, and so much capital has already been made by the opponents of the medical education of women out of this fact, that, in justice to Miss Jex-Blake, I shall be glad if you will allow me to state what I believe was the true cause of her failure – i.e., her unselfish devotion to the interests of her fellow-students. Those

Illustration 10. Thomas William Jex-Blake (1832–1915). Sophia's brother, who was Headmaster of Rugby School from 1874 to 1886. (Reproduced by permission of Mr Thomas Jex-Blake of Gisborne, New Zealand.)

who had watched her career, read her books, seen the ease with which she passed the preliminary examination in Arts, and the honours she had gained in the class examinations, knew that with due preparation she could also reach the standard of proficiency required of medical students in the first professional examination. . . .

Had she consulted her own interest, she would have allowed all matters that distracted her attention from her studies to take their course; but, faithful to her purpose of allowing no personal interests to interfere with those of her fellow-students, she responded to the call upon her time and attention with the heartiness which always characterized her exertions on their behalf, and her preparation for her examination became, in consequence, a secondary consideration; hence it is not surprising that under these circumstances she failed to satisfy the examiners; but, while regretting our friend's non-success, we, her fellow-students, feel that it was devotion to our cause which led to her failure, and are more surprised at what she accomplished than at what she left undone.

I am, Sir, yours truly,
Isabel Thorne[6]

When Sophia saw Isabel's letter in *The Times* she reacted impulsively. Her utter rejection of her friend's defence appeared on 20 June.

Sir, – I regret extremely that my name has been brought, as I think most unnecessarily, before the public in connexion with my alleged failure to pass an examination held two years ago at Edinburgh University, and I regret still more that my friend and fellow student, Mrs Thorne, should in your columns have now given to the public an explanation of the circumstances which I feel constrained to say I believe to be entirely erroneous.

I think it due to myself to state that my preparation for the examination in question was not made secondary to any other object whatever, but was, on the contrary, as I still believe, thoroughly adequate; and, further, that my success in answering the papers set was, at any rate, not less than that which had in previous years enabled me, as Mrs Thorne truly asserts, to obtain a place in the prize lists (after examinations generally considered more difficult) in every one of the subjects in question. As, however, I was subsequently refused all information respecting the extent, and even the nature, of my alleged failure, and, as I found that the Examiners were practically quite irresponsible except to a Court of Law, I resolved, after much consideration at the time, to take no steps whatever with a view to my own vindication, and I am extremely sorry to have the matter brought up again, much to my surprise, at the present moment.

I had even resolved to take no notice of the allusion contained, Sir, in your leader of the 13th inst., but I feel that Mrs Thorne's letter (written, I am sure, with the kindest motives, but during my absence and without my knowledge) leaves me no choice but to express my own emphatic dissent from the explanation she suggests, and to say distinctly that it never has been the one generally accepted by those most competent to judge or who best know the circumstances of the case in Edinburgh at that time.

I am, Sir, yours obediently,
Sophia Jex-Blake[7]

In the most public way possible Sophia had accused a group of distinguished scholars of professional dishonesty. These gentlemen could not remain silent. *The Times* of 29 June carried a letter signed by five of the six examiners who had marked Sophia's papers; the sixth was travelling abroad with a scientific expedition and so could not defend himself. The others wrote:

Sir, – . . . It is unusual for an Examining Board to give a public account of what led to the rejection of a candidate examined by them. But ordinary customs must yield to extraordinary circumstances. For the first time in the history of our University its medical examiners have been openly charged with injustice to a rejected candidate. Miss Jex-Blake has insinuated – for no other meaning can be attached to her words – that our decision was at variance with the evidence furnished by her examination papers. We feel compelled publicly to declare the contrary. The subjects of examination were chemistry, botany, and natural history. Her papers were carefully examined by six examiners (three of whom were professors), and they unanimously agreed that the answers were extremely defective on every subject.

Miss Jex-Blake, however, insinuates that this was not the cause of her failure, but that there was another, "the one generally accepted by those most competent to judge, or who best know the circumstances of the case in Edinburgh at that time." But no one can be competent to judge who had not the opportunity of perusing her examination papers; and, to our certain knowledge, the only person, not a member of our Board, who has perused the papers delivered by her to her examiners is one of our colleagues, who is satisfied that the examiners did no more than their imperative duty.

Miss Jex-Blake further says she "found the examiners were practically quite irresponsible except to a Court of Law," to which, however, she declined to apply for redress. Had she done so she would have found how much she was mistaken. She would have been told that, by Act of Parliament, the University Court was established as a special Court, among other purposes, expressly to try and to punish any delinquencies on the part of professors in the discharge of University duty. Moreover, the older constitution of the University still remains so far in force that she might have appealed to the Medical Faculty or to the Senatus Academicus, either of which has power to deal with their erring brethren, and to put them right when in the wrong.[8]

The signatories to the letter were Alex. Crum Brown, W. Drumbeck, Benjamin Bell, William Robertson and J.H. Balfour; (the last-named was the Dean of the Medical Faculty, not the Dr George Balfour who had taught the women students). Of course Sophia replied. She challenged the examiners to submit her papers, along with those of all the candidates who had been granted passes, to an unbiased arbiter. She also demolished their argument that she could have appealed to the Senatus or the University Court. As they well knew, her appeal would have been dealt with by the very men she was accusing!

Sophia may have had the last word, but her friends feared that the unpleasant episode could have harmed the medical women's cause. Whether she herself later had any regrets is not known; she does not seem to have referred to the incident again.

With the bill delayed, and with the future as uncertain as ever, Sophia embarked on another project. For nearly a year she had contemplated the establishment of a separate medical school for women, but had feared that such a school would be regarded as second-rate because it was for women only. Now as she talked with some of her friends it seemed possible to forestall this criticism by ensuring that the school was conducted according to standards that were patently as high as, or even higher than, those of existing schools. Three noted medical men – Mr Arthur Norton, a surgeon of St Mary's Hospital; Dr Francis Anstie, a physician at the Westminster Hospital; and Dr King Chambers, who also taught at St Mary's – were willing to help. Although all of the established medical schools were still closed as firmly as ever to women, some of their teachers were prepared to teach women in a separate school. Mr Norton's preliminary enquiries suggested that there would be no difficulty in recruiting a complete staff of teachers, all of whom were already accredited by the various examining bodies.

The move to found a women's medical school rapidly gained momentum. Sophia moved to London and opened a temporary office in Wimpole Street as headquarters for the group. Edinburgh friends of the medical women's movement gave generous financial help when they heard of the plans, and additional contributions came from friends in other parts of the country. Almost the only adverse response was that of Elizabeth Garrett Anderson. She thought the move premature and doomed to failure, and for this reason she was reluctant to have her name associated with it. A letter Sophia wrote to her at this time shows how widely their views differed, and how frankly they dealt with each other:

145

Hampstead
21st August, 1874.

Dear Mrs Anderson,

If I kept a record of all the people who bring me cock and bull stories about you, and assure me that you are "greatly injuring the cause," I might fill as many pages with quotations as you have patience to read, but, beyond defending you on a good many occasions, I have never thought it needful to take much notice of such incidents, still less to retail them to you.

Nor do I much care to know whether or no certain anonymous individuals have confided to you that they lay at my door what you call "the failure at Edinburgh," – inasmuch as the only people really competent to judge of that point are my fellow-workers and fellow-students, such as Professor Masson, Professor Bennett, Miss Stevenson, Mrs Thorne, Miss Pechey, Dr Watson, and Dr Balfour, and I do not fancy that it is from any of these that you have heard the comments in question.

It can, as I say, serve no purpose whatever to go into this sort of gossip which is very rarely indeed founded on any knowledge of facts; but, quite apart from any such discussion, I am more than willing to say that if, in the opinion of a majority of those who are organizing this new school, my name appears likely to injure its chances of success, I will cheerfully stand aside, and let Mrs Thorne and Miss Pechey carry out the almost completed plans. . . .

In conclusion let me say that I never said it 'did not signify' whether you joined the Council (though I *did* say that I believed the School was already tolerably secure of ultimate success.) I think it of very great importance, both for your credit and ours, that there should, as you say, be no appearance of split in the camp, and I should greatly prefer that your name should appear on the Council with Dr Blackwell's and those of the medical men who are helping us.

Believe me,
Yours truly,
Sophia Jex-Blake[9]

Elizabeth did agree to join the Council of what was to be called the London School of Medicine for Women. She did so mainly to avoid the appearance of a 'split in the camp', and in the early days of the School's history she was an observer rather than an enthusiastic advocate.

The first formal meeting of the supporters of the London School of Medicine for Women was held at the home of Dr Anstie on 22 August 1874. Dr Anstie was elected the School's first Dean. A Provisional Council, consisting of twenty-one registered medical practitioners, was appointed. One of its members was Mr Ernest Hart, a surgeon, who was also the Editor of the *British Medical Journal*. Other famous names on the list of Council members were those of Professor Huxley, Dr Burdon-Sanderson, Dr Garrett Anderson, Dr Elizabeth Blackwell and Dr Hughlings Jackson. Soon afterwards Sophia was appointed one of the four Trustees, along with Dr King Chambers, Mr A.T. Norton and Mrs Thorne, but it was in her unofficial role of organizing secretary that she carried most of the responsibility for the establishment of the School. She later wrote an account of those weeks of planning and achievement that culminated in the opening of the School.

So rapidly was the work pushed forward, that our staff of lecturers was almost organized before we had succeeded in finding any local habitation for the School. After, however, an almost incredible amount of search, enquiry, and disappointment, I succeeded in finding wonderfully suitable premises, in the shape of a very old-fashioned house in Henrietta Street, Brunswick Square, with spacious ground-floor rooms, and long frontage to a walled garden of a size very unusual in the centre of London. On the upper floor were a series of rooms suitable for museums, library, reading-room, etc. I got a lease of the house in September, in conjunction with Mr Norton, and on October 12th, 1874, the School was actually opened.[10]

The disjointed notes in Sophia's diary give a more vivid impression of the hectic activity that preceded the opening day of the London School of Medicine for Women: 'Sept 15th. Actually signed lease and got possession of 30 Henrietta Street. Rigged up some kind of beds and slept there that night, – Alice coming from Wales to help me.'[11]

Alice and Sophia must have recalled those earlier occasions, in London, New York and Edinburgh, when they worked to transform various rented dwellings into homes. Sophia's thoughts would also have turned at times to the school she planned in Manchester, and to the colleges she saw in America – Oberlin, Hillsdale and Antioch. She would have remembered, too, Elizabeth Blackwell's medical school in New York, where she herself had studied for such a short time, and Surgeons' Hall in Edinburgh. Her own London School would be different from all of these, but it would have gained something from each of them. Certainly it was Sophia who planned the School in detail and supervised the work of the builders, carpenters and painters, as they rapidly converted the old residence into an up-to-date medical college.

Another entry in her diary at this time reads, 'Miss Irby also came for a night one day this month, – grand, quiet, strong.' Paulina Irby, like Sophia, had family roots in Norfolk, and it was in Norfolk that the two had met several years previously, when both were on holiday there. Paulina was now middle-aged. In her youth she had been an avid traveller, going to places that were rarely visited by English tourists, especially single ladies. One of her journeys took her to Bosnia-Herzegovina, in the Balkans, and at once she seemed to feel a deep affinity with the land and its people. The Christian Serbs of

Illustration 11. The London School of Medicine for Women, Henrietta Street, Brunswick Square. (Reproduced by permission of the Royal Free Hospital, London.)

Bosnia lived under Turkish rule and suffered great hardship. Paulina returned to help them by founding and maintaining schools for girls, who otherwise would have been deprived of education. This work kept her in the Balkans for the greater part of each year. Only in the summer did she come home briefly to visit her family and friends. Sophia was one she liked to see whenever time permitted.

The friends of the School were shocked by the sudden death of Dr Anstie, shortly before the opening date. At first his loss seemed irreparable; then Mr Norton agreed to assume the position of Dean and the preparations went ahead. The opening of the London School of Medicine for Women took place, as planned, in time for the beginning of the winter term of 1874–5. Mrs Thorne recorded the names of the fourteen women who were the School's original pupils. They were:

1. Mrs Thorne
2. Miss Sophia Jex-Blake
3. Miss Pechey
4. Mrs Marshall
5. Miss Ker
6. Miss Annie E. Clark
7. Mrs Foggo
8. Miss Vinson
9. Miss Rorison
10. Miss Shove
11. Miss Elizabeth Walker
12. Miss Agnes McLaren
13. Miss Waterston
14. Miss Fanny Butler[12]

The first twelve had all been members of the group who studied together in Edinburgh. Agnes McLaren, who did so much to help them, decided to join the medical classes herself during their last months in that city. Now she, too, was anxious to complete her training. Mrs Marshall was the former Mary Anderson, one of the three who had given up their studies in Edinburgh in order to marry. Only a few months after her marriage her husband had died, and the child born to her in her widowhood also died. Mrs Marshall was the sister of Elizabeth Garrett Anderson's husband, James Skelton Anderson. The two newcomers to the group were Miss Waterston, a South African, who later became famous for her pioneer medical work in her own country, and Miss Butler, who was to use her training as a medical missionary in India. All were single-minded in their determination to become doctors, so their teachers had no need to coerce them into working. From the outset the School was a cheerful hive of industry, even though everyone associated with it was aware that its survival depended on the solution of two problems: first, it had to become affiliated with a major hospital so that its students could receive practical training and, second, women students had to be given access to examinations that would qualify them for registration. No solution to either of these problems was in sight.

On 3 March 1875 Mr Cowper Temple's bill to empower the Scottish universities to admit women was at last put to the vote. Dr Lyon Playfair's delaying tactic of the previous year had achieved his objective of allowing public interest in the matter to decline – the bill was defeated by 196 votes to 153. But Cowper Temple was not a man to accept defeat easily. Three weeks later he gave notice of a bill to amend the Medical Act of 1858, so that women holding medical degrees from the universities of France, Leipzig, Berne and Zurich would be eligible for registration, even though men would still be required to hold a British qualification. It was appropriate that such a radical modification of the law should have as its proposer Mr Cowper Temple, since he was one of the principal architects of the original Act. Cowper Temple always maintained that he and his colleagues had had no intention of excluding women from the medical profession when drafting the legislation; they had simply overlooked the possibility of women being candidates for registration. But now the Government refused to support his amending bill, so it had to be abandoned.

Sophia was not just a passive observer of these Parliamentary events. Cowper Temple and other Members interested in helping the medical women's cause constantly turned to her for advice and information. She knew the history of the campaign better than anyone else did, and she could supply accurate records whenever they were required. Sophia meanwhile was becoming uncommonly well informed on Parliamentary procedure and the drafting of bills, as well as continuing to play a key role in the conduct of the School.

The next development involved the General Medical Council, the body that presided over the Medical Register. The Council had twenty-three members who were all qualified medical practitioners, six of them nominated by the Crown, the remainder representing the various examining bodies; it was responsible to the Privy Council. When Mr Cowper Temple's bill failed, the President of the Privy Council sent a request to the General Medical Council that at its next meeting, to be held in June 1875, it would review the subject of registration of female practitioners, and submit a report.

The Council had allowed six days in which to deal with the whole of its agenda; the debate on medicine as a profession for women occupied three of them. The old arguments against women as doctors were again aired, but Professor Turner, one of Sophia's adversaries at Edinburgh University, struck a new note with his statement that women's brains were smaller than men's, so they were incapable of sustained intellectual effort! It was pointed out to the Professor that the ratio of brain size to body size is the same in women as it is in men. A wit observed that according to Turner's reasoning the best students of medicine would be elephants and whales! Professor Rolleston was refreshingly practical. He noted that many women wished to be doctors, and that many more wished to be treated by doctors of their own sex; these facts in themselves were sufficient reason to allow women to become registered practitioners. The report submitted by the General Medical Council had to represent a range of opinions, so its recommendations were necessarily rather tentative. Nevertheless, its first statement established that the Council would not actively oppose the registration of women:

> The Medical Council are of opinion that the study and practice of medicine and surgery, instead of affording a field of exertion well fitted to women, do, on the contrary, present special difficulties which cannot be safely disregarded; but the Council are not prepared to say that women ought to be excluded from the profession.[13]

The report then acknowledged that the examining bodies might refuse to accept women candidates. If this happened a separate qualification for women would be required, but 'the examination of female candidates for a licence entitling their names to be placed on the "Register" should be equivalent to those of male candidates'.

Sophia and her friends were elated. Two of their principal aims now had the approval of the General Medical Council, the body that could have been their most powerful adversary. On this occasion Providence had been on their side. Sir Robert Christison, who had been a Crown representative on the Council since its foundation in 1858, retired at the end of 1873. If he had still been a member, the report would probably have read very differently.

A few weeks after the Medical Council completed its report, the British Medical Association held its Annual General Meeting. The President for that year was Sir Robert Christison, and the Meeting was held in his home city of

Edinburgh. Sir Robert was shocked to find that the Association now had a lady member who expected not only to attend the meeting but also to present a scientific paper. The lady was Elizabeth Garrett Anderson. Her London colleagues had successfully nominated her for membership of the Metropolitan branch, having previously ascertained that nothing in the Association's charter specifically excluded women. But at the Annual Meeting she faced open hostility. Some of the members tried to prevent her from reading her paper, but after prolonged discussion she was allowed to proceed.

Observers might have wondered why so many men felt themselves threatened by the presence of just one woman. The only other woman to have her name on the Register was Elizabeth Blackwell, and Dr Blackwell was not clamouring for admission to the British Medical Association. Perhaps it was the General Medical Council's recent decision not to debar women from registration that had alarmed the women's opponents. Sir Robert Christison's historic victory of only two years ago was already being undermined.

The General Medical Council's suggestion of a 'different but equivalent' qualification for women prompted the women students to try a new approach. The Royal College of Surgeons of England offered a Licence in Midwifery, the holders of which were eligible for registration. The requirements with regard to hospital training and attendance at lectures were exactly the same as for the Membership of the College, but very few candidates had ever presented for the Licence examination, most preferring the Membership. Thus, the Licence would appear 'different', but its standards had been set for male candidates, so there could be no suggestion that it was an inferior qualification designed for women.

In December 1875 Sophia, Isabel Thorne and Edith Pechey applied to be examined for the Licence in Midwifery. Taken by surprise, the College authorities consulted legal opinion, and were informed that the College had no valid grounds for refusing the women's applications. In January 1876 the three women submitted their Edinburgh certificates of attendance at lectures and hospital classes. These were found to exceed the College's requirements. In March they were formally accepted as examination candidates. Then the opposition that had been simmering suddenly reached boiling point.

The *Lancet* attacked the notion of these 'persons' being able to use the Licence in Midwifery as an easy route to registration.[14] It ignored the fact that the women's preparation met all the requirements for the College Membership. The *Lancet* was not only opposed to women doctors, it was also at the forefront of a strong reform movement working for a 'single portal of entry' into the profession. This movement had the laudable aim of improving the standards of basic medical training by requiring all candidates to be examined in all three branches of practice – medicine, surgery and obstetrics. Thus its attacks on the 'persons' now preparing for the Licence in Midwifery appeared to have only the good of the profession at heart.

For two months the three women candidates worked hard to be ready for this vital examination. Then, a few days before it was due to begin, they were informed that it had been cancelled. All three examiners had resigned! Doctors Barnes, Farre and Priestley had consulted with their colleagues in the Obstetrical Society and had been urged to resist all attempts to have their specialty of obstetrics made the path by which women could gain entry to the medical profession. The action they took was bizarre, but effective. No substitute examiners came forward, so the Licence in Midwifery was unattainable by anyone, male or female, and remained so for a number of years.

Sir James Paget, the President of the Royal College of Surgeons, was embarrassed. His views on the medical aspirations of women were ambivalent. He believed them to be 'sadly mistaken' in their wish to enter a 'masculine' profession, but he would not oppose them actively.[15] Indeed, he had been the first consultant to come to Dr Elizabeth Garrett's aid when she was a newcomer to medical practice. Sir James issued a statement in which he dissociated the College from the unjustified and regrettable action taken by the examiners.[16] Sophia thought that, although most of the Members and Fellows of the College would not publicly disagree with their President, privately they applauded the men who had so adroitly foiled the women's ambitions.

Meanwhile, the London School of Medicine for Women was approaching a crisis. Although the number of enrolled students had doubled during the eighteen months since it opened, support for it would decline if its students could not soon be assured of access to hospital training and to qualifying examinations. Some of the students who had been at Edinburgh with Sophia were now studying abroad, where they could at least gain some practical experience. Edith Pechey found an opening nearer to home. After the débâcle of the midwifery examination she went to Birmingham, where she was permitted to work at the Women's Hospital under the supervision of the eminent surgeon, Mr Lawson Tait. Sophia could not leave London. Not only did she feel responsible for the day-to-day running of the School, but she needed to be available to assist the Members of Parliament who were working for the women's cause.

Lord Sandon, of the ruling Conservative Party, had intimated that the Government was sympathetic, and would not oppose a bill aimed at securing their rights to a qualifying examination, but he could give no assurance that his party would itself introduce such a bill. The next step was to send a deputation to the Duke of Richmond and Gordon, Lord President of the Privy Council. The members of the deputation were Lord Aberdare (himself a former Lord President), Mr Stansfeld, Mr Forsyth, Dr Garrett Anderson and Miss Jex-Blake. Mr Forsyth MP was a prominent member of the Conservative Party. James Stansfeld, now that his Liberal Party was in opposition, had more time to devote to feminist causes, such as the movement for the repeal of the Contagious Diseases Acts, and the medical women's campaign. He accepted the post of Honorary Treasurer of the London School of Medicine for Women, and was soon to play a key role in the history of the School. The gentlemen of the deputation put up an excellent case (based largely on data supplied by Sophia), but they could not extract from the Lord President a promise of positive action.

Mr Cowper Temple was about to revive his Foreign Degrees Bill when a different approach was suggested by another MP, Mr Russell Gurney. He proposed a bill that would give *all* of the medical examining bodies the power to admit women as candidates, subject to the same conditions and requirements as those already imposed on men. The General Medical Council, after considering the proposed bill, suggested two amendments: first, it must be made clear that the various bodies were being *enabled*, not *compelled*, to admit women and, second, it should also be stated that women who obtained such qualifications would not be entitled to participate in the administration of any of the examining bodies. When these amendments were accepted, the General Medical Council undertook not to oppose the bill, which became known as the Russell Gurney Enabling Bill.

The terms of the bill sounded rather weak, since the examining bodies could all choose to ignore their new powers. Sophia was assured by her parliamentary friends that this was an unlikely outcome, but if it did happen, the Government would be in a strong position to bring in legislation enforcing the admission of women. It was much more likely that one of the bodies would promptly open its doors to women, thus solving the immediate problem. In time the others would follow suit.

The Russell Gurney Enabling Bill was to be treated as a private member's bill and, as such, was unlikely to be allocated an early date in the House. At worst it could be postponed indefinitely. These were anxious times for Sophia, and it was at this juncture that she received a most disturbing letter from a friend. Paulina Irby wrote from Bosnia, telling her about the armed revolt the Serbs were waging against the Turks. Serbian casualties were high and many of the wounded were dying because of the gross inadequacy of their hospital facilities. Paulina urged Sophia to come to Sarajevo and establish a military hospital there. The idea was certainly attractive. Sophia wrote in her diary:

> Oh, dear, how I should love to go! It would probably be just the making of me as a surgeon, . . . I feel as if it would be an intense relief to break right away into half savage parts and do rough hard work – and breathe! . . .
> I suppose the constant worry and constant thwarting have made me almost wild to break away for a bit. I feel somehow as if my mind were all strained, and this better than anything would give it back its tone.[17]

But a little reflection convinced her that she must put Sarajevo out of her mind. She would be foolish to leave London now that her political campaign was at a critical stage. Her friend Ursula Du Pre warned her that British public opinion was just beginning to accept that there was a need for women doctors to care for women patients; she could alienate support by rushing off now to treat wounded soldiers. So Sophia remained at her post. She was pleased to observe that within a short time public appeals in Britain raised funds that enabled the Red Cross to give effective aid to the wounded in Serbia.

It was well that Sophia remained in London, because soon there were indications that the Russell Gurney Bill would be dealt with expeditiously. It passed through the various stages without delay or serious opposition, and was passed on 11 August 1876. Here, at last, after seven years of fighting, she had won a victory that could not be snatched away!

Now it was a matter of urgency to find an examining body that was prepared to act on its new powers and admit women. In England and Scotland the same old opponents were still entrenched in positions of power, so the women decided to make their first appeals to two Irish institutions – Queen's University, and the King's and Queen's College of Physicians. In September 1876 Edith Pechey, accompanied by Edith Shove, a student at the London School of Medicine for Women, went to Dublin to present the women's case. Sophia might have been expected to undertake this important mission herself. Perhaps she thought that she was too closely associated with the long history of confrontation and lawsuits, and that two personable young women who had no record of militancy could achieve more on this occasion.

The two Ediths were cordially received at both institutions. But they found that at Queen's University there was one man who intended to oppose them, so they decided to concentrate their efforts on the College of Physicians. There negotiations proceeded smoothly. The College was prepared to admit women to examinations, provided they met with all its ordinary requirements. This was exactly what Sophia had always sought – 'a fair field and no favour'. The College also had no difficulty in granting its recognition to the London School of Medicine for Women, since the School's lecturers had all previously been accredited by the College.

Six Englishwomen were immediately eligible to take advantage of this development. Three of the Edinburgh group – Sophia Jex-Blake, Edith Pechey and Isabel Thorne – had certificates of attendance at the Edinburgh Royal Infirmary as well as at all the prescribed courses of lectures. The others – Eliza Dunbar, Frances Hoggan and Louisa Atkins – were protégées of Dr Garrett Anderson. They had followed her advice and gone to Europe to study, each eventually obtaining the MD Zurich – Frances in 1870, and Eliza and Louisa in 1872. When the College of Physicians in Dublin accepted their training as meeting College requirements they, too, were ready to present themselves for examination.

Sophia felt the need for a period of intense revision before she attempted the examination. She had been so preoccupied with the establishment of the School, and with the political campaign, that her studies had been neglected. She arranged to spend two months in Switzerland, attending lectures and visiting hospitals, and then to take the examination for the MD Berne. This would be valuable practice for the Dublin examination. Edith Pechey decided to join her. Unfortunately, Isabel Thorne's family commitments kept her at home, and for the time being she had to forego any attempt at obtaining a qualification.

Sophia and Edith arrived in Switzerland at the beginning of November, 1876. They brought with them letters of introduction from their Edinburgh friend Professor Masson, and they were soon enrolled for lectures and practical classes. In addition to taking the examination, each candidate for the MD Berne had to submit a thesis. Sophia chose to write on the subject of puerperal fever because she had seen an outbreak of this dreaded disease while she was working in Boston. Pasteur's discovery of the bacterial cause of puerperal fever was not made until 1879, so Sophia's thesis, while considered a sound review of medical knowledge at the time, made no lasting contribution to this subject.

The final preparations for a professional examination are a strain for any earnest candidate, but Sophia was more anxious than most. Her foes at home would be exultant if she failed and, although she probably did not admit it even to herself, the failure at Edinburgh had shaken her confidence. She was not helped by some of the letters received from well-meaning friends, such as Ursula Du Pre, who begged her not to be in too great a hurry to take the examination, because if she failed, it couldn't be kept a secret. 'Are they all in league to shake my nerves?' Sophia asked herself. It was not surprising that she was troubled by neuralgia and insomnia for the first few weeks in Switzerland. Then her cheerfulness returned and she began to enjoy the luxury of being able to concentrate on her studies, although even here the concerns of the London School of Medicine could not be entirely ignored. Mr Stansfeld kept her informed of the progress of his efforts to obtain a hospital affiliation for the School. He wrote, 'I met Mrs Garrett Anderson at dinner the other day; she did not seem to have much hope or plan about the School in any way.'[18] But he went on to say that recently, while travelling abroad, he had met Mr Hopgood, Chairman of the Weekly Board of the Royal Free Hospital, London. The School's previous formal approach to this hospital had not been fruitful, but when the two senior administrators were able to discuss the matter informally, Mr Hopgood became more sympathetic. Stansfeld told Sophia, 'I am to send Mr Hopgood something to read, and he is to consider whether anything is possible there; he does not appear to be in awe of the [medical] staff.'

Sophia completed the examination for the MD Berne on 10 January 1877, and was informed that she had passed. With obvious relief she wrote in her diary, 'Now to see how much better an MD sleeps than other people!' A few weeks later, Edith Pechey also passed. It was a jubilant Sophia who returned to England to face the problems awaiting her there. For the next two months she divided her time between the London School and her mother's home in

Brighton, evidently because Mrs Jex-Blake's health was again causing concern.

Efforts to secure a hospital affiliation for the School were now centred on the Royal Free Hospital. This highly respected institution was founded in 1828, for the purpose of providing treatment for the poor. Its charter stipulated that nobody in need of care would be turned away because he had neither money nor a letter of recommendation from a reputable citizen. Originally called the London General Institution for the Gratuitous Cure of Malignant Diseases, it changed its name in 1853 to the Free Hospital. Two years later it became the Royal Free Hospital. In 1842 it moved·from its original site in Hatton Gardens to Gray's Inn Road, where it continued to grow. Although it had never been a teaching hospital for medical students, the Royal Free was well able to assume this additional function. It provided a comprehensive service, and its medical staff included a number of distinguished members of the profession. If it became affiliated with the London School, all its facilities would be available to the women students, since there were no male students claiming rights of priority. It was even conveniently close to the School.

In the negotiations James Stansfeld and Sophia represented the London School, and Mr Hopgood represented the Royal Free Hospital. On Thursday, 9 February 1877, Stansfeld wrote to tell Sophia of an important meeting he had arranged for the three of them for the following Sunday. He enclosed a copy of a letter from Mr Hopgood confirming the appointment, and commenting in the most optimistic vein about the probable outcome:

> I see my way so far clear that on receiving a formal application from your Association it shall be without delay submitted to our Weekly Board, – and I think they will forthwith summon a special meeting of the Committee of Management, whose *decision will be final for the current year*! My wish may be father to the thought, but I think that if you can make some such proposition as that we talked of we have a good prospect of success.
>
> My wife feels such a deep interest in the success of the movement that she wished me to say that if you think it desirable to form a guarantee fund, her name may be put down as a subscriber or guarantor to the extent of £100.[19]

Sophia must have acquitted herself well at that important meeting; a few days later she received a letter from Mr Hopgood in which he said, 'I heartily wish that every success may attend this movement – if so, I know to whom it will be chiefly due.'

Many supporters of the Hospital were aware that affiliation with a medical school would enhance the status of their institution, and would stimulate its medical staff to aim for higher levels of professional achievement. But there was also a risk that the proposal would alienate some financial contributors who objected to the presence of women students. The Hospital representatives therefore pressed for exacting financial arrangements with the School, as a protection against loss.

An agreement was reached on 15 March. James Stansfeld sent a telegram to Sophia, who was in Brighton, 'London Free Hospital have unanimously accepted my proposal.' The School had been saved! Women who wished to study medicine were now assured of complete theoretical and practical training, as well as the right to qualify and become registered. Sophia's eight years of striving had been rewarded. Elizabeth Garrett Anderson, who was recovering from the birth of her third child, wrote Stansfeld a cordial note of congratulation, which he sent on to Sophia.

Sophia still had to obtain the Licence of the King's and Queen's College of Physicians of Ireland in order to be registered, but by now her confidence was restored and the battle wounds were healing. For several weeks she and Edith Pechey visited the Brompton Hospital to be coached by the kindly Dr Symes Thompson. Then, in May, they were ready to face the examiners. They would be joined by a third woman candidate, Louisa Atkins. On the eve of her departure for Dublin Sophia wrote in her diary:

The various tests loom vague and large. Diagnosis at bedside, – horrible, – though enormously helped by Brompton experience. Recognition of drugs and things under microscope. 4 written exams. 2 hrs oral, etc., etc.

I feel as if I really had fairly mastered my subjects and must know more than the average medical practitioner just fledged, – not to say have more sense.

But the stake is so enormous. A pluck would be so perfectly awful after all antecedents. But in spite of my work, my brain is wonderfully well and clear.[20]

A few days later Sophia was able to send her mother a telegram bearing the joyous message that all three of the women had passed. Since 1866 the Medical Register had listed the names of only two women – Elizabeth Blackwell and Elizabeth Garrett Anderson. In 1877 five more were added. Sophia's was not the first of the new entries. Eliza Dunbar and Frances Hoggan had passed the Dublin examination three months earlier, and so appeared ahead of her, a detail that she did not mind in the slightest.

It was now eleven years since Dr Lucy Sewall had inspired Sophia to make medicine, rather than teaching, her life's work. Sophia had not then known that the realization of her own ambition would become less important to her than the victory she eventually won for all women. She was justly proud of her achievement, but later in life, when recalling those troubled years in Edinburgh and London, she would often add one of her favourite sayings, 'Efforts are ours, results are God's.'

One more success was soon to follow. Late in 1876 Edith Shove applied to London University for admission to its medical degree examination when she had completed her training at the London School of Medicine for Women. In 1862, when the young Elizabeth Garrett had applied, opinion in the University Senate was so evenly divided that the motion in favour of her admission was defeated on the casting vote of the Chancellor, Lord Granville. Now Lord Granville, with a majority of the Senate, supported Edith Shove's submission.

When the matter was discussed in Convocation, the opposition by a group of medical graduates led to prolonged debate, and the familiar pattern of motions, counter-motions and suggestions for deferral was again evident. Mr William Savory, an eminent surgeon of St Bartholomew's Hospital, was strongly opposed to the opening of the profession to women. He used the delaying tactic of moving that the Senate should take no action on the matter of medical degrees until the larger question of admitting women to *all* degrees had been fully considered.

But the tide of feeling was turning in favour of the women's cause, so on 20 June 1877 the Senate voted to proceed with its original resolution to admit women candidates to medical examinations. Savory's action not only failed in its purpose, it facilitated an even greater victory for the women's cause. It engendered so much public interest in the subject of higher education for women that, when Convocation met in January 1878 to consider changes to the University charter, it voted for the admission of women to all degee examinations! Four years later Edith Shove was awarded the MB of London University. She was the first woman to obtain a degree in medicine from a British university.

Although in the year 1877 Sophia had reasons to rejoice, it was also then that she experienced one of her most bitter disappointments. A key administrative position at the London School of Medicine for Women, a position that she had expected would be hers, was given to another. The School was Sophia's brainchild, the fulfilment of her childhood dreams of Sackermena; she had assumed that she would guide its development for the rest of her working life. She would have had her own medical practice as well, but the School would have been her major interest. Now this was not to be.

In the early months of 1877 Sophia was obliged to spend more time than usual away from London – there were the examinations in Switzerland and Ireland, and more frequent visits to Brighton to care for her ailing mother. The School's Executive Council was able to take a more detached view of her role. In any case, some change in Sophia's position at the School was necessary. Previously much of her work was done in an unofficial capacity, but now that the School was firmly established, a more formal allocation of responsibility was required.

The minutes of a meeting of the Executive Council held on 7 May 1877 contain the following entry:

Appointment of Honorary Secretary. The Chairman Mr Stansfeld explained that the time had now arrived when it was requisite to consider the appointment of a person or persons to carry on the important work which was before the School. It would require the possession of various qualities such as power of organization to ensure the success of the public meeting to raise the large funds now needed, and tact and judgment to enable the arrangements connected with the working of the School and its students to go on smoothly with the Hospital.[21]

Although Stansfeld well knew how much the School owed to Sophia, he seemed to be suggesting, with his reference to tact, that she was not the ideal person for the permanent appointment of Honorary Secretary. Perhaps the School now needed a diplomat, rather than a warrior, as its leader.

The minutes record further discussions of the subject at each of the next three meetings of the Council. It was decided to appoint a paid secretary to do the clerical work, so that the Honorary Secretary would have time to attend to administration. The divergence of views of Council members was illustrated by Elizabeth Garrett Anderson's questioning whether an Honorary Secretary was really needed, followed by Sophia's listing of the onerous duties that would fall to the lot of the person appointed. The matter was finally resolved at the meeting of 30 May, when it was moved by Dr Chambers and seconded by Dr Jex-Blake that 'Mrs Thorne be urgently requested to undertake the office of Honorary Secretary'. Voting was deferred until the next meeting, on 12 June, when Mrs Thorne was elected unanimously.

The minutes do not record all the events leading to Isabel Thorne's appointment, nor do they convey the emotional strain suffered by the three women principally concerned. The full story was told by Dr Margaret Todd, a friend of Sophia in her later years. Dr Todd not only heard the story from Sophia herself, but she had access to her letters and diaries. She tells how, at that first meeting on 7 May, when Sophia was in Dublin taking her examinations, Isabel Thorne nominated her for the position of Honorary Secretary. But a second nomination was immediately brought forward, that of Elizabeth Garrett Anderson.

Elizabeth certainly did not wish to be Secretary. She had a busy practice and was the mother of a young family. She accepted the nomination only because she feared that Sophia's autocratic temperament could jeopardize the School's future. James Stansfeld, as Chairman, faced a dilemma. In the hope that some other solution could be found, he deferred the matter for discussion at later meetings. The two nominations were not even recorded in the minutes.

Sophia returned from Dublin elated with her success in the College examinations, only to find her position at the School seriously threatened. It seemed that if a vote had been taken at that meeting on 7 May, Elizabeth would have won. Sophia could not bear to think of the School being entrusted to a woman who had tried to discourage its founders. If she herself had to stand aside, then let her place be taken by one who shared her sense of dedication to the School.

Sophia turned to her old friend Isabel Thorne, in whom she had complete trust. Isabel had been a campaigner ever since the early days in Edinburgh. Her loyalty to the School was beyond doubt. She was also intellectually gifted, industrious and well liked by all who knew her. Isabel seemed ideal for the position, but if she accepted it she would have to sacrifice her own medical career. Since leaving Edinburgh she had had no time to continue her studies, or even to maintain the level of knowledge she had gained there. Now that her family commitments had diminished she had hoped to repeat much of the course in order to be thoroughly prepared for the examinations. Such a plan was incompatible with the duties of the Honorary Secretary. Dr Lucy Sewall had once commented that, of all the women students at Edinburgh, Isabel Thorne would probably make the best doctor. Now Isabel unselfishly chose instead to accept nomination for the position of Honorary Secretary. Her election on 12 June was unanimous. Sophia's diary contained the comment, 'About the best possible, with her excellent sense and perfect temper. So much better than I.'

Much as Sophia and Elizabeth admired each other's achievements, they never understood each other. Elizabeth worked for the women's cause through the medium of her own success. Sophia, on the other hand, constantly risked personal failure while fighting for the rights of others. Whereas Elizabeth was usually discreet and cautious, Sophia was often domineering and impetuous. Elizabeth was reserved and had few close friends. Sophia was warm-hearted; although a few thought her unbearable, she had a large number of friends whose affection for her grew stronger with the passage of time.

These differences were observed by so many of their associates that they must have been real. Perhaps the circumstances of their lives partly explained them. Elizabeth was never goaded and publicly humiliated as Sophia was in Edinburgh. In her student days Elizabeth had the support of a strong-minded father who was prepared, if need be, to take her opponents to court on her behalf. Sophia, although helped by many friends, had to fight her own battles. The publicity, even notoriety, that attended her campaign was unavoidable because she had to win the support of the public. The quiet, dignified approach that succeeded for Elizabeth was not possible for those who came after her.

James Stansfeld, who had been so closely associated with the London campaign, wrote a brief history of the events that led to the victories of 1876–7. His article, 'Medical women', appeared in the journal *Nineteenth Century* for July 1877. He began:

The movement whose object has been to permit and to enable women to pursue the study of medicine . . . dates, practically speaking, from the month of March 1869, when Miss Jex-Blake first made application to the University of Edinburgh to be allowed to attend the lectures of the Medical Faculty with a view to obtaining the degree of Doctor of Medicine, which would have carried with it the right to registration under the act. . . .

I have not dated the movement from Mrs Garrett Anderson's personally successful attempt, because its immediate consequence was the closing of the door through which she had forced her way. . . . Her honourable place appears to me to be that of a forerunner of the movement, which she has, however, continuously aided, and now aids, by personal service and pecuniary help, and by the prestige of her own character and repute.

After recounting the story of the hard-fought battles in Edinburgh and London, Stansfeld concluded:

Such struggles do not persist and succeed, according to my experience, without the accompanying fact, the continuous thread as it were, of one constant purpose and dominant will. Dr Sophia Jex-Blake has made that greatest of all contributions to the end attained. I do not say that she has been the ultimate cause of success. The ultimate cause has been simply this, that the time was at hand. It is one of the lessons of the history of progress that when the time for a reform has come you cannot resist it, though, if you make the attempt, what you may do is to widen its character or precipitate its advent. Opponents, when the time has come, are not merely dragged at the chariot wheels of progress – they help to turn them. The strongest force, whichever way it seems to work, does most to aid. The forces of greatest concentration here have been, in my view, on the one hand the Edinburgh University led by Sir Robert Christison, on the other the women claimants led by Dr Sophia Jex-Blake. Defeated at Edinburgh, she carried her appeal to the highest court, that most able to decide and to redress, the High Court of Parliament representing the nation itself. The result we see at last. Those who hail it as the answer which they sought have both to thank, in senses and proportions which they may for themselves decide.[22]

Sir Robert must have been startled by the suggestion that he had actually hastened Sophia's victory!

Notes

1. *The Times*, 5 August 1873.
2. *The Times*, 5 August 1873.
3. *The Times*, 23 August 1873.
4. *Life of Sir Robert Christison* (edited by his sons), London and Edinburgh: 1885–6, vol II, p. 43.
5. *The Times*, 13 June 1874.
6. *The Times*, 18 June 1874.
7. *The Times*, 20 June 1874.
8. *The Times*, 29 June 1874.
9. M. Todd, *The Life of Sophia Jex-Blake*, London: Macmillan, 1918, p. 424.
10. S. Jex-Blake, *Medical Women*, Edinburgh and London: Macmillan, 1886, p. 178.
11. Todd, op. cit., p. 421.
12. I. Thorne, *Sketch of the Foundation and Development of the London School of Medicine for Women*, London: Women's Printing Society, 1915, p. 23.
13. Jex-Blake, op. cit., p. 190.
14. *Lancet*, 6 May 1876.
15. Todd, op. cit., p. 444.
16. Jex-Blake, op. cit., p. 198. See also, the *Scotsman*, 19 May 1876.
17. Todd, op. cit., p. 432.
18. ibid., p. 441.
19. ibid., p. 443.
20. ibid., p. 439.
21. Archives of the Medical School, Royal Free Hospital, London.
22. J. Stansfeld, 'Medical women', in *Nineteenth Century*, July 1877.

10

The years in practice

The dramatic events of the first half of 1877 restored Sophia's freedom to lead a life of her own, but she had difficulty in adjusting to her changed circumstances. While Edith Pechey was establishing a successful practice in Leeds, Sophia's career was at a standstill. Instead of going into practice she occupied her time with further medical studies and with visits to several hospitals. She stayed in London, still living in the rooms she had taken near the School, during those hectic days when the house in Henrietta Street was being prepared for its new function. She was still a Trustee and a Governor of the School, so for nearly a year she continued to attend its Executive Council meetings, although with declining interest, now that she had no personal responsibility for the management of the School. She needed this time to rest, before she could plan the next phase of her life.

Early in 1878 Sophia decided to return to Edinburgh. Some of her London friends were surprised that she chose to begin her professional career in the city where she had suffered such hardship and ignominy. But staunch friends far outnumbered her old foes in Edinburgh. Besides, now that the victory had been won, the setbacks the women had suffered there were to be seen as milestones along the road to success.

She could not make the move at once, since it involved her mother as well. Mrs Jex-Blake would give up the family home at Brighton so that in future she could divide her time between Edinburgh and Rugby. Sophia had to help her complete her arrangements; then all was ready for her departure. At its meeting on 6 May 1878 the Executive Council of the London School of Medicine for Women formally thanked Sophia for her services to the School. There was unanimous support for a motion to appoint Drs Sophia Jex-Blake and Edith Pechey joint lecturers in hygiene. The course in this subject was not held every year, so it would not be difficult for the two lecturers to spend enough time in London to fulfil their obligations.

Ursula Du Pre and Agnes McLaren were the closest of the many friends who welcomed Sophia back to Edinburgh in 1878. Later in the year Agnes successfully completed her studies and was duly registered as a medical

Illustration 12. Sir Robert Christison (1797–1882). The most powerful opponent of the women medical students at Edinburgh University. Portrait by W. Hole. (Reproduced by permission from *The Life of Sir Robert Christison, Vol. II*, edited by his sons, Edinburgh and London: William Blackwood, 1886.)

practitioner. Mrs Russel, who had been one of the original five students in 1869, was another who was delighted at Sophia's return. Sophia had been shocked to hear of her husband's sudden death from a heart attack in 1876. Helen Russel was now the mother of three children; she had no thought of returning to medical studies, but she retained her enthusiasm for the cause and her regard for Sophia.

Time had also changed the lives of some of Sophia's former adversaries. In 1877 Sir Robert Christison retired from the academic staff of Edinburgh University. Although he was 80 years old he retained his place on the University Court, and his interest in University affairs. Professor Joseph Lister had left Edinburgh in the same year to take the Chair of Clinical Surgery at King's College, London.

Sophia leased a house at 4 Manor Place, and it was here that in June 1878 she put up her brass plate. Scotland now had its first woman doctor! Her early days in practice were not without anxiety, but she had the support of several of Edinburgh's leading consultants. Drs Heron Watson and George Balfour, who had taught the women students at the Royal Infirmary, were now equally willing to help a woman colleague become established.

Her practice grew steadily, and was as busy as she could wish, although she lacked some of the aids to easy success. She could never bring herself to waste time talking pleasantries with rich ladies who were consulting her only because they were bored; after a few minutes she would look pointedly at her watch and move towards the door. She rarely gave or attended formal dinner parties. Some people were astonished to observe that she often left her coachman at home to work in the garden, and took the reins herself when she went to visit her patients. For these reasons society ladies thought Sophia rather eccentric, and few of them consulted her. But working-class women were grateful for her help. As well as giving them expert medical care, she would try to ease the burdens of work and poverty that sometimes retarded their recovery.

Three months after beginning practice at Manor Place, Sophia opened an outpatient clinic at 73 Grove Street, Fountainbridge; here poor women could receive medical attention for a fee of a few pence. In a letter to her mother she reported the gratifying success of both aspects of her practice:

> I know you will be pleased to hear that I yesterday received fees which just completed my first £50, – earned in Edinburgh in less than three months, – and that in what they call the 'empty' season. And what pleases me still better is that everyone of my patients has done well. Several have left my hands practically recovered, and those who are still there are all going on satisfactorily. And as among them were two cases to which I was called when the patient was described as 'dying' (and both got well) I think I may very well be content. I have had 23 patients (nearly 100 visits) at my private house, and about as many more at my

Dispensary, which has only been open a fortnight; so I don't think there is much doubt about the 'demand' nor about my prospects.[1]

A little later she wrote to a friend:

> I have full as much work at my Dispensary as I can manage, indeed I am pretty well used up on those days, but I always enjoy them.
> I am just going to begin a course of lectures which I hope may be successful.
> It is hard work altogether, but nothing to the old worries.[2]

Sophia's house at 4 Manor Place was comfortable and well kept. She no longer had Alice's expert help – Alice was enjoying a well-earned retirement in Wales – but she employed a cook, a housemaid, a coachman and several other servants. She often shared their work so that she could be sure that they were keeping to her well-tried methods. Her home was always open to her friends, and many of them came to stay with her from time to time.

She delighted in letter-writing, and by this means kept alive her friendships with people who now lived far away. Her letters sometimes sparkled with humour, at other times dealt with serious topics, but the warmth of her friendship was always there. She had not seen Isabel Thorne for over a year when she wrote:

> I hear that your two girls are coming to Morton next week. Don't you think it would be very wrong to let them travel so far all alone? Don't you think it is clearly your duty to come and stay a week or two with me when you arrive? I should like so very much to see you again at something like leisure, and also to show you my Dispensary and all and sundry I am doing here. *So* many Edinbro' friends would like to see you! *Do* try to come if only for a week or two![3]

Edith Pechey wrote frequently from Leeds. Paulina Irby, on a brief holiday from the Balkans, came to stay with Sophia in Edinburgh. Lucy Sewall had not been to Britain since her visit of 1871, but they kept up a lively correspondence. In October 1879 Sophia wrote to Lucy:

> I have a very charming little brougham, which my Mother gave me; and a beautiful horse, quiet as a lamb and strong as a bull, from Miss Du Pre. Altogether it is an extremely smart turn-out, and I should like so much to show it to you! I hope I shall this summer. You *must* come then if possible, – it is so hard to be apart so many years!
> I am so sorry my Father's carriage is worn out. That little gift was such a pleasure to him and almost the last thing he did. I think the letter in which he told me he had paid the money to my bankers was the very last I had from him – dear old man![4]

166

Not long afterwards she wrote to Lucy again, this time with sad news:

> I have rather a sore heart today, for dear old Turk has just died in my
> arms. . . . He seemed about as usual today, but rose from where he was
> by the kitchen fire, walked into the scullery and fell over. They fetched
> me, and he gave just two gasps in my arms and died. It seems a bit of
> one's life gone, when he had been in it for 13 years! – and a Boston bit
> too.[5]

Sophia still found time to follow the progress of the London School of Medicine
for Women. A brief visit she made to London in October 1879 coincided with
the beginning of the academic year at the School. She attended the opening
ceremony and was asked to move the vote of thanks to her friend, Dr King
Chambers, who gave the address. Although it was a happy occasion, for
Sophia it must have been tinged with sadness.

She continued to keep a close watch on political developments that could
threaten the status of medical women. In 1878 there was a bill before Parliament that would make it compulsory for medical practitioners to obtain basic
qualifications in both internal medicine and surgery; previously a single qualification in either was sufficient for registration. The proposed change would
improve the standard of medical practice, but it posed a serious threat to
women doctors. Neither of the examining bodies to which women candidates
had access offered qualifications in surgery. An early passage of the bill would
either prevent more women from being registered, or would place them in a
separate, inferior category. The professional equality of medical men and
women was one of the important principles established in 1876. Sophia would
not see it undermined. She wrote to James Stansfeld and other friends in
London, warning them of the danger. She also wrote to Elizabeth Garrett
Anderson, suggesting that the eight women then registered should send a
protest to their friends in Parliament. The bill of 1878 was deferred, and then
dropped, but it was not until 1885, when it became possible for women to
qualify in surgery, that the threat was at last removed.

Although Sophia was never one of the leaders of the women's suffrage
movement, she supported it wholeheartedly. In 1879, in response to a request
from Paulina Irby, she wrote some notes setting out the arguments in favour
of giving the vote to women:

> If I correctly understand the British Constitution, one of its fundamental
> principles is that Taxation and Representation should go together, and
> that every person taxed should have a voice in the election of those by
> whom taxes are imposed. If this is a wrong principle, it should be
> exchanged as soon as possible for some other, so that we may know what
> is the real basis of representation in this country; if it is a right principle,
> it must admit of general application, and I am unable to see that the sex
> of the tax-paying householder should enter into the question at all.

The argument respecting the 'virtual representation' of women under the present system seems to me especially worthless, as it can be answered alternatively thus: – If women as a sex have exactly the same interests as men, their votes can do no harm, and indeed will not affect the ultimate result; if they have interests more or less divergent from men, it is obviously essential that such interests should be directly represented in the councils of the nation. My own belief is that in the highest sense, the interests of the two sexes are identical, and that the noblest and most enlightened men and women will always feel them to be so; and, in that case, a country must surely be most politically healthy where all phases of thought and experience find legitimate expression in the selection of its parliamentary representatives.[6]

Sophia continued to cram into her life enough activity for three ordinary women. She seemed to have come through the years of strife unscathed, with her energy and courage as boundless as ever. But this was not the case. She was soon to be severely tested again, and this time her strength would fail her.

Mrs Jex-Blake spent the winter of 1880–1 with Sophia in Edinburgh. In April she left for Rugby. She was now 80 years old, and in quite good health for her age, although she still had occasional episodes of fever caused by the stone in her kidney. Towards the end of June she had one of these attacks and her condition suddenly became critical. Sophia received a telegram asking her to come immediately. Accompanied by Ursula Du Pre she set off at once, arriving at Rugby in the early hours of the morning. Mrs Jex-Blake was close to death, but Sophia tended her night and day, and her condition seemed to improve. Dr King Chambers came from London in response to Sophia's call. He agreed with the treatment being given and thought that, although the patient was very frail, she would probably survive this attack. But a few days later Mrs Jex-Blake's condition suddenly worsened, and her life was ended. In a letter to a friend Sophia wrote:

> It was a hard battle, – it was bitter to fail just when we seemed winning, but I believe it was her wish to go. On Thursday I heard her murmur quietly, 'Oh, Father, I pray Thee take me home,' – and now all is peace.[7]

Sophia felt her loss severely. She never blamed her mother for the unhappiness of her childhood, thinking of her only as a loving and understanding parent. Certainly it was to her mother that the adult Sophia instinctively turned for comfort in times of trouble and, no matter how hard-pressed she was, Sophia would at once leave her other commitments if her mother needed her. Her friends and associates knew how she would grieve. Elizabeth Garrett Anderson wrote a warmly sympathetic letter:

I have seen with very great regret the notice of your sorrow. Knowing as I do how very close and tender was the tie between you and your Mother and also what a fine and enobling influence she must have been to all within her range I am very full of sympathy for you. It is always very sad to break away from the past by losing one of those main links with it, but in your case there is very much to increase your sense of this. You have not (as so many others unhappily allow themselves to do) outlived the tenderness of the relationship. I hope that after a time it will be a comfort to you to remember this and to recall how happy she was in having so much affection from you. I was very sorry to find I had written on business last Sunday at such a time.[8]

Sophia squared her shoulders and pressed on with the letter-writing and other formalities associated with a bereavement. But another calamity quickly followed. A young woman who had been her assistant at the Dispensary for over a year also died quite suddenly. She had been extremely hard-working, and Sophia blamed herself for not noticing that her assistant needed more rest and leisure. To add to Sophia's distress there were rumours that the young woman's death was partly caused by her work in the Dispensary, where she could have been exposed to high concentrations of ether fumes. Sophia's courage suddenly failed. She could no longer meet the demands of her profession, and instead of being the rescuer she herself had to be rescued.

Her friends came to her aid. They closed the practice at Manor Place and arranged for others to carry on the work of the Dispensary. Ursula Du Pre took her away for a long rest in the country. There are no letters or diaries to tell her innermost thoughts during this dark period, which must have tested her courage and religious faith to their limits. Slowly the agony of depression resolved, but two years were to pass before Sophia could return to her normal life.

Her illness removed her from public life at a time when several controversial issues came to the fore, issues on which she would normally have expressed firm opinions. In August 1881 the Seventh International Congress of Medicine was held in London, bringing together for a week three thousand doctors and scientists from Britain, Europe and the United States.[9] The importance of the event is evident from the names of some of those who attended – Pasteur, Charcot, Virchow, Koch, Osler, Lister, Huxley and Darwin. Surely no medical conference before or since has been honoured by the presence of so many great men. But not all members of the medical profession were able to enjoy the experience – women doctors were excluded. The organizing committee, headed by Sir James Paget, feared that the presence of even a small number of women would so offend some of the men that the Congress could be marred by disputation. They were not prepared to take the risk.

The committee could not, however, prevent another controversy that was sparked by the Congress and lasted for several months. Six years previously supporters of the antivivisection movement, led by Sophia's friend Frances Power Cobbe, had campaigned for the prohibition of scientific experimentation in which live animals were used as subjects.[10] Physiology, bacteriology and pathology were then rapidly expanding fields of medicine, but their progress depended on laboratory research. The debate did not involve most members of the profession, so a small group of scientists faced a large and very vocal group of antivivisectionists. In 1876 a truce was achieved with the passage of the Cruelty to Animals Act. This Act required scientists who carried out experiments on animals to be licensed by the Home Secretary. They were required to use anaesthetics whenever possible, and their laboratories could be inspected at any time. Thus animal experimentation would be limited and controlled, but the antivivisectionists were not satisfied with this compromise.

The Medical Congress provided Miss Cobbe and her supporters with an opportunity to trap their opponents. They studied all the published papers and found what they believed to be a glaring breach of the Act. Dr David Ferrier of King's College Hospital reported the results of his experiments on the brains of monkeys, but inquiry revealed that he did not have a licence for this work. Ferrier was brought to trial. In his defence he stated that although he was in charge of the research the practical experiments were performed by his assistant, and the assistant had the requisite licence. Dr Ferrier was acquitted, but the antivivisectionists felt that the inadequacy of the Act had been demonstrated. The controversy continued to smoulder.

In this debate Elizabeth Garrett Anderson strongly supported the scientists, but Sophia's views are not known. In 1876, when the Cruelty to Animals Bill was before Parliament, the medical women's campaign was also at a crucial stage and needed her undivided attention; in 1881 illness forced her temporarily into a life of seclusion. Thus, we can only guess at her views on animal experimentation. She was certainly fond of animals and on more than one occasion she came to the defence of domestic animals that she saw being ill-treated. She was also a friend of Frances Power Cobbe. But Sophia would have been well aware of the urgent need to extend scientific knowledge in order to alleviate human suffering, so it is at least as likely that she was on the side of the scientists in this debate.

Another event of this period had more personal significance for Sophia. On 27 January 1882 Sir Robert Christison died, at the age of 84. His academic achievements and service to the people of Edinburgh were recorded in the long list of honours awarded to him during his lifetime. Large crowds gathered in the winter cold to pay their last respects as his coffin was borne through the streets of his beloved city. If his treatment of Edinburgh's first women medical students was out of character, it was an episode that most now preferred to forget. Even Sophia, so recently reminded of the transience of life, probably could nor harbour any bitterness against Sir Robert Christison.

Before she had fully recovered she was involved in another unfortunate episode at the London School of Medicine for Women, an episode that showed that she had still not forgiven Elizabeth Garrett Anderson. In February 1883 Mr Arthur Norton, who had been Dean since the opening of the School, announced his resignation. At the next meeting of the Executive Council, held on 13 March, there were fifteen members present instead of the usual six or seven. Sophia came down from Edinburgh to attend, but Elizabeth, who probably had some inkling of what would happen, stayed away.

The meeting dealt first with such routine matters as the financial statement and the appointment of lecturers for the summer term. The minutes give a succinct account of the next item of business:

> The following resolution was proposed by Dr Donkin, seconded by Mrs Atkins MD: That Mrs Garrett Anderson MD., be nominated by this Council to the Governing Body for election to the Deanship of the School vacated by the resignation of Mr Norton.
>
> Dr S Jex-Blake and Dr T K Chambers seconded the following amendment: That Dr Edith Pechey be proposed for election as Dean of the School. The amendment was put to the meeting and lost. The original resolution was then put and carried by 14 votes to 1.[11]

Sophia continued to be associated with the School as a Trustee and as a Governor, but she never attended another meeting of the Executive Council.

Later in the year she again established a home for herself in Edinburgh. Bruntsfield Lodge, in Whitehouse Loan, was spacious and comfortable with a view over the green expanse of the Links; it was an ideal place in which to complete her recovery. The Lodge belonged to her friends Mr and Mrs Burn Murdoch, from whom she rented it for six years. It was then agreed that she could purchase the property.

In September 1883 Sophia returned to medical practice, and soon was seeing more patients at Bruntsfield Lodge than she had at Manor Place. The work of the Dispensary also expanded. In 1885 it was moved to larger premises at 6 Grove Street, and a small five-bed ward was added. The little outpatient clinic thus became the Edinburgh Hospital and Dispensary for Women. The opening of the ward required the employment of a resident Matron, and a year later Dr Catherine Urquhart, who had trained at the London School, was appointed the first Resident Medical Officer. The Edinburgh Hospital and Dispensary was Scotland's first hospital for women staffed by women.

While Sophia was busy with her growing practice and the Hospital, she was also watching some other developments with great satisfaction. In 1885 the Royal College of Surgeons in Ireland opened its lectures and examinations to women. A year later the Faculty of Physicians and Surgeons of Glasgow, and the Royal Colleges of Physicians and Surgeons of Edinburgh announced the formation of their Conjoint Board, which would examine candidates in both

Illustration 13. In this house overlooking Bruntsfield Links
Sophia lived and conducted her practice for sixteen years;
the house was then known as Bruntsfield Lodge. When
Sophia retired in 1889 the Edinburgh Hospital and
Dispensary for women moved to this site, and changed its
name to Bruntsfield Hospital. The Bruntsfield Hospital
continued to function until 1989.

internal medicine and surgery. Successful candidates would receive the
Colleges' combined diploma and, furthermore, women would be permitted to
take the examination. The threat of being relegated to inferior status because
they could qualify in only one branch of medicine was at last removed.

In London the Royal Colleges of Physicians and Surgeons were less pro-
gressive. They also established their Conjoint examination in 1885, but they
remained adamant that women candidates would not be accepted. They were
to maintain this attitude for nearly twenty years.

These events marked the beginning of another episode in Sophia's career, one which made the strengths and weaknesses in her character very evident. The opening of the Scottish Royal Colleges' examinations to women encouraged Scottish women to study medicine in their own country, but they encountered some of the difficulties the Edinburgh Seven had faced seventeen years previously. Most of the extramural lecturers still refused to admit women to their ordinary classes. To be able to arrange separate classes the women needed an organization to represent them as a group. Some of them wrote to Sophia appealing for help, and she responded generously. She negotiated with two lecturers who were prepared to conduct classes for women at Surgeons' Hall, provided she would give her personal guarantee that their fees would be met if the contributions from the students were inadequate. Eight women were enrolled for the beginning of the winter term of 1886–7.

Sophia invited the group to dine with her at Bruntsfield Lodge. Among them were two whose personalities contrasted strongly. Margaret Todd was a scholarly young woman who had previously worked as a teacher; she hovered in the background, observing her colleagues and her hostess with amused interest. The lively and outspoken Grace Cadell had been enrolled at the London School of Medicine for Women, but family problems compelled her to return to Edinburgh. She, perhaps even more than the others, was anxious to be able to complete her studies without interruption. In reply to questions about their prospects Sophia promised to stand by the group, and to do her best to ensure that they were able to complete their training in Edinburgh.

All went well during the first winter term. Grace Cadell's sister Ina and several other new students joined the classes. A more formal organization was needed for the management of the women students' interests. Sophia could not continue to carry financial responsibility for them all. Besides, they needed much more than admission tickets to lectures – the familiar problem of hospital training had to be solved. They also needed a library, and laboratories for practical classes. Fate seemed to be asking Sophia to found another medical school for women. She was older now, and less energetic, but the prospect was irresistible. Six of her friends agreed to form an Executive Committee for the school; they were Dr G.W. Balfour, Dr Agnes McLaren, Mr White-Miller, Mrs Alexander Russel, Dr Heron Watson and Miss Ursula Du Pre. The Committee did not have to search for premises. In 1876 Sophia, Ursula and Louisa Stevenson had joined forces to buy a property in Surgeon Square, and this was now vacant.

Surgeon Square has a place in the history of medicine. In the eighteenth and nineteenth centuries generations of students walked along Infirmary Street and crossed High School Yards to reach the Square's picturesque old houses, most of which had been converted to function as lecture rooms and dissecting laboratories. Here they were taught by extramural lecturers whose fame extended far beyond Edinburgh. One of the most famous names associated with Surgeon Square is that of the anatomist Robert Knox. In the early 1820s Knox attracted large audiences to his lectures, but in 1828 his career was ruined by a scandal. The 'body snatchers' William Burke and William Hare were accused of murdering the men and women whose corpses they sold to the anatomy teachers for dissection. Knox was known to have bought a number of bodies from Burke and Hare. Hare saved his own life by turning King's Evidence, but Burke was hanged. Although a committee of inquiry absolved Knox from complicity in the crimes, he never regained his professional standing. (The house used by Knox for his lectures was No 10, in the south-west corner of the Square. Sophia's property was No 1, in the north-east corner. Both have since been demolished.)

It is not clear why Sophia and her friends made their purchase in May 1876. The passage of the Russell Gurney Enabling Bill was then an uncertain prospect, so they could not have known that ten years later they would be establishing a women's medical school in Edinburgh. But whatever their intentions had been, Sophia was now very glad to have the building at her disposal.

Under her practised guidance tradesmen restored the lecture rooms and laboratories to good condition. A library and a comfortable sitting-room were added. Progress was so satisfactory that early in 1887 the school was formally designated the Edinburgh School of Medicine for Women, with Sophia as its Dean.

One of the Dean's first tasks was to arrange hospital training for her students. The Edinburgh Royal Infirmary had moved to new and larger premises since Sophia and her colleagues worked in its wards as students, but the number of male students had also increased. Many members of the medical staff would still oppose the setting aside of any of the wards for the teaching of women only. Rather than waste time in fruitless discussion with the Infirmary Managers, Sophia applied to the Leith Hospital. In 1871, when the women students were desperately seeking hospital training, she had been given a sympathetic hearing there. Unfortunately, the Hospital could not then afford to meet all the requirements of the examiners. Since then the Leith Hospital had been enlarged and was accredited by the Royal Colleges of Physicians and Surgeons. The staff realized that affiliation with a medical school would be in the best interests of the Hospital, so they welcomed the women students. The Edinburgh School of Medicine for Women could now offer complete professional training, and was recognized by the Royal Colleges. Dr Balfour persuaded Sophia to fill the post of lecturer in midwifery, so she had the distinction of being the first accredited woman lecturer in the extramural system.

She received many congratulatory messages. One was from Edith Pechey, who was now living in Bombay. In 1883 Edith had accepted an invitation to take charge of an Indian hospital for women and children, staffed by women doctors; this was the beginning of a project that was to be her life's work. Edith's letter must have brought a smile of pleasure to Sophia's face:

Hip Hip Hooray!!
Hip Hip Hooray!!!
Hip Hip Hooray!!!!!
In the very place where we were stoned and beaten 18 years ago. Well, I
am glad to have lived to see the day. . . .
I don't know when I have felt so pleased and elated and especially that it
should happen to *you*, it is so appropriate. Isn't Mrs Thorne very pleased
and everybody else?[12]

In fact, Mrs Thorne was one of the few who were *not* very pleased. She said
that Sophia and her friends in Edinburgh would have been wiser if they had
given all their support to the London School, instead of founding a second
medical school for women. Sophia thought that her colleagues in London did
not understand the difficulty some Scottish women had in moving so far from
home to begin their training.

In October 1887 the house in Surgeon Square was ready for occupation. A
description of the interior of the School appears in a novel called *Growth*,
written by Graham Travers and published in 1906. The hero of the story,
young Mr Dalgleish, visits the School one evening and inadvertently enters
the dissecting room:

> He pushed open a door to find himself in a spacious room that looked
> even larger than it was, in contrast with the dark little by-ways through
> which he had come.
> All the daylight there was streamed down through two great rows of
> windows in the roof. . . . The walls were lined with anatomical drawings
> and preparations; a skeleton hung from a bracket; and, on the great zinc
> tables were things ill-defined, swathed in wrappings, ghastly to his over-
> stimulated imagination.

A lady member of the staff rescues Dalgleish and conducts him to the students'
sitting-room:

> The room was small but comfortably furnished. The window looked out
> on the chimneys and roofs of the Pleasaunce, dark against a stormy sky.
> The uncertain firelight fell on pictures that seemed to invite a nearer
> acquaintance. . . . Later in the evening crimson curtains were drawn
> over the door and window, and a pretty lamp called into prominence
> bright notes of colour here and there, suggestive-looking books, a deeper
> meaning in the pictures.[13]

This description is probably accurate, because it was written by someone
whose knowledge of the subject was second only to Sophia's; 'Graham
Travers' was the pen-name of Margaret Todd, one of the first students at the
School.

175

Margaret was the daughter of a Glasgow merchant, James Cameron Todd, who spent much of his working life in the Far East. She was 27 years old when the Scottish Royal Colleges of Physicians and Surgeons opened their examinations to women. Margaret then decided to give up the occupation of teacher in order to begin the study of medicine. Not having a family home in Edinburgh, she was delighted to accept Sophia's invitation to stay at Bruntsfield Lodge. The two became close friends, although Margaret was eighteen years younger than Sophia.

Margaret Todd did not qualify in medicine until 1894. Why she took eight years to complete a four-year course is a matter for conjecture. The fact that in 1894 she obtained the MD Bruxelles, as well as the Licences of the Edinburgh Royal Colleges, indicates that her academic ability was more than adequate. She was probably deflected from her studies for part of this time by her other major interest, writing. In 1892 her most successful novel, *Mona Maclean*, was published. This, like *Growth*, is based in part on her own experiences as a medical student.

Margaret Todd also made a small contribution to the history of science. In 1913 the scientist Frederick Soddy reported his discovery that the atoms of some elements, although chemically identical, have different atomic weights. He called them 'isotopes', from the Greek *isos topos*, because they occupy the 'same place' in the periodic table. It seems that shortly before Soddy published his report he attended a dinner party where Dr Todd was also a guest. While describing his discovery Soddy mentioned that he was still seeking a name for these chemically identical atoms of different atomic weight. Margaret Todd suggested the name isotope, which Soddy at once adopted.[14]

Despite Sophia's tendency to adopt a 'Mother-knows-best' attitude to her students, some of them, like Margaret Todd, were grateful to her and regarded her with affection. But Sophia was now close to fifty, and the attitudes of the average young woman had changed since her own student days. Several of those at her School had a strong sense of independence and resented her tendency to impose strict rules. They did not understand that the rules reflected her anxiety to protect their hard-won access to the world of masculine privilege. In the early months there were several minor disagreements, but the first serious trouble at the School occurred in 1888.

The School's agreement with the Leith Hospital directors required the students to leave the wards by 5 p.m. each day, so that they would not interfere with the work of the nurses. At this hour the patients were given their evening meal and were made comfortable for the night. At first the rule was not strictly enforced, but as the number of students increased, their presence in the wards in the evenings became more of a nuisance and there were occasional complaints from Miss Perry, the Lady Superintendent.

The trouble came to a head on 8 June. At 5 p.m., just as the Misses Cadell and two other students were leaving the Hospital, an accident case was brought in. The house surgeon, Dr Juckes, told the students that the patient

Illustration 14. Sophia Jex-Blake in middle age. (Reproduced by permission of the Edinburgh University Library.)

had an interesting head injury, so they returned to the ward to watch him carry out his examination. Miss Perry came into the ward some time later and was vexed to find four students clustered round a bed, although it was then well after five o'clock. She told them to leave at once, but Grace Cadell retorted that she had no business to interfere as the students were there at the invitation of Dr Juckes.

That night Miss Perry wrote to Sophia complaining about the students' behaviour and saying that if they did not mend their ways she would take her complaint to the Hospital Directors. The School's association with Leith Hospital was threatened. Anxiety heightened the authoritarian element in Sophia's personality. Instead of discussing the matter with the four students privately, she reprimanded them in the presence of the whole class, and drafted an apology to Miss Perry for them to sign. They signed it, but one of the four, Ina Cadell, later regretted that she had allowed herself to be coerced; she wrote again to Miss Perry, retracting her apology. A minor episode had become a crisis. For several weeks an atmosphere of tension prevailed until, with the exchange of more letters between the School and the Hospital, and the submission of another apology from Ina Cadell, peace was restored. After this the students observed the 5 o'clock rule.

The Leith Hospital episode was hardly over when another dispute erupted. In April one of the junior students, Miss Sinclair, had failed the preliminary examinations in English and arithmetic. Sophia sympathized with her and helped to rearrange her programme of lectures so that she would be able to take the examination again in July. But on the examination day Miss Sinclair did not appear. On making enquiries Sophia discovered that at some time between April and July the examiners had reviewed her papers and had issued her with a pass certificate. They had done this in response to an appeal from one of Miss Sinclair's friends, who told them that she had been unwell when she took the examination.

Sophia was strongly opposed to the granting of any special privileges to women students. Furthermore, Miss Sinclair's secrecy about the certificate suggested a sense of guilt on her part. At her next weekly meeting with all the students Sophia expressed her views bluntly, referring to Miss Sinclair's action as 'a mean thing'. These comments were not well received by some of the students. There were angry murmurs from those who thought that Sophia was exceeding her authority and victimizing Miss Sinclair.

After this episode the School was divided into two factions. The Cadell sisters were the most outspoken of the group who were hostile to Sophia; Margaret Todd was one of those who remained loyal to her. For several weeks the work of the School was disrupted by the dispute. When Sophia addressed the students she sometimes had to speak above a background of murmured dissent. Her pride and her sense of order were affronted. At the meeting of the Executive Council held on 26 July she recounted the story of the dispute and its effect on the School. She said that she could not continue as Dean if the

Misses Caddell returned for the winter term. The Committee resolved that the Misses Caddell should be informed that they would not be accepted again as students.

When Grace and Ina Cadell received the Secretary's letter telling them that they had been expelled from the School, they immediately sought legal advice. The Committee was served with notice of an action for damages, in which the Misses Cadell each claimed £500 from the School as compensation for the interruption of their studies. For the second time Sophia, who had borne so much, was accused of inflicting on others injuries to the extent of £1000!

The case was not heard until a year later, in July 1889. It lasted for two days, during which nineteen witnesses recounted in detail the events that had led to the expulsion of the Cadell sisters.[15] When made the subject of a formal legal inquiry the dispute seemed ridiculously trivial. How easily the trouble could have been averted if both sides had shown just a little more tolerance and humour! Throughout the hearing the courtroom was packed, mostly with ladies who were amused by this split in the ranks of the medical women.

The court's final decision was delivered on 15 July 1890. The judges found in favour of the complainants, the Misses Cadell, but awarded each of them only £50 instead of the £500 originally sought. Neither side in the dispute could claim outright victory. The aftermath was to be borne by the Edinburgh School of Medicine for Women.

Shortly after the exclusion of the Cadell sisters, another student, Elsie Inglis, emerged as the leader of the rebel group. She was regarded as the School's most gifted pupil, so her opposition was especially hurtful to Sophia. Encouraged by rich and influential friends, Elsie left Sophia's School and established Edinburgh's second medical school for women. The Medical College for Women, as it was called, was housed in rented premises at 30 Chambers Street. It lacked many of the facilities Sophia provided at her School, but its fees were lower and its rules less restrictive. When the new College opened for the winter term of 1889–90 its students included Elsie Inglis, the Cadell sisters and several other former students of the School. For the first three years of its existence, the Chambers Street College could not provide its students with hospital training in Edinburgh; they had to travel to the Glasgow Royal Infirmary. Even so, the College attracted students in sufficient numbers for it to be a serious rival of the School in Surgeon Square.

In July 1892 the Chambers Street College gained a significant advantage when it concluded an agreement with the Edinburgh Royal Infirmary for the clinical training of its students. The Infirmary was generous; none of the dis-advantages suffered by the first women students in 1873 would be borne by the students from the College. Although they would work in separate wards from those frequented by the male students, they would have access to all the opportunities for learning available to the men. This striking reversal of the policy of the Infirmary's administrators and medical staff was largely due to changes in social attitudes, changes that had developed slowly, but were now being openly expressed. The Chambers Street College had an additional powerful weapon – two of the members of its Committee were also members of the Infirmary's Board of Managers. It must have seemed a bitter irony to Sophia that one of these two gentlemen was Sir Alexander Christison, the late Sir Robert's son!

The School in Surgeon Square still had loyal supporters. The women who enrolled there now were happy to accept Sophia's firm leadership, and many of them remained her friends long after they had finished their studies. Among these were a group of Indian women who were introduced to the School by Dr Edith Pechey. Sophia gave Edith's students a special welcome. Several of them were guests at Bruntsfield Lodge for the duration of their studies; all were grateful for her kindly interest.

In her roles as campaigner for medical women's rights and Dean of the School, Sophia appeared stern and aggressive, but those who knew her well saw the other side of her nature. Her home was a haven, where friends were assured of generous hospitality enlivened by her joyous sense of humour. She would nurse them back to health, sympathize with them in times of trouble or celebrate a happy occasion, always with selfless concern. Friendship played an important part in Sophia's life. She still remembered Octavia Hill with affection; for many years after their estrangement she had named Octavia as a beneficiary in her will. But Margaret Todd was now filling her need for companionship. In 1887 Margaret had bought Louisa Stevenson's share of the ownership of the School building. When she became a registered medical practitioner in 1894 Margaret was appointed an assistant physician to the Hospital and Dispensary for Women and Children. She thus became Sophia's professional assistant as well as her closest friend.

In 1890 Sophia lost a friend who had changed the course of her life. She wrote to Mrs Brander (Isabel Bain), her travelling companion during the trip to America in 1865, telling her of the death of Lucy Sewall:

> My dear friend Dr Sewall, has been as you know in bad health for the last 4 or 5 years, and last month she was seized with a very severe attack of bronchitis, from which she never regained strength, and she passed away 'very peacefully' on Feb. 13th 1890.
>
> Though I have seen so little of her for some years back, it is a great blow to me, – the greatest I have felt since 1881.
>
> *How* I hope that she is again with the mother and father she loved so very dearly. Indeed she has never really rallied, I believe, from her father's death (at 90) a year ago.
>
> A whiter sweeter soul never lived, and her memory 'smells sweet and blossoms in the dust.'
>
> I cannot write more today, but I could not let you hear it from anyone else. I hope you got the little book I sent you at Christmas. I could not write but it carried much affection to you.[16]

In 1892 Sophia was visited by Edith Pechey, who had married three years previously and was now known as Dr Pechey-Phipson. Her husband, Herbert Phipson, was a merchant whose trade in wine and herbs was conducted in Bombay. Edith was still the medical officer in charge of the Cama Hospital, a large hospital for women. Recently, she had been appointed to the Senate of the University of Bombay; she was the first woman to hold such a position in India. Her visit to Edinburgh coincided with the end of an academic term at Sophia's School, so Edith attended the ceremony and distributed the prizes.

The two friends probably rejoiced together over another victory for medical women, when the British Medical Association at last opened its membership to all registered women doctors. For nearly twenty years Elizabeth Garrett Anderson had been the Association's only woman member, and at times she had faced open hostility to her presence at meetings. But now the number of women's names on the General Medical Register was approaching 200, and even their enemies had to admit that they were providing a valuable service to the community. Clearly, the woman doctor had come to stay. When the British Medical Association held its Annual General Meeting at Nottingham in 1892 the vote in favour of admitting women members was almost unanimous.

London University opened its doors to women in 1878, but ten years later it was still the only British university to have done so. Although public opinion was in favour of giving women access to higher education, some decisive action was needed to accelerate progress. In 1888 the Government appointed a Commission to review the charters of the Scottish universities, and submissions from the public were invited. Any event of significance to the medical women's cause still received Sophia's close attention, so she seized on this opportunity. Not only did she make her own submissions, but she provided information and advice to others who were prepared to present the medical women's case. The work of the Commission extended over six years, during which Sophia appeared before it on a number of occasions. She described one of these in a letter to a friend:

> The Scottish Universities Commission has been issuing some 'Ordinances' to which serious objections are taken, and among others a flaw has been found in the Women's Ordinance, which we want to have remedied. All the objecting bodies were to meet together, so Dr Balfour and I were summoned by enclosed solemn document to appear to represent our School, and it *was* amusing to find myself an invited delegate, at whose entrance the Chairman rose and came forward with outstretched hand, in the awful University Court Room, where our case had over and over again been tried by a hostile authority, and lost, without an opportunity for a word in our own defence.
> Sir Robert Christison looked down from the wall, and it made me almost chuckle to think what *he* would have said!
> Sic transit! *How* the world moves![17]

In 1894, as the result of the Commission's findings, Edinburgh University opened its medical degree examinations to women. Women students were still debarred from the University's medical classes, but the alternative sources of instruction, the two medical schools for women, were recognized by the University. Sophia's friends shared her pleasure. At a reception held in her honour on 3 November 1894 she was presented with an address bearing more than thirty signatures. It read:

> We, the undersigned, women members of the original National Association for the Medical Education of Women, resident at this time in Edinburgh, desire to offer to you our warm and hearty congratulations on the brilliant success you have achieved in securing the opening of the Edinburgh University medical examinations and degrees to women students. We know that it was largely due to your great ability and knowledge that the enabling Bill of 1876 was passed, which put it into the power, if they so willed, of each of the nineteen examining bodies of the United Kingdom to admit women to qualifying examinations, and which was the foundation of the success on which we congratulate you today. Many who worked with you and under you in the old days have passed away. We who are left take this opportunity of expressing to you our appreciation of the great sacrifice you have made of time, and strength, and money, to win for younger women in their own country a complete medical education crowned by a degree. To have done this in Edinburgh we regard as a success of which you may be justly proud.[18]

The first women medical graduates of Edinburgh University were Jessie Macgregor (from the Surgeon Square School) and Mona Geddes (from the Chambers Street College). They both received their degrees on 1 August 1896.

The Edinburgh School of Medicine for Women was no longer wracked by disagreements between students and Dean, but its days were numbered. There was room for only one such institution in Edinburgh, and the rival College had the advantage of being affiliated with the famous Edinburgh Royal Infirmary. Each year the School enrolled fewer students and had increasing difficulty in paying its way. Some of the lecturers offered to teach for reduced fees, or for no fees at all, but by 1896 the end appeared inevitable, and two years later the School was closed. It was a bitter defeat for Sophia, who had spared no effort to make the School a success. Perhaps if she had cared about it less she would not have provoked the Cadell sisters and Elsie Inglis into open rebellion. But Sophia could neither see her own faults nor change her nature.

It was a cruel trick of fate that 1896 was also the year in which the Executive Council of the London School of Medicine for Women announced plans for a much larger new building. The School was enjoying such success that it had

Illustration 15. Elizabeth Garrett Anderson (1836–1917).
(Reproduced by permission of the Archives Section, The
Royal Free Hospital, London.)

outgrown its original premises. The proposal was initiated by the Dean,
Elizabeth Garrett Anderson, but she had the full support of the Council; it was
a confident Elizabeth who wrote to *The Times* inviting the public to contribute
to a fund to finance the project.

To Sophia, struggling with her problems in Edinburgh, this seemed like
reckless extravagance. Eight years previously she had objected to some aspects
of the financial management of the London School. Her protests then had
been to no avail. Now she wrote to the Council again, arguing that the
increase in number of students was probably only a temporary phenomenon,
which justified nothing more than minor alterations to the old building. Again
she failed to win any support from the Council. When the Council met on 26
May it received Sophia's letter of resignation. Thus, she severed her last

connection with the School she had founded twenty-four years before. Perhaps her indignation temporarily numbed the pain, but the wound probably never healed completely.

While the Edinburgh School of Medicine for Women was foundering, the Hospital and Dispensary for Women and Children flourished. In 1895 a building sub-committee was formed to begin planning a move to a larger site. In 1897, the year of the Queen's Diamond Jubilee, a public appeal was launched in the Scottish newspapers:

> The Edinburgh Hospital and Dispensary for Women and Children now in Grove Street has existed first as a Dispensary then as a Hospital for nearly 20 years. The Dispensary in the first 16 years was attended by 2,621 patients who paid 25,773 visits. The present building affords one large ward of 4 beds and another small private ward. In the first 10 years the Hospital admitted 340 patients. It is now proposed to raise a fund of £10,000 in order to build a really adequate and satisfactory hospital and it has been suggested that in honour of the present year a special Jubilee Ward should be erected to be free to all needy patients.[19]

The fund grew slowly, and at the same time Sophia's personal plans were changing. Soon she would be 60 years old, and her energy was failing. After the closure of the School her practice could have absorbed more of her time, but now that there were well-trained young women able to take over the work she gradually reduced her own commitments. She thought longingly of rest and of having leisure to enjoy a garden and her large collection of books. After a prolonged search she found a house that appealed to her as a home in her retirement. It was in Sussex, near the village of Mark Cross, and about five miles south of Tunbridge Wells. She called the house Windydene. 'It was built probably some 50 years ago', she wrote to a friend, 'very comfortable and airy, and with pleasant garden and shrubberies, a good kitchen garden (much neglected of late) and about 8 acres for pasture and hay.'

The Committee of the Hospital and Dispensary decided that Bruntsfield Lodge, with some minor alterations, was ideally suited to house their new Hospital. Sophia was prepared to sell it for this purpose at a price the Committee could easily afford. On 27 March 1899 a new Constitution for the Hospital was signed.[20] The name was changed to the Bruntsfield Hospital, but the original policy of appointing women doctors only, to care for women and children, was reaffirmed. Dr Sophia Jex-Blake was appointed a consultant physician to the Bruntsfield Hospital.

A few days later Sophia's friends arranged a large farewell reception in her honour. Distinguished ladies and gentlemen mingled with former patients of the Dispensary. Speakers eloquently praised her courage and achievements, but formality was soon swept aside in a surge of emotion, as guests clustered around Sophia to shake her hand and wish her well. Margaret Todd, when writing of these events some years later, paid her own tribute to her friend:

> For years she had lived among the Edinburgh people, driving about in her quiet brougham or unpretentious pony-chaise, and retiring to the high-walled garden. In a way they could not but get to know her. They might like or dislike her, but she went on her way, doing her work absolutely without ostentation, welcoming publicity when it seemed likely to forward her aims or the welfare of the community, shunning it absolutely as a matter of private taste.
>
> With most of those whose opinion was worth having, opposition and dislike were simply worn down. She was impulsive, she made mistakes and would do so to the end of her life: her naturally hasty temper and imperious disposition had been chastened indeed, but the chastening fire had been far too fierce to produce perfection. She held out at times about trifles, – failed to see that they *were* trifles – and at times she terrified people more than she knew. Above all she cared nothing for the praise and blame of any but those whom she respected or loved. Of her indeed it might be said that she heard the beat of a different drummer. But there was another side to the picture after all. Many of those who regretted and criticised details were yet forced to bow before the big transparent honesty, the fine unflinching consistency, of her life.[21]

Notes

1. M. Todd, *The Life of Sophia Jex-Blake*, London: Macmillan, 1918, p. 459.
2. ibid., p. 461.
3. ibid., p. 462.
4. ibid., p. 464.
5. ibid., p. 464.
6. ibid., p. 465.
7. ibid., p. 473.
8. ibid., p. 473.
9. S. Paget, *The Memoirs and Letters of Sir James Paget*, 3rd edn, London: Fisher, Unwin, 1903, pp. 298, 310–18.
10. R.D. French, *Vivisection and Medical Science in Victorian Society*, Princeton NJ: Princeton University Press, 1975.
11. Archives of the Medical School, Royal Free Hospital, London.
12. Todd, op. cit., p. 505.
13. G. Travers, *Growth*, London: Archibald Constable, 1906, p. 228.
14. *Endeavour*, 1964, 23: p. 54 (Editorial).
15. Before Lord Kyllachy. Proof in Causa. Miss Grace Cadell and Miss Martha G.I. Cadell against the Executive Committee and Secretary of the Edinburgh School of Medicine for Women. July 18th, 19th, 1889. Officially reported by William Lindsay, Shorthand Writer.
16. Todd, op. cit., p. 506.
17. ibid., p. 508.
18. ibid., p. 510.

19.   Document SA/MWF/C23, Contemporary Medical Archives Centre, Wellcome Institute for the History of Medicine, London.
20.   Archives of Bruntsfield Hospital.
21.   Todd, op. cit., p. 525.

11

The return to Sussex

Sophia's move from Edinburgh to Mark Cross was quite an undertaking. She had always been an enthusiastic collector of books, and a hoarder of letters and documents. Furthermore, she could rarely bring herself to throw away old items of household equipment if they were still usable, so there was a great deal of sorting, discarding and packing to be done before Bruntsfield Lodge could be handed over to its new owners. Fortunately, Margaret Todd was there to help her; after only five years in medical practice she was retiring and coming to share Sophia's home in Sussex. Margaret may have decided to devote her time to writing, or her health may have become a problem – the reason for her early retirement is not recorded.

Margaret wrote of Sophia's contentment at Windydene, the last and the most carefully chosen of her homes. Now that she owned 'eight acres for pasture and hay' she could at last satisfy her yearning to be a farmer. She kept a herd of cows and had her own dairy, and there was an orchard where her gardeners grew peaches, figs and grapes. The house overlooked broad expanses of lawn and well-kept flower beds. Sophia enjoyed overseeing the care and improvement of her property.

The farm in Sussex seemed far removed from the world of medicine, but she still followed with interest events that reminded her of earlier days. In 1903 she read of Elizabeth Garrett Anderson's retirement from the post of Dean of the London School of Medicine for Women. Three years later Sophia's old friend Isabel Thorne also retired, having served the School for thirty years as its Honorary Secretary.

One of the functions Isabel attended during her last year in office was the School's end-of year ceremony in 1905, when the eminent surgeon Mr Henry Butlin was the guest speaker.[1] This was the same Henry Butlin who, forty years previously, had led the medical students of St Bartholomew's Hospital in their unequal battle with Ellen Colborne. Then there had been only two registered women doctors. Now there were over seven hundred, and the London School of Medicine had more than one hundred and fifty students enrolled for the following year.[2] Mr Butlin was able to assure the audience at the prize-giving ceremony that women had not only demonstrated their ability to complete medical training, but they were successfully meeting all the demands of practice!

If Sophia enjoyed reading the report of this function, she would have been even more pleased by another event that occurred three years later. In 1908 the Royal College of Surgeons of England and the Royal College of Physicians of London decided to admit women to their Conjoint examination in medicine and surgery. The surgeons went even further and made their higher qualification, the Fellowship, also available to women. (The physicians did not take this step until 1925.)

As always, Sophia's home was a meeting place for her friends. Often there would be an old comrade from the Edinburgh campaign, or a friend from even earlier times, spending a few days or several weeks at Windydene. Agnes McLaren was one of the regular visitors. She arrived each spring on her way home from the Riviera, where she conducted a medical practice during the winter. In 1906 Edith Pechey-Phipson and her husband handed over to others their responsibilities in India, and returned to England permanently. Sophia was delighted to welcome them to Windydene and looked forward to many more reunions with her old friend.

She also came to know the local people well. Margaret Todd wrote of the friendship that developed between Sophia and the Catholic priest:

> The Revd. Father Duggan became one of the most welcome guests at Windydene. He and his dog, Caesar, used to drop in almost every Sunday afternoon for strawberries on the lawn or tea round the study fire. . . . There were great talks on those Sunday afternoons; it was no uncommon thing to see three versions of the Bible and half a dozen volumes of the *Encyclopaedia* lying about at the end to witness to the interest of the discussion. There was much borrowing and lending of books, – and no obvious change of view on the part of anyone except in the direction of increased tolerance and brotherly kindness.[3]

Retirement brought Sophia peace and contentment; only one episode recalled the stresses of her earlier life. In 1905 there was a vacancy on the medical staff of the Bruntsfield Hospital. Sophia was still nominally a member of the Hospital Board, so she was informed of the steps being taken to fill the vacancy. The best applicant for the post was Dr Elsie Inglis, but the Board members knew that Sophia would object strongly to her appointment. As a conciliatory gesture they invited Sophia to become Vice-President of the Hospital. But Sophia was not so easily mollified. She replied that she would resign from the Hospital Board rather than acquiesce in the appointment of Dr Inglis. Her resignation was accepted and the appointment was made. So Sophia, who had founded two medical schools and a hospital, now had no association with any of them. Elsie Inglis was later to earn an honoured place

Illustration 16. Sophia Jex-Blake in retirement. The initials MGT suggest that the original photograph was taken by Sophia's friend Margaret Georgina Todd. (Reproduced by permission of the State Reference Library of Victoria, Australia.)

from a photograph by M.G.T.   Emery Walker ph.

in medical history, Sophia had already done so. The bitterness of their dispute revealed in each of them the human weakness of pride, which could sometimes overshadow their many noble qualities.

The softer side of Sophia's nature is apparent in the story of her last communication with Octavia Hill. In July 1910 Octavia wrote a letter to *The Times* in which she argued against women's suffrage. She said that women would be giving more valuable service to the community by caring for the sick, the old, the young and the erring, than by entering the already overcrowded world of politics. Sophia, of course, disagreed with this view, so she wrote a reply, but *The Times* did not publish it. Sophia then wrote directly to Octavia:

> I wrote enclosed mainly as an answer to yours in the *Times*, and as it has been sent back to me, crowded out, I send it to you, – to show you another old woman's point of view.
>
> I am rheumatic and lame now, and cannot go about much, but I wish you would come down and spend two or three days with me here on the Sussex hills, and we would thrash out this Suffrage question – surely one of us ought to be able to convince the other! And I *should* like to see you again![4]

Octavia replied, but did not accept Sophia's invitation, probably for several reasons – her age and infirmity, as well as her innate dread of emotional crises. Sophia was disappointed, but other losses were now affecting her more deeply.

In 1908 Edith Pechey-Phipson became seriously ill. When she was operated on by Dr May Thorne (Isabel Thorne's daughter) her condition was found to be incurable and she died not long afterwards. Isabel Thorne and Elizabeth Blackwell, Sophia's friends for forty years, both died in 1910.

But while she was losing her old friends, Margaret Todd was taking their place in her affections. Sophia encouraged Margaret with her writing. She enjoyed reliving the experiences of her earlier life as she recounted them to Margaret, who was an absorbed and intelligent listener. Sophia kept in touch with her brother and his family, and from time to time her sister Caroline came to stay at Windydene, but it was Margaret who shared her enthusiasms and brightened her declining years.

A failing heart increasingly limited Sophia's activities after she reached the age of 70. She never lost interest in the farm and watched over it as carefully as ever, but she herself was able to do less and less. She still liked to be taken for her daily drive, although she would often drift off to sleep in her carriage. Her life ended peacefully on 7 January, 1912.

Notes

1. I. Thorne, *Sketch of the Foundation and Development of London School of Medicine for Women*, London: Women's Printing Society, 1915, p. 50.

2. These figures are derived from those for the year 1906, quoted in *The History of the Royal College of Surgeons of England*, by Sir Zachary Cope, London: Anthony Blond, 1959, p. 124.

3. M. Todd, *The Life of Sophia Jex-Blake*, London: Macmillan, 1918, p. 530.

4. ibid., p. 538.

Bibliography

Contemporary sources

Contemporary books and articles

Before Lord Kyllachy. Proof in Causa. Miss Grace Cadell and Miss Martha G.I. Cadell against the Executive Committee and Secretary of the Edinburgh School of Medicine for Women. July 18th, 19th, 1889. Officially reported by William Lindsay, Shorthand Writer.

Blackwell, E. *The Influence of Women in the Profession of Medicine*, London: George Bell & Sons, 1889.

Blackwell, E. *Pioneer Work in Opening the Medical Profession to Women*, London: Longmans Green & Co., 1895.

Butler, J. (ed.) *Woman's Work and Woman's Culture*, London: Macmillan, 1869.

Life of Sir Robert Christison, Bart (edited by his sons), Edinburgh and London: William Blackwood & Sons, 1885–6.

Jex-Blake, S. *A Visit to Some American Schools and Colleges*, London: Macmillan, 1867.

Jex-Blake, S. 'The practice of medicine by women', in *Fortnightly Review*, 1875, pp. 392–407.

Jex-Blake, S. *Medical Women*, London: Macmillan, 1886.

Jex-Blake, S. 'Medical women', *The Nineteenth Century*, Nov. 1887, pp. 692–707.

Jex-Blake, S. 'Medical women in fiction', *The Nineteenth Century*, Feb. 1893, pp. 261–72.

Rouse, W.H.D. *A History of Rugby School*, London: Duckworth & Co., 1898.

Rye, W. *A History of the Family of Cubitt*, Norwich: Samuel Butler & Co., 1873.

Stanfeld, J. 'Medical women', *The Nineteenth Century*, July 1877.

Thorne, I. *Sketch of the Foundation and Development of the London School of Medicine for Women*, London: Women's Printing Society, 1915.

Todd, M. *The Life of Sophia Jex-Blake*, London: Macmillan, 1918.

Travers, G. *Mona Maclean, Medical Student*, London: William Blackwood & Sons, 1893.

Travers, G. *Growth*, London: Constable, 1906.

Wilson, R. *Aesculapia Victrix*, London: Chapman & Hall, 1886.

Archives

Bruntsfield Hospital
Central Library of Edinburgh
Fawcett Library, City of London Polytechnic

Bibliography

Francis A. Countway Library of Medicine, Boston, USA
Lothian Health Board Medical Archive Centre
Medical Library, Edinburgh University
Medical School, Royal Free Hospital, London
National Library of Scotland, Edinburgh
Wellcome Institute for the History of Medicine, London

Newspapers and journals

Bulletin of the New York Academy of Medicine
Edinburgh Medical Journal
Fortnightly Review
Lancet
Nineteenth Century
Postgraduate Medical Journal
St Bartholomew's Hospital Journal
Scots Magazine
Scotsman
Spectator
The Times

Later books and articles

Cooke, A.M. *A History of the Royal College of Physicians of London*, Vol. III. Oxford: Clarendon Press, 1972.

Cope, Z. *The Royal College of Surgeons of England – A History*, London: Anthony Blond, 1959.

Darley, G. *Octavia Hill – A Life*, London: Constable, 1990.

Donaldson, G. (ed.) *Four Centuries; Edinburgh University Life 1583–1983*, Edinburgh: University of Edinburgh, 1983.

Edwards, O.D. *A Quest for Sherlock Holmes*, Edinburgh: Mainstream Publishing Co., 1983.

Fisher, R.B. *Joseph Lister*, London: Macdonald & James, 1977.

Godlee, Sir R.J. *Lord Lister*, 3rd edn, Oxford: Clarendon Press, 1924.

Guthrie, D. *A History of Medicine*, London: Nelson & Sons, 1958.

Guthrie, D. *Extramural Medical Education in Edinburgh*, Edinburgh and London: E. & S. Livingstone, 1965.

Hobhouse, H. *Thomas Cubitt: Master Builder*, London: Macmillan, 1971.

Horn, D.B. *A Short History of the University of Edinburgh*, Edinburgh: Edinburgh University Press, 1967.

Kamm, J. *Hope Deferred*, London: Methuen, 1965.

Kaye, E. *A History of Queen's College, London*, London: Chatto & Windus, 1972.

Lawrence, M. *Shadow of Swords – A Biography of Elsie Inglis*, London: Michael Joseph, 1971.

Levin, B.S. *Women and Medicine*, Metuchen, New Jersey and London: Scarecrow Press, 1980.

Logan Turner, B.A. *The Story of a Great Hospital: The Royal Infirmary of Edinburgh 1729–1929*, Edinburgh: Oliver & Boyd, 1937.

Lutzker, E. *Women Gain a Place in Medicine*, New York: McGraw Hill, 1973.

Manton, J. *Elizabeth Garrett Anderson*, London: Methuen, 1965.

Bibliography

Marti, B.M. *The Spanish College in Bologna in the Fourteenth Century*, Philadelphia: University of Pennsylvania Press, 1966.

Mitchell, B.R. and Deane, P. *Abstract of British Historical Statistics*, Cambridge: Cambridge University Press, 1962.

Moberly Bell, E. *Octavia Hill*, London: Constable, 1942.

Morantz-Sanchez, R.M. *Sympathy and Science – Women Physicians in American Medicine*, New York: Oxford University Press, 1985.

Rae, I. *Knox the Anatomist*, Edinburgh and London: Oliver & Boyd, 1964.

Ross, I. *Child of Destiny (Elizabeth Blackwell)*, New York: Harper & Bros, 1949.

Stock, P. *Better Than Rubies: A History of Women's Education*, New York: Putnam, 1978.

Underwood, E.A. (ed.) *Science, Medicine and History*, London: Oxford University Press, 1953.

Wilson, D.C. *Lone Woman (Elizabeth Blackwell)*, Boston and Toronto: Little, Brown & Co., 1970.

Index